BUILD INCOME, INFLUENCE, & IMMORTALITY BEFORE IT'S TOO LATE!

#1 BESTSELLER

HOW YOU CAN BECOME A BESTSELLING AUTHOR IN ONLY 30 MINUTES A DAY

#1 NEW YORK TIMES BESTSELLING AUTHOR
ROBERT G. ALLEN
LYNDSEY MERRYMAN & AARON WATSON

Copyright © 2025 by Robert G. Allen, Lyndsey Merryman, and Aaron Watson

All rights reserved.

No part of this book may be reproduced or transmitted in any form or by any means, electronic or mechanical, including photocopying, recording, or by any information storage and retrieval system, without written permission from the author, except for the inclusion of brief quotations in a review.

This book is a work of non-fiction. The views and opinions expressed in this book are those of the author and do not necessarily reflect the official policy or position of any organization or entity mentioned within.

Editing and typesetting by Katie Carter

Published by Rosellón Publishing

To all who dream of becoming a bestselling author.

A GIFT FOR YOU—FROM ONE AUTHOR TO ANOTHER

Before you dive in, we want to give you something I wish I had when I was writing my first book. The kind of stuff that turns "I hope this works" into "Oh wow—this is happening."

That's why we put together a bundle of our favorite author tools, cheat sheets, and exclusive behind-the-scenes resources—including:

- Our AI Bestseller Coach – It's like having a 24/7 co-pilot to help you shape your message, sharpen your strategy, and stay on track.
- A Free Masterclass – You'll sit in with me and the team as we walk through the same process that helped us and so many others hit #1.

And that's just the beginning…

To claim your free gift, simply visit AuthorGifts.com or scan the QR code. It's 100% free and waiting for you. We're rooting for you, and we can't wait to celebrate your success.

See you inside,

– Robert, Lyndsey & Aaron

CONTENTS

In the Beginning   11
Do You Have a Book in You?

Before You Write a Single Word   16
12 "Stoopid" Mistakes That All Beginning Authors Make

Step 1. Your Irresistible Message   28
The Veins of Gold in the Goldmine of You

Step 2. Your Perfect Avatar   48
Riches Are in the Niches

Step 3. Your Success Map   55
The Right Picture Is Worth Millions

Step 4. Your Revolutionary Brand   69
How to "You-niquify" Yourself

Step 5. Your Word Forge   81
How to Make Your Words Irresistible

Step 6. Your Bold Book Cover   101
Crafting the Hook of Hooks

Step 7. Your Impressive Layout 115
Making Your Book Interior "Sticky"

Step 8. Your Opt-in to Wealth 124
A License to Print Money

Step 9. Your Succession Stack 135
Earn $100 for Every Word You Write

Step 10. Your Bestselling Buzz 159
Free & Paid Ways to Get the Word Out

Step 11. Your Guaranteed Launch 186
Becoming a #1 Bestselling Author

Step 12. Your Exponential Scalability 213
Adding Zeros

30 Magic Minutes 231
Your Commitment to Succeed

Let's Stay Connected 237

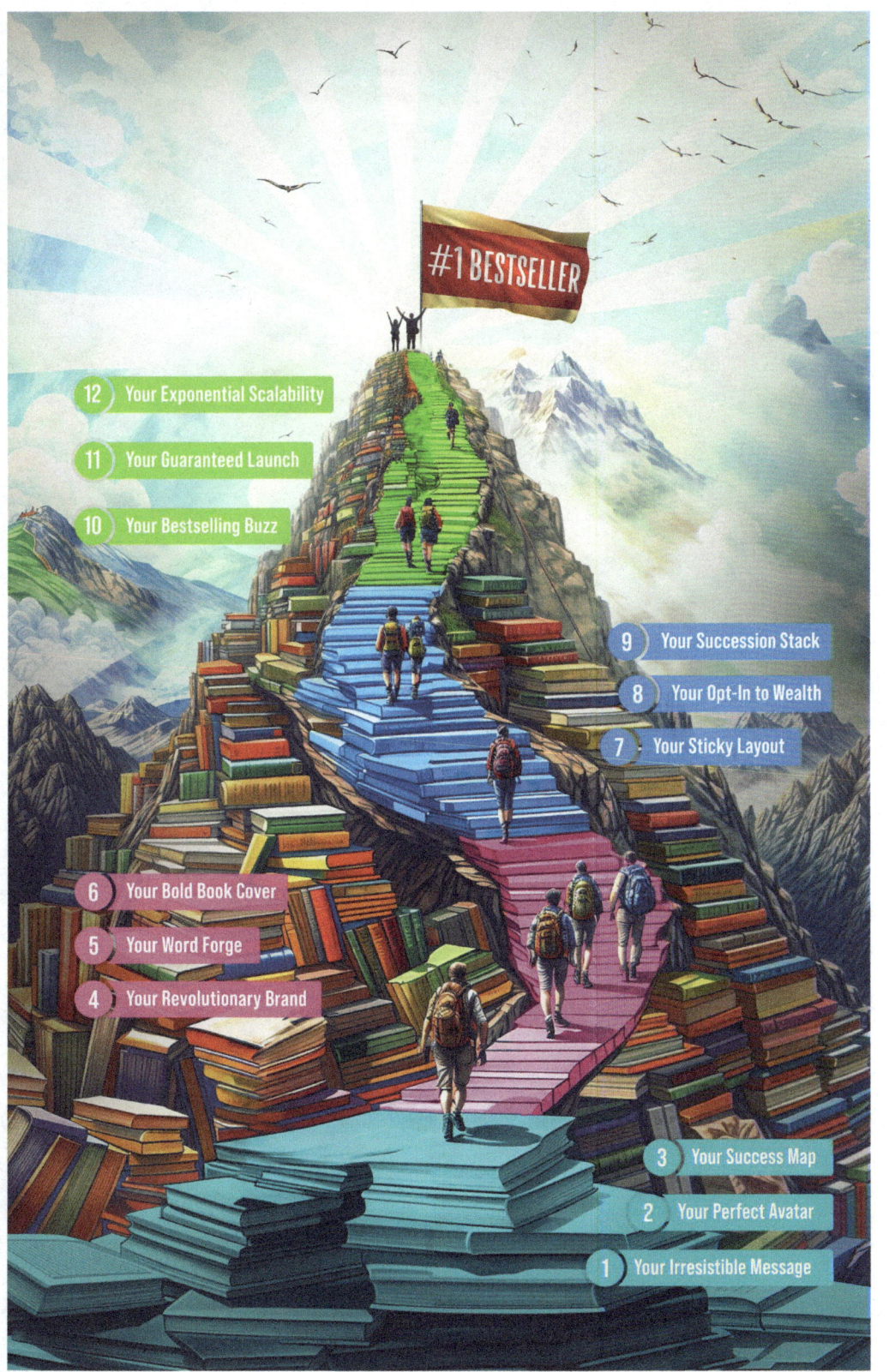

IS BEING A BESTSELLING AUTHOR IMPORTANT TO YOU?

If so, let me introduce myself. My name is Robert Allen. I know what it's like to want to write a book—to be a published author. But I had *no idea* what would happen when my first book—*Nothing Down*—hit number one on the *New York Times* bestseller list. It was a game changer! It stayed on the list for fifty-eight weeks! My second book–*Creating Wealth*—also hit number one and stayed on the list for twenty-six weeks. Since then, I've authored or co-authored fifteen other books that have sold in the millions.

Although I've taught millions of people in my worldwide seminars and speeches on real estate and financial success, I get the most pleasure in teaching people like you how to become a number-one bestselling author. Trust me, when you see your book hit number one on *any* bestseller list, the rest of your life is forever altered using any metric—money, prestige, respect, relationships, opportunity—it's a game changer!

That's why I didn't write this one alone.

In this book, I'm joined by two of the most brilliant marketing minds—my trusted partners, Lyndsey Merryman and Aaron Watson.

Lyndsey is a creative powerhouse—part strategist, part storyteller, and a master at turning ideas into movements. Aaron is a world-class marketing architect—one of the top one percent strategic thinkers I've worked with—able to build systems and momentum that take books (and businesses) to the next level. They're the quiet legends behind over eight figures in online sales—and now they're here to help you do the same.

Together, we've helped thousands of authors find their voice, write their books, and launch them to number one.

You're about to discover how.

I want to show YOU how to get YOUR book onto the bestseller lists so YOU can become a bestselling author. We've devised a twelve-step plan for showing you how to go from no book to a number-one bestselling book. This book will show you the entire system. Because if you don't know what you're doing, you could make a fool of yourself on the world's stage, and your dream of being a bestselling author may go up in flames—but not with my team and this book in your arsenal.

Onward,

Robert G. Allen

"We are the opening verse of the opening page of the chapter of endless possibilities."

– Rudyard Kipling

IN THE BEGINNING

Do You Have a Book in You?

Have you ever wanted to write a book? If so, you're not alone. Many people feel they have a book inside of them waiting to be written. According to the *New York Times*, over eighty percent of us would love to add the word *author* to our resumes.[1]

Over three million people will publish a book this year.[2] But only a tiny fraction will become bestsellers. Ninety-nine percent of these new books will sell just a few hundred copies during the author's lifetime.

If you want to be an ordinary author with an ordinary book that sells a few hundred copies, then please put this book down now. If you're ready to follow through on your goal and publish a number one bestselling book within the next year, then keep reading!

I want to show you how—with just a little smart strategy and extra effort—you can become a bestselling author with a bestselling book that sells tens of thousands of copies a year and perhaps a million copies over its lifetime.[3]

---

1. Epstein, Joseph. "Think You Have a Book in You? Think Again," *The New York Times*, Sep 2002. https://www.nytimes.com/2002/09/28/opinion/think-you-have-a-book-in-you-think-again.html

2. Errera, Rob. "How Many Books are Published Each Year?" Toner Buzz. https://www.tonerbuzz.com/blog/how-many-books-are-published-each-year/

3. Anderson, Chris. "A Bookselling Tale," *Publisher's Weekly*, Jul 2016. https://www.publishersweekly.com/pw/by-topic/columns-and-blogs/soapbox/article/6153-a-bookselling-tail.html

What—Me? A Bestselling Author? You've Gotta Be Kidding!

Yes, absolutely! You—a number one bestselling author. Look into the future. Leapfrog over all the hassle of writing and publishing your book, and imagine this scenario:

FedEx brings a package to your door. Inside is the very first copy of your newly-released book. You hold it in your hands. This is *your* book with *your* name on the cover. You place it carefully on your bookshelf to admire. You're a legitimate author—you did it!

> "The mass of men lead lives of quiet desperation and go to the grave with the song still in them."
> – Henry David Thoreau

Imagine sharing your new book with family, friends, associates, and customers. Imagine your book climbing the bestseller lists. There is absolutely nothing that compares to that feeling. (I know—I've done it seventeen times and counting.)

From this moment on, when someone asks you what you do, you can add the title "bestselling author" to your curriculum vitae. This title carries such prestige in our society. Trust me—when you drop those words alongside your name, people immediately treat you differently. They raise their eyebrows and tip their heads with an extra modicum of respect. Like there's something special about you.

Do you want to experience that firsthand? It will change your life. If you've ever read or listened to a book that had a profound impact on you, then imagine writing something that does that for someone else. How would that feel?

But wait, we're getting ahead of ourselves! There are twelve steps you need to take before you earn the privilege of using that title and experiencing that satisfaction. Before you read another word, let me ask you a few questions to determine if writing a book—becoming a bestselling author—is realistic for you.

Do I Have What It Takes?

Would you like to know if you have what it takes to accomplish your goal? Put a check mark next to every question in the following list that resonates with you:

As far as your DREAMS go...

_____ Do you feel you have a book in you?

_____ Is writing a book on your bucket list?

_____ Are you an expert in something who senses a need to contribute your expertise?

_____ Do you have a message that you feel "called" or destined to share?

_____ Do you want to be an author? Is earning that title important to you?

_____ Do you want to leave a legacy—a record of your valuable life experiences?

As far as your DOUBTS go...

_____ Have you been putting off writing your book for years—even decades?

_____ Do you question yourself—your abilities, credentials, or writing skills?

_____ Are you just too busy to fit writing a book into your busy schedule?

_____ Do you wonder how to discover your message and put it into words?

_____ Are you afraid of investing time and money and ending up with a book that won't sell?

_____ Do you want to ensure you don't go to your grave with your "song still in you?"

Now, count the checks you made next to the previous twelve questions. If you checked seven or fewer, this book probably isn't for you. Your goals likely won't align with the knowledge and expertise I'm about to share. It will be like I speak French, and you speak Japanese. We won't be on the same page, and you won't be ready to commit to the process outlined within these pages.

If you checked seven or more of these questions, then this book will probably be right up your alley. You "get it"—you're dedicated to becoming an author and are ready to overcome your doubts to get it done!

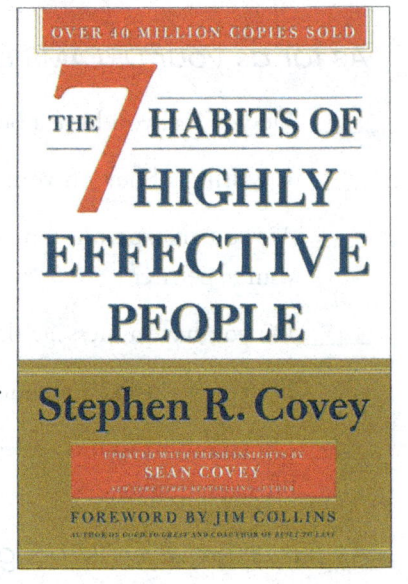

I want to teach you the twelve steps you'll need to take if you want to become a successful author—a bestselling author. But let me ask—when did you first realize that becoming an author was an important goal for you?

For me, it started in 1971 during a university class taught by Stephen R. Covey. Professor Covey was a popular author of several spiritually oriented books in my region. His massive worldwide bestseller, *The 7 Habits of Highly Effective People*, wouldn't hit the bookstores for another eighteen years.

In the class, Professor Covey challenged us to write down our goals. One of the three goals I chose was to write a book. I have no idea why that goal appeared in my mind. I had no special knowledge or experience and no career direction. It was just something I knew intuitively I would do—one day.

It wasn't until seven years later, during my real estate investing heyday, that the thought popped into my head, *It's time to write your book now.* That led me to quit my career as a real estate investment advisor and spend the next year writing my book *Nothing Down: A Proven Program that Shows You How to Buy Real Estate with Little or No Money Down.* Little did I know that writing this one book would change everything!

Nothing Down was published in January of 1980, eventually hitting the number-one spot on the *New York Times* bestseller list. It remained on the list for fifty-six weeks and went on to sell over a million

> "The elevator to success is out of order. You'll have to use the stairs... one step at a time."
>
> – Joe Girard

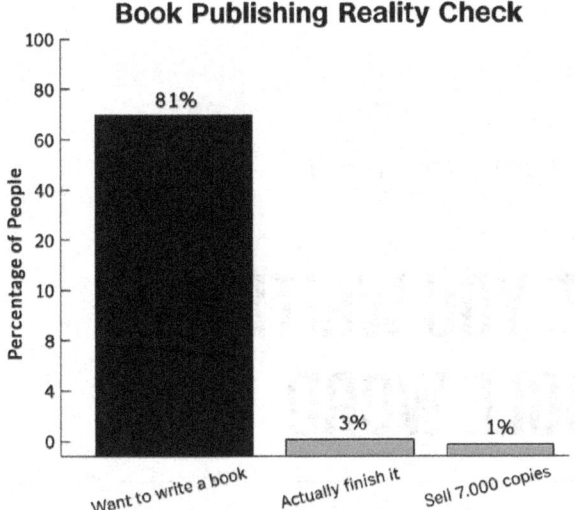

copies and be translated into multiple foreign languages. In fact, it's still generating royalties for me almost fifty years later. So, I know what it's like to dream of being an author and then win the Super Bowl of publishing.

Although I have sold millions of books since and earned millions of dollars in book royalties, please don't assume that your path to success will match mine. I'd rather keep your expectations low—for now. But wouldn't it be nice to make an extra thousand bucks a month in royalties—with gusts of five to ten thousand or more?

Well, with the right guidance, that's entirely realistic. And, if you play your cards right, who knows? Maybe you'll also beat the odds and become an international number-one bestseller. How long will it take? If you're driven and focused, it shouldn't take longer than ninety days. But if you're juggling a job and other responsibilities, I would hope you'd reach the top in a year or less. How does that sound?

> "The best way to predict the future is to create it."
> – Peter Drucker

You could be a number-one bestselling author this year! But not unless you avoid these twelve stupid beginner mistakes I'm about to share.

FREE GIFT: Top Money-Making Niches PDF

If you've been wondering whether your book idea is worth pursuing, I put together a simple PDF to help you decide. It breaks down the most profitable niches right now and includes prompts to help you pick one that sells. You can download it free at AuthorGifts.com or scan the QR code.

"To make mistakes is human; to stumble is commonplace; to be able to laugh at yourself is maturity."

– William Arthur Ward

BEFORE YOU WRITE A SINGLE WORD

Avoid These 12 "Stoopid" Mistakes that Most New Authors Make

So, you want to write a book—congratulations! Join the club. It's a big club. There are millions of wannabe authors. And yet, only a fraction of us will ever follow through on this wish. Still, those who do succeed in writing and publishing are in for a rude shock. Writing a book—the messaging—is the easy part. Selling the book—the marketing—is hard. And to be a bestselling author, you need to do both well.

Although this book is primarily focused on writing non-fiction, how-to books—my specialty—the concepts in this book can also apply to fiction—especially the later chapters that discuss book marketing. If you've already been fortunate to publish your book—in either non-fiction or fiction—but have been disappointed with the resulting sales, then you'll probably recognize some of the pitfalls outlined in this chapter that you've already stumbled into and need to avoid in the future.

If you've dreamed of being an author but haven't gotten around to writing anything yet, then *good*. I'm glad you haven't started because you'll be able to avoid some of these stupid mistakes that beginning authors *always* seem to make. If you do what I suggest, you might just pull off your goal successfully.

But don't expect that your book will make you rich or famous. The average traditionally published author sells less than five thousand copies over the lifetime of the book.[1] The typical self-published author sells a fraction of that. But let's be positive. Assume you finish your book and find a publisher who launches it to the world. Assume you do better than expected by selling five thousand copies over the next five years. How much can you expect to earn in royalties?

> "How do you make a small fortune as an author? First, you start with a large fortune."
> – Unknown

The average traditionally published author receives a royalty of between ten and fifteen percent of the book's cover price. If you publish with Amazon, the royalties can be much higher—thirty-five percent to seventy percent (minus printing costs) depending upon whether your book is digital or physical. Why the disparity? A major publisher assigns you an editor to help with the writing. They create a cover and handle sales and distribution of your book through major booksellers and independent bookstores. Amazon is only one bookstore, albeit the largest bookstore in the world.

This book is designed to share twelve insider secrets on how your book *can* lead to respect, honor, influence, money, and—who knows?—possibly wealth and success. You might even win the bestseller lottery and have your book top the *New York Times* bestseller list. If that's important to you, read on.

Consider the following as a checklist of things *not* to do!

Stupid Mistake #1: Writing Your Autobiography

You want to be a bestselling author, right? If you're like most beginners, you want to start by telling your personal story. It's what you're most familiar with and what comes naturally. You're ready to share the lessons you've learned and the experiences that taught you along the way. This is only natural.

But can we talk?

Nobody cares about your story yet—except you, perhaps a few family members, some close friends, and maybe a few business customers. Sorry. Save your full story for later. With very, very few exceptions, a book about you and your story will never be a bestseller. Let's talk about why.

---

1. Anderson, Chris. "A Bookselling Tale," Publisher's Weekly, Jul 2016. https://www.publishersweekly.com/pw/by-topic/columns-and-blogs/soapbox/article/6153-a-bookselling-tail.html

Most people with successful autobiographies are already rich, famous, or notable. Readers usually pick up their books because they have previous knowledge about the person featured.

What Readers Actually Want
- To solve a problem
- To feel inspired
- To learn something quickly
- To see results in their own life

Unless you're already a well-known, popular figure, *your* first item of business is to show your reader *why* they should care about your message. People read books to gain something from them. If they can't clearly see how your book will improve their own lives, they won't keep reading. If you spend most of your book's content talking about yourself, you'll likely lose your reader, and your book will never fly off the shelves like you hoped.

Instead, your objective is to write a how-to book—a book that *uses* your story to teach readers how to create their own success by implementing your strategies. This is what I call "messaging": crafting a magnetic message that resonates with your reader. I'll show you how to do that in the next chapter titled "Step 1. Your Irresistible Message: The Veins of Gold in the Goldmine of You."

Stupid Mistake #2: Trying to Change the World

I feel sorry for someone who says, "My book is going to change the world." It's highly unlikely to make a scratch, let alone a dent. Don't write to the broadest possible audience!

Writing to everyone means you'll probably reach no one. Don't attempt to change the whole world. Instead, change one slim sliver of the world. Pick a unique "avatar"—or your ideal reader—and write for them alone. In other words, don't go wide—go deep.

Amazon is one of the largest retailers in the world of *everything* you can think of. But they started by capturing the narrow niche of book sales. Once they owned that niche, they broadened their business from there.

> "You're never going to please everyone, and if you do, there's something wrong."
> – Constance Wu

Start by being a big frog in a little pond. Riches are in the niches. What is your niche? In Step 2, I'll explain *why* riches are in the niches, and I'll show you how to identify your niche and *own it*.

Stupid Mistake #3: Getting Writer's Block

Does this scenario seem familiar? You write a few words. You stop. You start again. You stop. You ponder. You fuss. You delete whole sections of what you just wrote. That little voice in your head is shouting, *Who do you think you are? You're not a writer!*

Weeks pass with meager progress. You get frustrated. You begin to doubt yourself. You *thought* you had "a book in you" but you just can't seem to find it. You want the words to flow from your fingers, but you keep getting distracted. This is called writer's block.

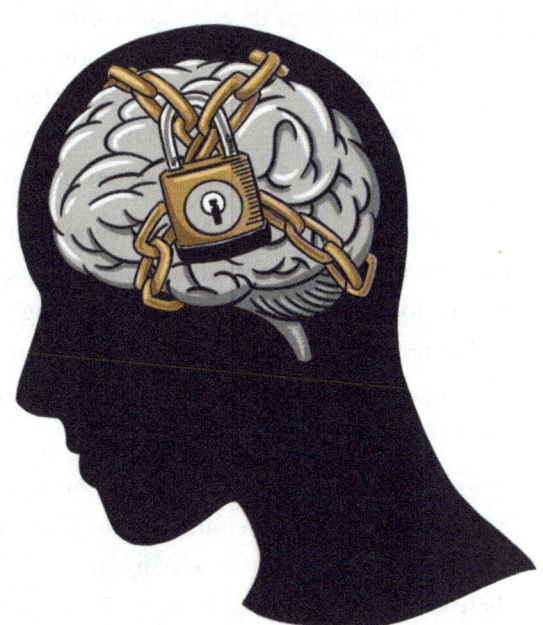

Here's the secret to blasting through writer's block: You need a simple yet powerful visual tool to organize your ideas into a road map or a "success map" because the right picture is worth millions! In Step 3, I'll teach you this efficient process to help you see the big picture and organize your book material into a simple, no-brainer system. Once you learn it, you'll *never* have writer's block again.

Stupid Mistake #4: Being a Cliché

With just one look at a book's cover and table of contents, I can tell whether it's a winner or a loser. I just count the number of boring, clichéd chapter titles. Then, I flip through and read a few pages. If there are clichés everywhere, the book is bound to be a loser—boring.

Can I tell you a secret? Most of today's current bestselling books are not sharing anything new or revolutionary. It's generally the same, basic old ideas repackaged to look like new ideas. Don't believe me? Look in your personal library. If you're like me, you'll find that the books you collect are clumped into four or five broad categories—personal growth, money, cookbooks, biographies, politics, etc.

My library contains fifty books on marketing—a favorite interest of mine. There are also fifty books on all kinds of entrepreneurship, a bunch on personal growth, a collection of biographies, and about five hundred books on spiritual themes. That topic really resonates with me.

> "I would rather read a poorly structured story that has fresh ideas than a tightly structured one with clichés."
> – Douglas Wood

I'm always buying the same book—over and over again—with just a few nuances between the various titles. Why? Because I still like the same things I've always liked, but I want to think about them differently. The key to catching a reader's attention is to present them with a topic that matters to them in a way they haven't considered before.

When I come across books that are likely to be losers, they all start with the basic foundational material, and they all use the same boring ways to describe it. It's rare to find an old subject totally reimagined in new, refreshing ways. But, new and refreshing is the only way to catch the interest of a reader who is likely to buy a book on your chosen topic. The last thing you want the reader to think is, *Been there—read that.*

You want them to think, *Now, this is different. Maybe this has something new to teach me.* Make your content fresh. Make it look new! If you don't, your readers will probably have seen too many other books like yours already. People are addicted to *new, interesting* stuff. So, if you want to stand out, don't look like *old* stuff.

If we ever get the opportunity to work together live in a Zoom class, I won't let you be a cliché.

> "To write a quality cliché, you have to come up with something new."
> – Jenny Holzer

In Step 4, I'll teach you the secrets to building your revolutionary brand in a unique way that will make you stand out.

Stupid Mistake #5: Writing Boring Words

Wandering through a bookstore or scrolling through the book section of Amazon or another prominent book retailer can be a discouraging experience. You roam the area where your wannabe book would be found, and you notice that there are already dozens of books on your topic—some might even have the same title or subtitle you were hoping to use for your own book. You assume it's too late. Someone has already filled your niche. Darn. I guess it's back to your boring job.

Not so fast!

Most of those other books will never sell more than a handful of copies a month. You can leapfrog over *all* of them, land in the top spot, and stay there—because words are *not* just words. You can turn your future book—and the info business that grows out of it—into a cash cow. Other authors might have a head start, but your audience is still out there waiting for you to get your act together and deliver your message. And new readers are born every day.

Besides, you can't copyright a title. So, shake off your disappointment and move forward relentlessly. Don't be discouraged! I'll show you how to make your words so irresistible that readers keep reading and start telling their friends.

In Step 5, you'll learn the secrets of the Word Forge and how to make your words irresistible.

Stupid Mistake #6: Picking a Bland Title with a Weak Promise

Most beginning authors just think up a title—usually a boring or worn-out cliché—and assume it will be a winner. When beginning authors bounce their favorite titles off me, they are often shocked when I tell them their title is a dud—a loser.

You must *not* have a bad title.

I know firsthand how disastrous this mistake can be. Four of my books are number one bestsellers—each selling over a million copies. A few of my books are "worst-sellers"—they have sold a tiny fraction compared to my bestsellers. Do you think their titles have anything to do with their worst-selling status? Absolutely!

The few words that make up your title are what I call "Marketing Words." They attract the reader like a news headline attracts attention. If the headline doesn't pique your interest, you probably won't invest any time reading the article.

> "Here's something to think about: How come you never see a headline like 'Psychic Wins Lottery'?"
> – Jay Leno

It's the same with a book. Your title must be difficult to ignore, and your subtitle must make a clear promise. Even your chapter titles must be attention grabbers. Don't pick a boring title with a weak promise!

In Step 6, you'll learn about the power of a bestselling title and how to incorporate it into an unforgettable book cover. Working together, they'll be the hook of all hooks.

I'll show you how to "hook 'em."

Stupid Mistake #7: Looking Like Self-Published Crap

They say you can't judge a book by its cover. What nonsense! Of *course* you can judge a book by its cover. *All* books are judged by their covers. Bookstore owners will tell you that most of a book's success can be attributed to the cover. The most important words are found in the book's title, but it doesn't stop there. The rest of the cover is important, too. Do you want to slave late nights and early mornings for months on the message inside of your book just to have the *outside* appearance shut the door to your future without people reading a single word?

If most of your future success can be linked to your cover, then you'd better take it seriously. Your cover is prime real estate. Don't make it look like a slum! That's just plain stupid. If I ever have an opportunity to discuss your book design with you, I won't let you release your message to the world with a cheap, self-published-looking cover.

Now, about the inside of the book.

When you open most self-published books, you can immediately tell they haven't been published professionally. They don't look right. The layout is off, the font is off, the spacing is off, the illustrations are off, and it just feels like someone didn't care enough to do it correctly. There is a *flood* of bad self-published books pouring into the world. In 2021, Bowker issued over two million ISBNs for self-published books.[2] I'm not railing against *all* self-published books. Some of the biggest titles in the industry were first launched as self-published books. But they looked professional, they had great titles, and they were backed by smart marketing.

You can probably tell that a shoddy self-published book is my *pet peeve*. This is your legacy—don't let it look like self-published crap. Make it a book you can be proud of. It's easier than you think to ensure your book has the right look inside and out. In Step 7, you'll learn how to create an impressive layout so the insides of your book are "sticky" and keep your reader interested.

Stupid Mistake #8: Forgetting to Build a Database

A book is a Trojan horse. It looks like a book, but hidden inside is a small army of soldiers with only one task: to capture the name and email of the reader. If you don't have a way to gather your readers' names, you lose the opportunity to communicate with them and to continue influencing their lives.

My first book sold a million copies. I didn't have a way to capture names because I didn't know I should ask my publisher to include a way for readers to connect with me—a million dollar mistake. If I'd had the names of those readers, I could have invited them to my seminars to learn more. People are addicted to information. They always want more. If you don't offer it, they'll go get it from someone else.

Not gathering names from my first book meant I threw away millions of dollars in ongoing revenue from readers who would have loved to form a relationship

---

2. Milliot, Jim. "Self Publishing Is Thriving, According to Bowker Report," *Publishers Weekly*. Feb 17, 2023. https://www.publishersweekly.com/pw/by-topic/industry-news/publisher-news/article/91574-self-publishing-is-thriving-according-to-bowker-report.html

with me as the author. So don't forget to build a database. In Step 8, I'll show you how to build a database and "opt-in" to wealth.

Stupid Mistake #9: Thinking Your Book Is Just a Book

Around four million new books will be published globally this year,[3] including the two million self-published books I've already mentioned. They join the millions of books that were published in previous years. As we've discussed previously, the vast majority of these new books will only sell a few hundred copies after years of suffering. The authors think their books will be their path to respect and financial freedom, but instead, their dreams will be dashed.

"I'm writing a book about reverse psychology. Please don't buy it."
– Unknown

For most, it's a path to frustration, disappointment, and some extra debts they'll have to get a second job to pay off. Not cool. Why does it end this way for so many authors? Because they thought of their book as "just" a book.

So, burn this into your brain: A book is not just a book—it's a business.

When you're writing your "how to" book, you should envision the long-term relationship you're building with your reader blossoming into lifetime streams of income. Most likely, your book alone won't make you rich. But if you position your book properly, it will become the gateway into an info business. That business can then open doors to a lifestyle that most only dream of but few achieve. Besides, if you're in business, a book can help you double your income. If you don't have a book to boost your bottom line, you're throwing money away.

In Step 9, we'll discuss twelve ways to earn multiple streams of income from the information in your book. I call it the Succession Stack. If you use one, you'll soon be earning one hundred dollars for every word you write. A book is never just a book. A book can be a gateway to anything you want.

Stupid Mistake #10: Being Afraid to Look Like a Fool

Are you afraid of what people might think if your plans to become an author don't go as planned? Are you worried you might look like a fool to the world?

---

3. Talbot, Dean. "Number of Books Published Per Year." WordsRated, Feb 2, 2022. https://wordsrated.com/number-of-books-published-per-year-2021/

Are you concerned your readers will notice every typo or grammatical error in your published work and think less of you?

Get over it. If you want your book to be a bestseller, you need to get comfortable broadcasting your message. You'll be exposing yourself—warts and all. Typos, grammatical errors, repetitions, outright falsehoods, and stupidities included. Yup. That list probably created a few more fears you hadn't even thought of yet!

> "Life has no remote... get up and change it yourself!"
> – Mark A. Cooper

Actually, there has never been a better time to showcase your imperfections. It's called radical transparency, "being real," showing your humanity, or however else you prefer to say it.

If you're not immersed in social media, maybe this will get your greed glands going. What if every word you wrote in a social media post earned you ten dollars a word? Would that incentivize you to start writing? Or if you're shy of shooting some video, what if every minute of video you posted earned you one thousand dollars? Wouldn't you grab your camera right now?

> "Your harshest critic is always going to be yourself. Don't ignore that critic but don't give it more attention than it deserves."
> – Michael Ian Black

Are you nervous about spending money to advertise on Facebook or Instagram? What if every one hundred dollars you spent on advertising would rebound three hundred dollars right back to you immediately? We call that 3X. Would you shell out the money then? If I could show you how to spend one hundred dollars on Facebook ads and earn three hundred dollars back, how much money would you want to spend? In Step 10, we'll discuss how to create "Your Bestselling Buzz" and utilize free and paid ways to expose yourself.

Stupid Mistake #11: Procrastinating

Are you a procrastinator? Have you been putting off writing your book for years and years? You know you need to write it—it's on your bucket list. Why can't you get it done?

Let's face it—you're likely overwhelmed with opportunity. You have too much on your plate already without adding "write my book" to your to-do list.

But we've already established that this is an important life goal, so you've got to get it done. You need to prioritize. Learn to say "no" to something, like that extra hour of sleep, that TV program, or that leisurely lunch hour. Get those words down—one way or another.

Every author has had the same challenge, and they pulled it off. They got their name on that book—they're published! But you don't *just* want to be a published author. You want to be a number one bestselling author by investing as little as thirty minutes a day!

In Step 11, I'll show you how to stop procrastinating and make it happen. You'll learn how to launch your book to bestseller status on the #1 bookstore in the world—Amazon.

Every day you wait, your story fades.

Stupid Mistake #12: Thinking Small

This advice seems contradictory. I told you earlier not to expect your book to make you rich or famous. At first, the royalties can seem small, but if you follow my advice and create a marketing platform with your own growing database, your little book emporium can become an empire pretty quickly. I'll show you how to make this happen in "Step 12. Your Exponential Scalability: Adding Zeros."

Following a Smarter Path

This book is designed to show you how to avoid these twelve stupid mistakes. These are the major biggies, but there's far more to learn about escaping these pitfalls, and I'm eager to share all of it with you.

Ordinary authors write ordinary words to deliver information to their ordinary readers. As I said before, that's fine if you want to write a book that sells a typical number of copies. If that's your goal, find a traditional publisher. I've heard that only one in ten thousand manuscripts sent to publishers

> "The future depends on what you do today."
> – *Mahatma Gandhi*

actually makes it to the bookstore. Those odds are not good, so I wouldn't recommend going that route—at least not yet. ☺

You could choose to self-publish your book instead. It's not that hard to upload a book to Amazon. But since the average self-published book only sells a few hundred copies, this isn't likely to help you reach your goal, either.

Or you can hire one of the many "vanity" publishers who charge from ten thousand to fifty thousand dollars to publish your book. Lots of people go this route. I call these publishers pseudo-publishers. They do the normal publishing tasks—editing, organizing, designing, and distributing your book to bookstores online and offline—and they charge you big dollars for the privilege of getting your name on the cover. They might even help you reach the number one spot in your narrow niche on Amazon—for one day. But thereafter, it's up to you to continue selling it—not smart.

You've got big potential. Stop riding small ideas.

There's got to be a better way—and there is! If you follow the twelve steps I've outlined in the remainder of this book, I'll see you at the top of the bestseller lists soon, and you'll possibly be enjoying streams of income to last a lifetime. Now, let's get started with Step 1.

FREE GIFT: New Author Cheatsheet

To help you avoid the most common (and expensive) mistakes new authors make, I created a one-page cheatsheet that walks you through the right steps to take—and the traps to dodge. Grab your copy at AuthorGifts.com or scan the QR code.

"The scariest moment is always just before you start."
— Stephen King, On Writing

STEP 1. YOUR IRRESISTIBLE MESSAGE

The Veins of Gold in the Gold Mine of You

Everyone has something to offer the world. What's your area of expertise or talent? You might think you don't have any knowledge valuable enough to contribute, but you're wrong. In this chapter, we'll explore your unique skills and abilities—your veins of gold—that you may not yet recognize.

You might ask, "Why is knowing my unique skills useful if I'm not supposed to write a book about myself?" That's easy—your veins of gold are not about telling your personal history and how you've learned everything you know. You can include some of those elements in your book, but they can't be the *subject* of your book.

If you're a little disappointed by this piece of advice, remember what it's going to feel like when your newly printed book arrives, and you've gained the title of bestselling author. Remember—people will only care about your story if it can help them directly somehow. Your goal is to write a how-to book using your unique knowledge. This may include applicable elements of your journey, but your book's focus should always be your reader and their needs, *not* yourself.

The first step in becoming an author—let alone a bestselling author—is deciding what to write about. Maybe you already have your book idea. Maybe you're absolutely clear about your message. Maybe you've been sharing it for years, and you just haven't put it down in book form.

If so, congratulations.

More than likely, you've been thinking about several book ideas, and you're trying to narrow them down to find the very best idea with the highest bestseller probability. Or maybe, you have *no* idea what to write about, and you just sense—like I did—that you're destined to write a book.

No matter which scenario matches your situation, you will gain insight and direction for your writing journey by spending a few minutes exploring your unique skills and natural talents.

Discovering Your Hidden Value

Next, I'll give you a few simple tests, and within minutes, we'll uncover together at least five marketable skills you possess that will be ideal book topics. These are your veins of gold. With the right coaching, you can turn several of these skill sets into a book that someone in the world will want to buy. Then, you can turn these buried assets into info products that can generate multiple streams of income. (Hey, that's the title of one of *my* books!)

There's gold in your story. You just have to dig for it.

For example, suppose a friend of yours—let's call her Barbara—has a lifelong weight problem. Finally, after serious research and experimentation, she discovers her own revolutionary way to lose weight—and it works for everyone who uses it!

The weight just falls off. Would this knowledge be valuable to share? Could she turn this into her own, unique weight-loss book? Certainly.

Suppose a middle-aged woman—let's call her Judy—lives in Barbara's city. Judy is getting ready for her big thirtieth high school reunion. She has procrastinated prioritizing her health, and now she desperately wants to lose thirty pounds in ninety days. She goes online and discovers Barbara's book about her astounding weight loss system. And Barbara's book is *free*! Judy orders it immediately. The book is digital and is delivered to her reading device within seconds. She devours it and loves it! Barbara's book offers some guaranteed advanced training for only one hundred dollars. Might this overweight woman with a looming deadline be willing to pay an extra one hundred dollars for Barbara's complete "secret" system?

Is that a "yes"? Duh!

Do you possess untapped information or skills like that? Absolutely! It's already in you, waiting to be excavated.

When I explain this, people immediately hit me with their "yabuts": "Yeah, but—I'm not famous. What information could I sell that a stranger would want to buy?"

I challenge these yabuts by asking, "Don't you know *something* that someone in the world would like to know? Don't you have at least one thing you're good at—one thing that you could teach someone if you were paid to do so?"

I call these areas of expertise your "Piece of Cake" topics. When you ask an expert to use their skill, they often say, "No problem—piece of cake." "Piece of Cake" is my fun way of representing the things you already know how to do—things that come easily to you that are second nature."

> "The only way to do great work is to love what you do."
> – Steve Jobs

What's your Piece of Cake? If someone paid you one hundred dollars to pick your brain on a skill that you've mastered, would you be willing to answer their questions? You'd probably give your advice away for free.

Remember what it took for you to acquire your specific knowledge or skill. It required hours of study and practice to learn and master it. You read books, completed courses, and watched videos. You spent money and time acquiring those skills. If someone could have shown you a shortcut before you started, would

> "Americans have been conditioned to respect newness, whatever it costs them."
>
> – *John Updike*

it have been worth one hundred dollars to you then? This knowledge could have saved you countless hours of study and research and could have helped you avoid many stupid mistakes.

Well, people are googling right now for the information that you've already acquired. Why can't you offer your solutions to the world for a fee? Isn't what you know worth at least one hundred dollars to somebody somewhere in the world?

"Yeah, but—I don't have a degree in the things I want to teach. Won't people know I'm a fraud?"

Breaking News! This just in—it's the 2020s! People value skills and actionable information far above degrees and diplomas. You don't need professional credentials. You just need information that works!

"Yeah, but—*everybody* knows how to do what I know how to do."

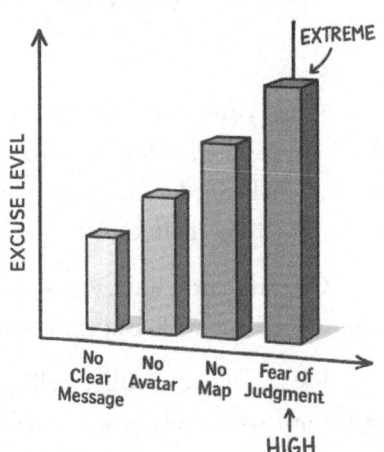

That's what I used to think about buying real estate using none of my own money. It was so second nature to me that I thought everyone had figured it out. I'm glad I followed my hunch to teach that very first one-hundred-dollar seminar. The book that was spawned out of that seminar became a number one *New York Times* bestseller and has sold a million copies!

I guarantee that you are a book-worthy expert at *something*. Maybe you have a forty-year marriage in an age where more than half of marriages fail. Maybe you have six-pack abs in your sixties. Maybe you've learned how to travel the world for less than a hundred dollars a day.

For example, a beginning author, Shinjuke Fujihiro, came to a Bestselling Author training I taught in Tokyo. I showed him how to turn his knowledge into a book called *How to Recover from Poverty*. It has already gone through four printings with more than ten thousand copies sold. It climbed to number two in the biggest and most famous bookstores in Japan, and it became a major lead generator for his online financial coaching business.

A few years ago, I was teaching a group of wannabe authors. I told them that they all possessed valuable skills and knowledge worthy of a book. To prove my point, I challenged them to earn one thousand dollars in the following twenty-four hours by selling their knowledge or expertise to somebody—anybody.

One student, Linda, was a part-time artist and painter. She was trying to sell her paintings to the world but with limited success—the definition of the starving artist.

I said, "Linda, you're selling the wrong thing. Instead of selling physical paintings, why don't you try selling your expertise on *how* to paint?" This had never crossed her mind, and she doubted that anyone would pay her one thousand dollars to learn how to paint.

I challenged her to try: "Send an email to your friend network and offer to teach one of them a sixteen-week course—over the Internet—on how to paint. The fee? One thousand dollars. But you only have one slot available."

> "Success is not something you can hide. Did you ever know a successful man who didn't tell you about it?"
>
> - *Kin Hubbard.*

Within twenty-four hours of sending that email, one of her friends, Debra Jo, responded excitedly, "Teach *me*. I've always wanted to learn how to paint!"

Linda was shocked at how easy it was!

Once Linda had "proof of concept," her next step was to write a book that she could give away for free. (For *free*!? Yes. Relax—I'll explain in a later chapter. ☺)

Wannabe painters are everywhere. Linda's free book would be an easy introduction to Linda's ongoing art classes taught online. Ironically, by giving away her book, she would find it easier to sell her paintings. Her growing list of students would be honored to have one of her paintings adorning a wall in their homes. Her apprentices would become ambassadors to let others know about their mentor's artwork. She would go from a starving artist to a financially secure and respected mentor.

> "Style is not how you write. It is how you do not write like anyone else."
> – *Charles Ghigna*

Yes, if Linda can do this, you can too.

"Yeah, but—I don't think my information is worth even ten dollars, let alone a thousand."

Actually, your information is worth a *lot more* than one thousand dollars—you're just not aware of how to market it. That's why you're reading this book.

"Yeah, but—my knowledge is so specialized, only one in a million people would want it."

One in a million? There are more than *eight billion* people on the planet. One in a million is *eight thousand* people! I can show you how accessing this tiny slice of humanity with your future book could generate multiple streams of income and financial freedom.

"Yeah, but—I'm not tech savvy."

"Yeah, but—I'm not good at selling."

"Yeah, but—I don't know the first thing about writing."

"Yeah, but—I'm too busy to fit this into my schedule."

Stop making excuses! Kill your yabuts!

You are reading these words because you've got a book in you. *This* book will show you how to get *that* book out of you and into the world.

When you take an inventory of your current skills and talents—your intellectual capital—there is no question that you know things some people anxiously want to know. As your mentor, I can help you narrow down your intellectual inventory into one simple list—your "Piece of Cake."

Finding Your Piece of Cake

Your Piece of Cake refers to the few skills that are easy, enjoyable, and almost effortless for you to do—things you can nearly do with your eyes closed. These are the areas of talent and expertise that set you apart. To discover them, I take students through a simple 230-question Piece of Cake process. Everyone who completes this assessment identifies at least five valuable areas of expertise or skill that could easily be converted into a book.

> "Respect your efforts, respect yourself. Self-respect leads to self-discipline. When you have both firmly under your belt, that's real power."
>
> – *Clint Eastwood*

The Piece of Cake assessment is segmented into twenty areas of competence, which are listed below. Put a mental check mark next to each category in which you possess knowledge or expertise:

___ Agriculture/Horticulture
___ Animal Care/Health
___ Art/Design
___ Business/Financial
___ Cosmetology/Esthetics
___ Craftsmanship
___ Family Care/Studies
___ Food Sciences
___ Health/Fitness
___ Home Maintenance/Care
___ Humanitarianism
___ Intellectual Skill
___ Language
___ Performance
___ Physical Skills/Athleticism
___ Scholarship
___ Science
___ Social/Cultural Arts
___ Spirituality
___ Technology

In my case, I've written eleven books about finances. That's my specialty. I've written one book in the category of intellectual skill. I have zero expertise in the areas of physical skills, agriculture/horticulture, animal care, or food sciences.

But I do have family care skills—I've been happily married for forty-eight years. As for language skills, I do a lot of public speaking, and I speak fluent French and passable Tahitian, which I learned while serving as a Christian missionary in French Polynesia. I have additional intellectual skills (mentoring and teaching) and spiritual skills in the form of wisdom gleaned over a lifetime.

> "In order to be irreplaceable, one must always be different."
>
> – *Coco Chanel*

Therefore, I have at least six *other* types of books in me, if I were so inclined. How many books do you have in you? If you don't feel you have skills in many of these twenty areas, don't worry! You likely possess more skills than you think you do. Complete the Piece of Cake checklist in the following pages to evaluate your personal skills, and you'll probably be surprised!

The 230-Question Piece of Cake Checklist

How do you discover your unique skills and talents? On the following pages is a list of skills and abilities segmented into the twenty competence categories previously outlined. Scan down this list and ask yourself which of these items you would have an interest in teaching or coaching to an interested "newbie."

This list is meant to help you brainstorm about the many skills you possess that you may not realize. It's not an exhaustive list of every topic imaginable, but it should get you thinking. Put a check next to each topic in which you feel you have some helpful knowledge:

Agriculture/Horticulture

____ container gardening
____ crop farming
____ fertilizing techniques
____ flower gardening
____ organic farming
____ pest control

____ ranching
____ tree care
____ urban agriculture
____ vegetable gardening
____ weed control

Animal Care/Health/Studies

____ adoption/fostering
____ animal nutrition
____ boarding
____ breeding
____ cats/dogs
____ equestrianism
____ fish/aquarist work

____ grooming
____ livestock
____ reptiles
____ small animals
____ training
____ veterinary skills
____ zookeeping

Art/Design

____ architecture
____ ceramics
____ drawing
____ fashion design
____ filmmaking
____ floral design
____ graphic design

____ industrial design
____ interior design
____ painting
____ photography/videography
____ sculpture
____ songwriting

Business/Financial

____ accounting
____ advertising
____ banking
____ business management
____ economics
____ finances
____ investments
____ legal expertise

____ marketing
____ organizational development
____ real estate
____ retail
____ sales
____ taxes

Cosmetology/Esthetics

- ____ cosmetics
- ____ hairstyling
- ____ manicures/pedicures
- ____ piercing
- ____ relaxation
- ____ salon/spa management
- ____ skincare
- ____ spa treatments

Craftsmanship

- ____ construction
- ____ crochet
- ____ glasswork
- ____ handicrafts
- ____ jewelry
- ____ knitting
- ____ leatherwork
- ____ macramé
- ____ manufacturing
- ____ mechanics
- ____ metalworking
- ____ needlework
- ____ textiles
- ____ woodworking

Family Care/Studies

- ____ adoption
- ____ blended families
- ____ child development
- ____ dating
- ____ divorce
- ____ family finances
- ____ family history
- ____ family recreation/trip planning
- ____ family scheduling
- ____ intimacy
- ____ marriage therapy
- ____ meal planning
- ____ parenting
- ____ relationship coaching
- ____ retirement planning
- ____ scrapbooking/personal history

Food Sciences

- ____ baking
- ____ butchering
- ____ cake decorating
- ____ catering
- ____ cooking
- ____ food safety
- ____ food chemistry
- ____ grocery
- ____ recipe creation
- ____ restaurant management
- ____ wine/chocolate tasting

(Continued)

Health/Fitness

____ addiction recovery
____ counseling
____ detox
____ disease prevention
____ health care
____ hospice
____ mental health
____ nursing
____ nutrition science
____ physical fitness
____ physical therapy
____ physical training
____ psychology
____ recuperation
____ weight loss/weight gain
____ weight training

Home Maintenance/Care

____ cleaning
____ decluttering
____ decorating
____ home repair/maintenance
____ home security
____ organization
____ renovation
____ simplifying/minimizing

Humanitarianism

____ advocacy
____ charitable outreach
____ community support
____ disaster relief
____ fundraising
____ nonprofit work
____ service opportunities
____ volunteering

Intellectual Skill

____ critical thinking
____ leadership
____ life coaching
____ mentoring
____ problem solving
____ seminars
____ strategy
____ teaching
____ time management

Language

____ editing
____ grammar
____ linguistics
____ literary study
____ public speaking
____ translation
____ writing

Performance

- ____ acrobatics
- ____ comedy
- ____ dance
- ____ drama
- ____ improv
- ____ music
- ____ theater

Physical Skills/Athleticism

- ____ aviation
- ____ body building
- ____ coaching
- ____ competitive sports
- ____ hiking/backpacking
- ____ hunting
- ____ martial arts
- ____ military training
- ____ obstacle courses
- ____ self defense
- ____ skilled driving
- ____ stunt work
- ____ team sports
- ____ water sports
- ____ wilderness survival
- ____ winter sports
- ____ yoga

Scholarship

- ____ education
- ____ effective study techniques
- ____ geography
- ____ history
- ____ mathematics
- ____ philosophy
- ____ research
- ____ scholarships/financial aid
- ____ teaching
- ____ tutoring

Science

- ____ anatomy
- ____ astronomy
- ____ biology
- ____ chemistry
- ____ earth science
- ____ physics
- ____ physiology

(Continued)

Social/Cultural Arts

_____ civic involvement
_____ communications
_____ etiquette
_____ entertaining
_____ event planning
_____ hospitality/vacation rentals
_____ hosting
_____ journalism
_____ mentoring
_____ politics
_____ social media
_____ social studies
_____ travel/tourism

Spirituality

_____ building whole-hearted connections
_____ following intuition
_____ increasing spiritual capacity
_____ journaling
_____ meditation
_____ mindfulness
_____ organizing spiritual meetings/retreats
_____ prayer
_____ religious studies
_____ spiritual writing
_____ strengthening wisdom
_____ study of sacred texts

Technology

_____ app creation
_____ artificial intelligence
_____ automotive design/repair
_____ coding
_____ computer science
_____ cybersecurity
_____ digital marketing
_____ engineering
_____ gaming
_____ home entertainment systems
_____ programming
_____ software design
_____ technical writing
_____ telecommunications
_____ web development

Now, scan the list again and consider any additional topics that may have popped into your mind. Write down the top five subjects that you would consider teaching someone, if properly compensated. Do you have a desire to write a book or create a course about any of these subjects?

1. _____
2. _____
3. _____
4. _____
5. _____

Narrow your list of five down to your top three possible book subjects.

1. _____
2. _____
3. _____

Okay, you've identified three skills that would be appropriate for a book. It's time for the Low-Hanging Fruit exercise. Your Low-Hanging Fruit represents the very few types of knowledge unique to you—with the highest probability for you to create a fast, easy, *sustainable*, long-term stream of income.

Your Low-Hanging Fruit

I call your most expert topic your Low-Hanging Fruit because there are so many things about it that you don't need to learn. You're already there. You're ripe, ready to be picked. You could talk about it endlessly. You like it. You're good at it. However, it's a little deeper than a Piece of Cake. You have a passion for it. It fits your values. It's important to you. It's something you stand for—or something you *won't* stand for. It feels like it's part of your purpose in life—your destiny.

You could write a book about a multitude of subjects. For example, I enjoy watching movies with my wife. But I don't see myself writing books about movies. I'm just an amateur. I don't obsess about plots and camera angles. However, some people are born to obsess about movies. Writing a book about it would be a natural extension of their passion for the cinema.

There are millions of unique ways to live a life and earn money, but there are fewer paths that fit *your* innate passions, talents, and values. When you think about the books you could write, do they align with who you are? You don't want to write a book just to make some extra money. You want a book that represents the real you—the authentic you—the purposeful you. When you are in alignment with your core passions and talents, you tap into a source of energy and drive that is often inexhaustible. It just feels right. That's why it's your Low-Hanging Fruit. It's what you were born to share.

So here are twelve questions to ask yourself as you grapple with discovering your Low-Hanging Fruit.

Passion

What do you love to do?

___

What excites you about life?

___

What is your secret ambition?

___

Talent

What are you especially good at?

___

What are your strengths?

___

Where have you succeeded?

___

Values

What is important to you?

_____

If money was no object, what would you do?

_____

What would you be willing to risk your life for?

_____

Destiny

What do you feel you were born to do?

_____

In what area are *you* uniquely situated to make a difference?

_____

What does the Universe want you to do?

_____

As you ponder these questions, notice if there might be a common theme that runs through them. For example, my Low-Hanging Fruit relates to success in financial subjects and real estate investing, but I've also created multiple streams of income from my many other businesses. So, that's why *Multiple Streams of Income* is one of my most popular books. I've also had multiple bestselling books, thus the subject of this book. These books fit my talents (skills), my passions (making money, entrepreneurship, and writing books), my values (freedom, independence, and contribution) and destiny. I believe I was born to do this. I can't see myself *not* teaching these things. This is who I am. This is my song.

> "Nothing is impossible—the word itself says 'I'm possible!'"
> – *Audrey Hepburn*

What's your song?

Which of the three book subjects you've narrowed down do you feel inspired by, drawn to, or "called" to create? Ask yourself, "Which *one* of these three subjects am I the *most* passionate about teaching?" Imagine that you could teach this to millions of people but would not be paid a single dollar for your work. Would you still want to do it?

That's the one!

Your psychological compensation is the joy of knowing you can improve lives by sharing your knowledge and skill. But there can also be financial compensation as well.

Write down your final subject below:

The subject of my bestselling book will be...

_____

_____

How does this feel? Can you imagine gifting this book to family, friends, and associates? Imagine it in a bookstore or on your bookshelf. Does this book feel like part of your legacy? Does it help your reader have a better life? Does it bring some extra money into *your* life? Do you feel that this is part of your destiny?

> "Convince yourself that you are working in clay, not marble—on paper, not eternal bronze; Let that first sentence be as stupid as it wishes."
> – Jacques Barzun

These are profound questions. But don't think too deeply about it. Aligning with your authentic message can be a lifetime pursuit. Frankly, your first book may just be a way to practice as you discover your voice and learn how to find your audience. Then again, your first book may be a blockbuster like my first bestseller. Or you might hit the jackpot like novelist Bryce Courtney.

At a writer's conference, I heard writer Bryce Courtney tell the story of writing his first fiction book. He'd heard that an author's first book is usually terrible. So, he assumed that his first book would just be a practice book—a throwaway. And that's exactly what he did. He wrote the complete manuscript, tied a string around it, and used it as a doorstop in his house. His daughter saw this unusual doorstop and asked about it. He said it was just his "practice book." She asked for permission to read it and was astounded by the story. She convinced him to publish it. It became the international bestseller *The Power of One*, which has been translated into eighteen languages and has sold over eight million copies.

Most beginning authors hope that their first book becomes a bestseller, but the odds of that happening are extremely small. I hope to guide you through the steps to dramatically improve your odds. One important way to do this is through effective messaging.

Crafting Effective Messaging

The first step in messaging is to decide your subject, which you've already done. The next step is to decide the basic *essence* of your message. Write your book's message below:

My book's message is...

_____
_____
_____
_____
_____
_____
_____

For example, the book you are now reading is about how to become a bestselling author. That is the basic description.

The next step would be to say the message in a new, enticing way that would cause someone to say, "Really? How can I get a copy of that book?" This is called your elevator pitch. How can you make your pitch sexy, provocative, compelling, captivating, or exciting?

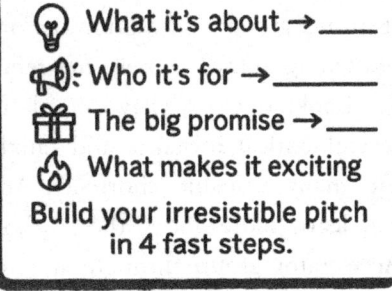

A good pitch takes a little longer to develop. It's something you test out every time you have a chance. If someone asks you what your book is about, what would you say? Practice different ways of saying it. Eventually, you'll come up with a way to explain your topic that grabs attention and keeps it. Once you've discovered it, write down you're your irresistible message below:

My elevator pitch is...

_____

_____

_____

_____

_____

If you need additional tips and feedback about how to do this, consider joining my Authors Accelerator class. In the class, I work with a small number of students on a live Zoom call to identify their Pieces of Cake and select from those the perfect Low-Hanging Fruit for their first book. You can continue as a solitary writer—as I did. Or you can join a support group of writers like my Authors Accelerator.

At the beginning of my career, I wish I'd had access to a brainstorming group led by a number one bestselling author to help me refine my book. It would have saved me several critical mistakes and taught me many valuable shortcuts. You can learn more about the Authors Accelerator group through my free author seminar, which you can sign up for at authorsummits.com.

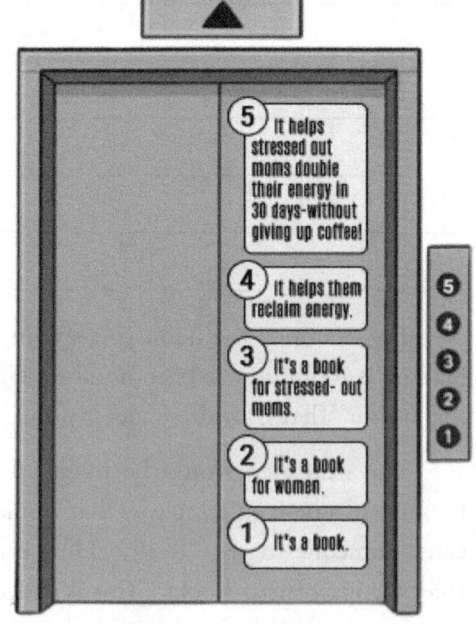

Building Your Elevator Pitch.

So, now you've discovered your subject—your Low-Hanging Fruit. You've written your basic message, or what you want to teach.

Next, go to the book section of the number one bookstore in the world—Amazon. Look at the current bestseller lists. The authors of these books are your peers. Imagine your book appearing on this list, and smile—I'll show you how to make it happen!

Now that you've chosen a topic and learned how to make your message irresistible, you've completed the first step. In Step 2, I'll help you find your ideal audience.

FREE GIFT: Low-Hanging Fruit Finder Worksheet

Not sure what your book should be about? Here is an exercise that helps you uncover your best—and most profitable—idea. It's the same one I use in coaching calls. Just go to AuthorGifts.com or scan the code.

"Even the worst message sent to the right people will do better than the most brilliant message sent to the wrong people."

– Drayton Bird

STEP 2: YOUR PERFECT AVATAR

Riches Are In the Niches

If you plan to publish a bestseller, you're probably assuming your book needs to appeal to as many people as possible. How else will you sell millions of copies? If this is what you're thinking right now, you need to change your goal. Writing a bestseller isn't about speaking to everyone. It's about finding a distinct community of readers who want or need your message.

As I shared in the second chapter, it's a stupid mistake to write to the broadest possible audience. I know that this goes against the prevailing wisdom. You'd think a larger audience (such as everyone on the planet) would generate more total sales. But it's just the opposite. Riches are in the niches.

In other words, you need to hone into a specialized market. Don't go *wide* by trying to catch the broadest amount of attention, go *deep* by capitalizing on the needs and desires of an audience who is already interested in your topic. The more your message speaks to a specific audience, the more that audience feels that the book was written precisely for them. This will transform you into a big frog in a little pond instead of a little frog in a pond that's already teeming with competition.

Narrow your target to a specific person belonging to a precise demographic such as age, sex, race, family relationship, interest, hobby, affiliation, geography, job description, etc. Keep this person in mind as you write. Imagine where they live. Imagine what they do for a living. Imagine what problems they're dealing with. What are their hobbies? Imagine them reading your book and finding inspiration for a better life through your words. Give your reader a name. Your words will resonate better if you feel as if you know them personally and you speak directly to them when you write.

When you understand your reader this way, you can target your advertising to exactly the right audience—what they read, what they watch, where they are surfing to find their information, and what social media they follow. The broader the message (generally speaking) the weaker the reach. The rays of the sun are more powerful when focused through a magnifying glass onto a single point on a piece of paper. Like Zig Ziglar used to say, "Don't become a wandering generality. Be a meaningful specific."

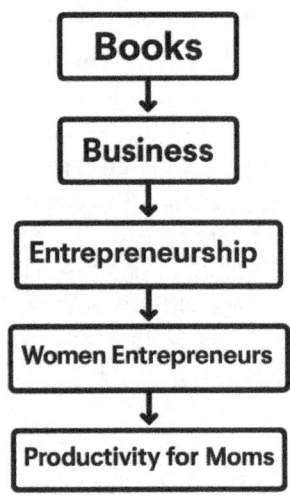

When ordering from a mail-order catalog, do you call the toll-free number and say, "There are so many amazing items in your catalog that I have a hard time deciding. Just send me something you think I might like."

No! You get very specific. You tell them the page number in the catalog, the item number, the size, the color, how to ship it, and the credit card number. You get minutely specific. You need to think the same when ordering up your ideal book reader.

Ask yourself, "Who is my ideal book reader?" In the book business, we call that person your "avatar." In addition to demographics, what are the distinct characteristics that you'd love your ideal avatar to have?

Marketing guru Gary Halbert posed this question in one of his newsletters: "If you and I both owned a hamburger stand, and we were in a contest to see who could sell the most hamburgers, what advantages would you most like to have on your side to help you win?" Most of us would want the advantage of a better burger, a better location, or a better price.

> "I think one of the bigger lessons the Internet has taught us is that 'niche' or 'subculture' are a lot bigger than anyone ever thought."
> – Warren Ellis

Then, he continues, "I'll give you every single advantage you have asked for. I, myself, only want one advantage and, if you will give it to me, I will (when it comes to selling burgers) whip the pants off all of you!" What advantage is that you might ask? He says, "The only advantage I want is a Starving Crowd!"[1] This is Marketing 101.

As a book marketer, you need to find readers who are starving. What does that mean? It means finding a reader who has an *urgent* problem and/or a *burning* passion. They are not just curious or interested—they are famished, ravenous, or obsessed.

Urgent Problems

Your ideal avatar has an urgent need to solve a pressing problem. Imagine your reader roaming through a bookstore or googling right now to find answers to an immediate problem such as intense back pain, an ugly divorce, a pending bankruptcy, a cancer diagnosis, or a desperate need to find meaning in life.

They have broken through procrastination. They've breached the pain threshold. They have a searing toothache, and they're looking for a dentist. Their pain has moved them to act. They want a solution today—now—ASAP! They notice your book. Does it promise to solve their urgent problem? If it does, they'll buy it.

---

1. Halbert, Gary. "The Gary Halbert Letter," https://thegaryhalbertletter.com/newsletters/direct_marketing_to_a_starving_crowd.htm

Passionate Desires

Your ideal avatar has an unreasonable interest in a subject—like a love of architecture, a drive to lower their golf handicap, an obsession with a particular sports team, a food fetish, a fascination with finances, or a zeal for travel. They are not just passively interested. They are actively, aggressively seeking to learn more.

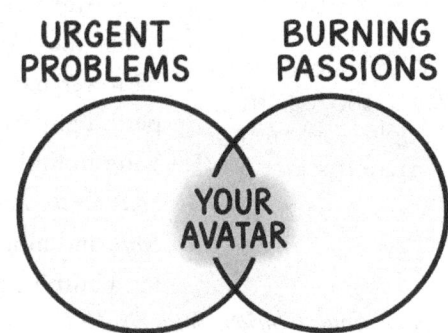

The sweet spot is where pain and passion meet.

You could say that they're positively addicted. Your book feeds their infatuation. They're at the boiling point. They're burning to act. Does your book scratch their itch? Does it move them from high-level interest into purposeful action toward their goals? If so, they'll buy it.

Most authors write books that give basic information about their subject, and they arrange it into ordinary chunks of content. But it's just organized information. The secret to making your book a bestseller is to reorganize your content into a series of steps that lead the reader to solve their *urgent* problem or satisfy their *burning* passion. If you do this, your reader will be ready to buy *right now*.

> "We are all experts in our own little niches."
> – *Alex Trebec*

Focus on these two "starving crowd" advantages, and you'll increase the chances of your book ending up on the bestseller lists.

Problems and passions. These are the biggies—the big kahunas.

A good example is my book *Nothing Down: How to Buy Real Estate with Little or No Money Down*. The American dream is to own a home—it's an ever-present passion. But most Americans have a problem—they don't have enough money! Along comes my book. It relieves the pain and shows people how to satisfy their desires. They buy that book ASAP, and it's a double whammy—pain gone, dream realized. They tell their friends about it, and it climbs the bestseller lists.

The ultimate example of niching avatars is the most successful series of books in the history of the world: *Chicken Soup for the Soul* by Jack Canfield and Mark Victor Hansen. The original *Chicken Soup* book was a compilation of 101 short stories. These weren't just ordinary stories. Each story was "vetted" for the goosebump factor. I challenge you to read through a *Chicken Soup* book and not have a goosebump experience.

> "If hard work is the key to success, most people would rather pick the lock."
> – Claude McDonald

After the word-of-mouth success of the original book, the *Chicken Soup* audience was segmented into narrower and narrower avatar niches. *Chicken Soup* is the perfect gift for someone dealing with an urgent problem. You can find *Chicken Soup for the Grieving Soul*, *Chicken Soup for the Recovering Soul*, *Chicken Soup for the Survivor's Soul*, and more! It's also an ideal gift for someone satisfying a burning passion, with titles like *Chicken Soup for the Golfer's Soul*, *Chicken Soup for the Dog Lover's Soul*, and *Chicken Soup for the Mother and Son Soul*. (In fact, you'll find the story of *my* mother in this last one.)

Here's a little secret that very few *Chicken Soup* fans know. I became aware of this while co-authoring three books with Mark Victor Hansen. When the first *Chicken Soup* book was launched in 1994, Jack and Mark set an audacious goal of selling *one billion* books by 2020. How ridiculous! Well, they didn't reach their objective. But as of this year, they're closing in on *six hundred million* books! In another twenty years, I'm sure they'll reach their bold target.

We should all learn from *Chicken Soup*. The narrower the niche, the more relevant the message to that specific audience. The more urgent or passionate the avatar, the more responsive they will be to your message.

"My great friend, Bob Allen, is one of the geniuses of geniuses in book creation, wordsmithing, and masterful marketing of books to become bestsellers. If you get a chance to work with him, Take it! I did. And we sold millions of books together. And I'm eternally grateful."
– Mark Victor Hansen

After the huge success of *Chicken Soup for the Soul*, Mark and I became friends. Together, we wrote the *New York Times* bestseller, *The One Minute Millionaire* plus *Cracking the Millionaire Code* and *Cash in a Flash*.

Superspreaders

It's also important to find the avatars in your audience who are "superspreaders." These are readers who are likely to spread your message far and wide, such as social media influencers, industry leaders, bloggers, or reviewers. If your avatar is a superspreader, they'll mention your book to dozens, often hundreds of people, saying, "You've gotta read this book!" They'll often give you a four- or five-star review. They'll mention you on social media and in conversations.

SUPERSPREADER
→ SOCIAL MEDIA
→ BOOK CLUB
→ AMAZON REVIEW
SHARE

Many book purchases are the result of word of mouth (or word of "mouse.") Think about your own reading habits—if someone whose opinion you trust tells you about a great book, you'll often buy it.

As a fun homework assignment, go to Amazon. Go to "shop by department" in the site's menu, and select "books." Then, along the left column, you'll find thirty-plus general book categories. Try to determine which category your potential book would be listed under.

> "If the book is true, it will find an audience that is meant to read it."
> – Wally Lamb

When you find your category, click on it. It will show narrower niches. Amazon calls these sub-genres. What is the narrowest niche where your book would fit? Then, notice the other books in the niche. What are the most popular books? These are generally the perennial bestsellers. Notice the titles. Why do you think these books are constantly selling? Your book will be competing against these titles. Our goal is to see your book listed as number one on this list.

Imagine that! This is where we're headed.

Once you know your ideal avatar, you'll need to win them over and keep their loyalty. Write a good book! Make it shareworthy. Find one thousand true fans—one at a time—as Kevin Kelly shares in his famous "1,000 True Fans" article originally published in 2008.[2] (Google it—there's a reason it's famous.) Make it easy for people to spread the buzz. Build value by giving them the "inside scoop" on your latest tips or products. Take care of them. I'll tell you more about how to accomplish this in a later chapter, so stay tuned.

Now, let's take the next step.

FREE GIFT: Avatar Clarity Worksheet

If you're unclear on who your book is actually for, this worksheet will fix that fast. It walks you through your audience's pain points, their desires, and what drives them to action. Download it now at AuthorGifts.com or scan the QR code.

---

2. Kelly, Kevin. "1,000 True Fans" *KK: The Technium.* https://kk.org/thetechnium/1000-true-fans/

"Begin with the Map in mind."
— Robert G. Allen

STEP 3: YOUR SUCCESS MAP

The Right Picture Is Worth Millions

Suppose you've narrowed down your book idea to one Low-Hanging Fruit concept and you've discovered your ideal avatar—now it's time to start writing. For me, writing is a piece of cake. But I realize that—for many—the job of putting down words on a blank page or screen can be daunting. It's called writer's block. Let me show you how to blast through writer's block forever.

As my mentor, Stephen Covey, taught me, it's a good idea to "Begin with the end in mind." I've added my twist to this statement: "Begin with the *Map* in mind." For me, a Map is a visual image that illustrates the steps outlined in your book. I sometimes call it a metaphor, a blueprint, or a big picture. This Map will guide you through the writing process and create a unique, memorable picture for your readers that could eventually be worth millions if you play your cards right.

The first thing I do when I work with authors is to help them create Maps for their books. Very few authors ever do this. They just start writing and—sooner or later—they're confused and overwhelmed.

Why should you go to this extra trouble of creating a Map? Because once the Map, or the big picture of your reader's journey, is clear in your own mind, you'll be a better guide. It will allow you to visualize exactly where you want to take your student and where they are currently along the path. It will help you identify and explain the challenges they might encounter at different stages.

WITHOUT A MAP: Lost in the Maze.   **WITH A MAP:** Straight to Success.

But more importantly, with your Map in front of you, it's easier to write your book. In fact, when your metaphor is clear and simple, you can talk your book out loud and have someone else clean up the text for you. Just write the description of walking your reader through the steps to success, much the same way as I'm walking you through these steps now. It shortens the time needed to write your book, and your written message will be much clearer.

How to Create a Map

To create a Map for your book, start with a vivid vision of what you want your reader to accomplish. Organize the transformation you promise into a series of steps. Each step will eventually become a chapter in your book. Then, link these steps to a memorable metaphor. If you lay out the reader's journey in your mind, the book almost writes itself—almost.

> "Visualize this thing you want. See it. Feel it. Believe in it. Make your mental blueprint and begin to build."
>
> – *Robert Collier*

To create the Map for this book, I started with a vivid vision of my reader (you) transforming from an aspiring writer to a bestselling author with a number one bestselling book. I asked myself, "What steps will my reader need to take to become a bestselling author?" I envisioned the process as a journey from point a to point b and created a metaphor to illustrate it. In this case, I imagined the journey to the top of the bestselling lists as a climb to the top of a mountain. The Map of your bestselling author journey is what I call the Author Accelerator.

You'll notice as you view the image of this journey on the previous page (which you can also find at the beginning of the book) that it includes twelve steps. Before I created this Map, I spent time deciding the order of these steps. The twelve steps outlined within these chapters describe each step I encourage you to take in the proper order.

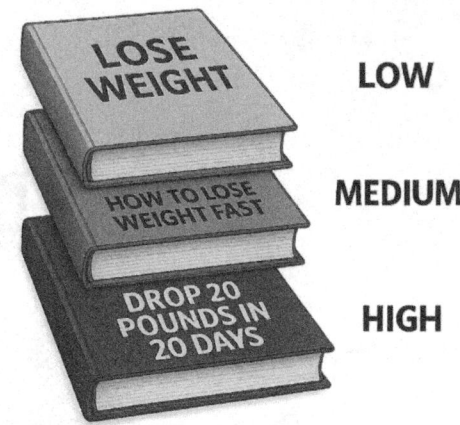

Create a Vivid Vision

As you begin writing, ask yourself what steps your reader must take to achieve the results they desire. As you ponder all that will be involved in this process and build upon your Low-Hanging Fruit idea, you'll soon build a vivid vision for your reader, and you'll be able to outline the necessary steps for your Map.

Just what is a vivid vision? What are you promising? Most ordinary books don't create a strong and tangible vision. They just inform. The author assumes that if you read the information in the book, you'll be able to pull together a successful plan and achieve what you want on your own. I'm encouraging you to go beyond this ordinary process. Be aggressive. Make a clear picture of the results you expect your reader to achieve. Decide on the specific time frame required to accomplish this goal.

So, my vivid vision is for you to be a number one bestselling author this year. It's clear. It's descriptive. It includes specific numbers and a precise time frame.

What is your vivid vision for your reader? Here are some examples:

- Lose twenty pounds in twenty days
- Find the love of your life by your next birthday
- Graduate in two years instead of four
- Hustle your way into two thousand dollars of additional income every month in six months or less

Once you can see your vision clearly, you can show your readers how to reach it.

Outline Steps

Next, in your mind or on a piece of paper, sketch out the journey you want your reader to take toward your vivid vision. What is your step-by-step process? What is your unique system? How many steps will it take for your reader to get the result you promise?

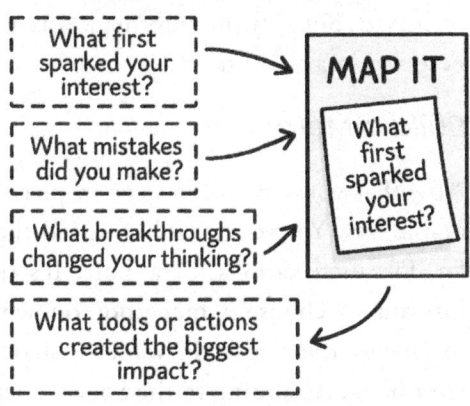

Many successful people have no idea what steps they took to achieve their mastery. They just grew their success instinctively and solved intervening problems as they moved forward. They might have read a book that kick-started them, but eventually they developed their own system. And for most of them, this process was unconscious—their knowledge grew organically from an acorn into a seedling into a sapling into a mighty oak. (Notice the metaphor? You'll need to think about that more in a moment.) If this sounds like you, it's time to do a little brainstorming:

- What first motivated you to learn about your chosen topic?
- What were the first actions you took to get involved?
- Where did you go and with whom did you collaborate to achieve your level of success?
- What skills did you need to develop?
- What mistakes did you make along the way?
- How much time and money did you invest?
- Is there anything you could share with your readers to help them navigate these steps more effectively and efficiently?
- What do you wish someone else had shared with you before you began?

After considering these questions, you'll likely have a greater appreciation for how far you've come. You can look back on your journey and identify the times when you surged forward and the times when your progress seemed more gradual—like a racecar driver speeding down a straightaway and slowing down on the sharp turns. Remembering these details will help you delineate the best routes up the mountain, over the cliffs, up the steep inclines, across the slippery shale, and onward to the ultimate goal.

With this new wisdom guiding you, you'll be able to articulate the principles, strategies, and "aha" moments that got you where you are now—the step-by-step process that can best teach a beginner how to navigate uncharted territory and claim their prize. Simplify this information as much as you can and outline the exact steps necessary in a clear list.

Build a Metaphor

Now that you have your steps in place, it's time to illustrate them in a memorable way. You've probably noticed that as I've described the Map process so far, I've used various metaphors. It's time for you to choose a metaphor on which to "hang" the steps you want to share in your book. According to the Social Science Research Network, sixty-five percent of us are visual learners.[1] Frankly, including a Map with visual cues and a metaphor will make you a more effective writer and a better teacher.

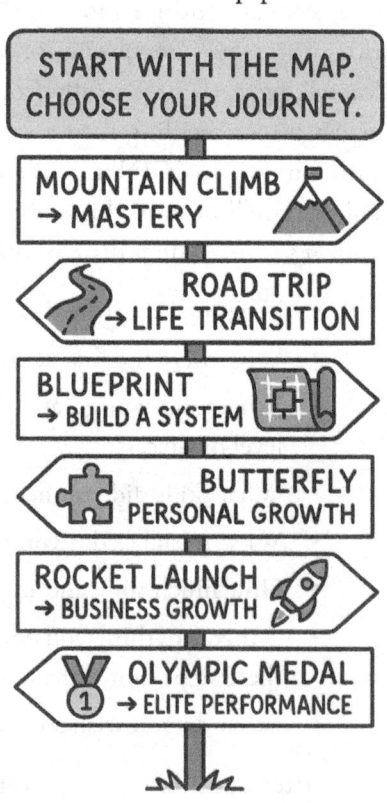

In my Authors Accelerator class and in this book, I use the metaphor of climbing a mountain. If you take each step following the trail to a mountain peak, you'll eventually reach the top. Becoming a bestselling author is similar. It's a challenging climb, it's difficult to reach the pinnacle, but the journey is worth it. There are many different possible paths to the top, but if you follow the most reliable trail outlined

---

1. Bradford, William C. "Reaching the Visual Learner: Teaching Property Through Art," *The Law Teacher Vol. 11*, 2004. https://papers.ssrn.com/sol3/papers.cfm?abstract_id=587201

by an expert who has been to the top before, you'll have an easier ascent, avoid hazards, and save time and energy.

Here are some examples. Suppose you have a dog-walking business that is extremely successful. You want to turn your expertise into an extra stream of income, so you decide to write a book about how someone can replace their income from a job they hate by starting their own pet-walking business in thirty days. Your metaphor could be a person leaving the prison of their hated job, taking off their shackles, and walking into a new world of wealth and freedom—going from a bad, dark world to a good, light world. You could say, "Walk away from that job you hate, and in less than thirty days, walk into more money and more time freedom by arranging to walk other people's dogs."

> "Leadership refers to the art of convincing someone else to do what you want because he is motivated to."
> – Dwight D. Eisenhower

Maybe your metaphor is a trip from Los Angeles to New York City. As part of your planning, wouldn't you buy a map? So, what is the first step or stage in the journey? It would be to travel from LA to Las Vegas, where you might spend the night and catch a show. Then, the next stage is to drive to Denver. Where will you stop for food and gas? Next, you'll go from Denver to St. Louis and stop to touch that iconic, metallic arch, and so on.

BUTTERFLY METAMORPHOSIS

STEP 1: START FROM SCRATCH → STEP 2: BUILD GOOD HABITS → STEP 3: BREAK THROUGH → STEP 4: SPREAD YOUR WINGS

Perhaps your metaphor could be a blueprint for building a house with a foundation, walls, and roof? Or a map to find treasure? Or the metamorphosis of a butterfly? Or polishing the many facets of a diamond? Or assembling a puzzle? Or planting a tree and growing fruit? The possibilities are endless. Here are a few more ideas to get you thinking:

- Climbing a staircase
- Floating down a river to the sea
- Taking flight in an airplane
- Climbing a mountain
- Participating in a sport such as basketball, football, soccer, tennis, etc.
- Creating a specific shape like a pyramid, circle, square, or rectangle
- Progressing through the four seasons
- Competing in the Olympics and earning a gold, silver, or bronze medal

Organize your system around this metaphor, and you'll find that your students will grasp lessons more quickly and you'll be able to teach them more efficiently.

Put It All Together

Sometimes it takes several hours of brainstorming to create a vivid vision, organize the step-by-step process, and identify the framework of a metaphor on which to hang the steps. But it's essential. It forces you to identify the steps that you, yourself, took to climb the ladder to your success.

Suppose your book is about how to quit smoking. You were a smoker for years and finally found a revolutionary, new way to break your habit. You've shared it with a few friends, and it's worked for them too. You wonder, "Is there a book in here somewhere?"

You organize what you've shared with your friends into a more professional, step-by-step system. You test your system out with a sample of strangers. Ninety-five percent of them also succeed. Your system is different from anything on the

MAP VS. NO MAP: WRITING RESULTS

Author A
- Frustration
- Wastes Time
- Tons of Revisions

Author B
- Faster writing
- Clearer direction
- Less stress

market. It's revolutionary. Could your book introduce people to more information about this important topic—and in the process save hundreds of thousands of lives? You feel that it's part of your purpose in life to share this message. This is your Low-Hanging Fruit.

So, you start to organize your book. You create a vivid vision for your reader. You plan to teach your readers how to become non-smokers in seven days or less, never to smoke again.

You create your step-by-step process. Each step—each chunk of information—takes your student closer to the success you've imagined for them.

> "If you can't explain it to a six-year-old, you don't understand it yourself. Make everything as simple as possible, but not simpler."
>
> –Albert Einstein

Then, you create a visual metaphor to lock in the process—perhaps something like five keys that will open the five locks of smoking addiction.

If you join me in my number one Bestselling Authors Accelerator Class, we'll work together to create and design your own Map using my proprietary mapping system. If you're doing this on your own, I strongly recommend that you complete your Map before you write a single word of your book. When you've completed the Map process, fill in your details:

What is my vivid vision for my avatar, and how much time will they need to reach it?

_____
_____
_____
_____

What are the steps of my unique system that readers will need to complete?

_____
_____
_____
_____

What metaphor will I use to illustrate this process?

_____
_____
_____
_____
_____
_____

You can find examples of other Maps at the end of this chapter.

The greatest compliment you can receive from one of your readers is, "I can do that. Your writing is so clear and so simple that I believe my success is not only possible but inevitable." Once they believe, it's easy for them to act. This is my strength, my skill—making a subject so simple, so clear, that the reader is not afraid to get started. And it can be yours too! You may have noticed that this entire book is an example of exactly how you should design your own bestselling book.

Let's climb onward up the mountain to "Step 4: Your Revolutionary Brand."

FREE GIFT: Map Your Framework – Lesson #1

If you're overwhelmed trying to organize your book, I made a short training that shows you how to map your method clearly and quickly. You can watch it at AuthorGifts.com or scan the code to get started.

Example I: A metaphor and map image created for *The One Minute Millionaire*.

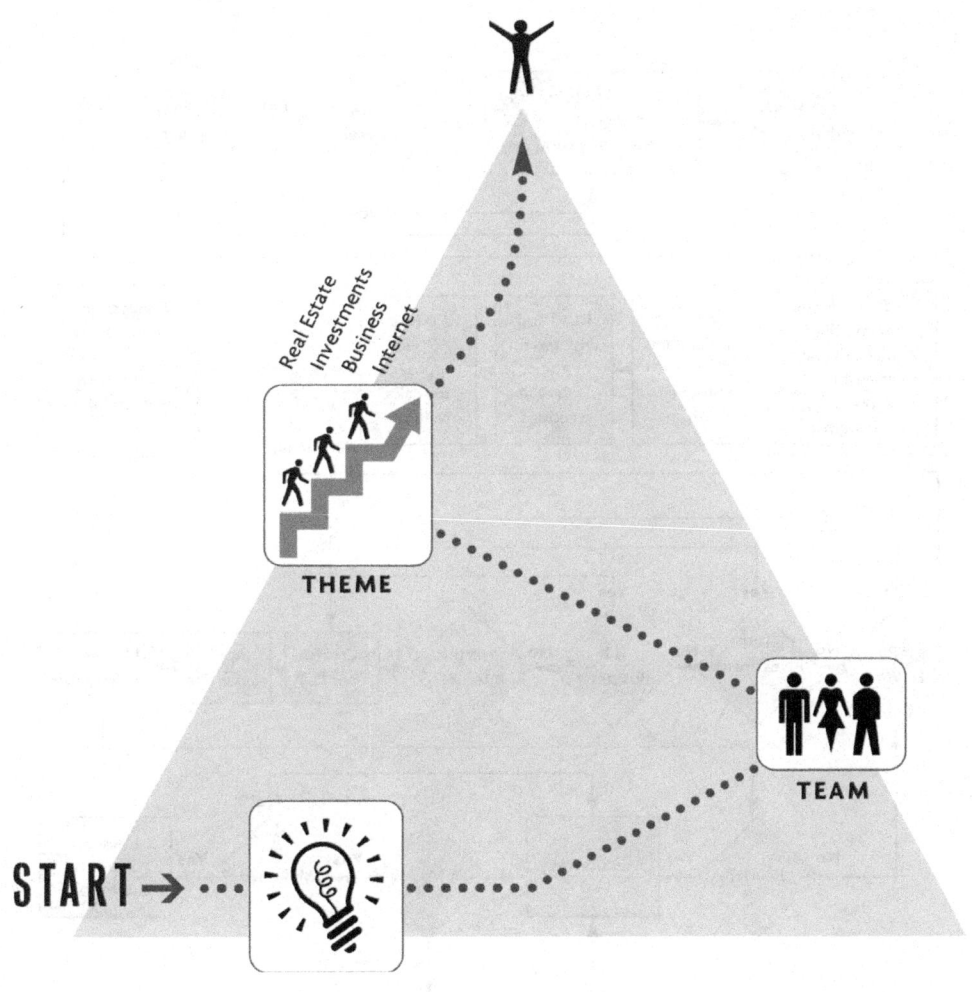

Example II: A system of steps created for *The One Minute Millionaire*.

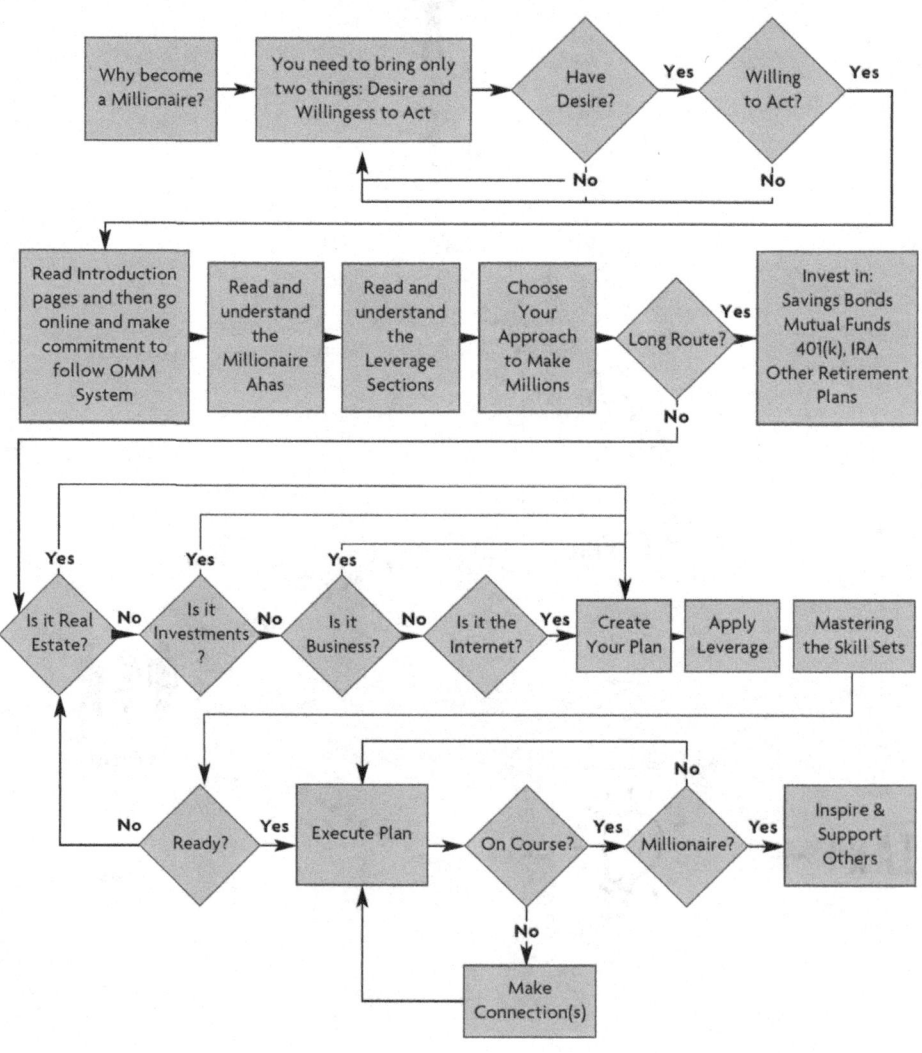

Example III: A Map for parents from *Raising Savant-Garde Kids: The Blueprint to Raising Legendary Leaders* by Eldon Grant.

> "The system Robert has taught me—step-by-step—is exactly what I needed. It makes the impossible feel possible. Without the structure of creating a Success Map, I would've never gotten this far. I would still be stuck writing lots of words but without a clear direction of where I wanted to take my reader. Robert's mentorship is more than tactical—it's spiritual. It's helped me align my purpose with my writing.
>
> – Eldon Grant

Example IV: A Map for retirees from *The Clueless Retiree: Safely Navigating the Steps to Enroll in Medicare* by Daniel Ortiz.

> "I was planning to write a boring book on how to enroll in Medicare. Robert opened my eyes to a more interesting approach. He showed me how to create a metaphor—a Map—to guide my readers through the danger zone of the complicated and tricky world that all 65-year-old seniors in the USA need to navigate. It was revolutionary. I know my business will skyrocket because of it."
>
> – Daniel Ortiz

"Think different!"

– Apple slogan 1997–2002

STEP 4: YOUR REVOLUTIONARY BRAND

How to You-niquify Yourself

When your book is published, it will enter a crowded field. More than three million new books and eBooks will be released this year to pile on top of millions of books from previous decades. Your topic will already have hundreds of books written about it. Imagine hundreds of authors in your space competing for the same avatar's attention. This can be discouraging.

Yet, you know there's a book in you, and you're the only one who can write it. Frankly, if your book doesn't top the bestseller lists, you still *have* to write it. Maybe you won't be discovered until a generation from now, like Vincent Van Gogh… no, scratch that idea! You want to reach bestseller status this year, don't you? To do that, you can't be a cliché—you need to stand out, and I can show you how.

Even before you start writing, there are questions you need to pause and ask yourself. How can my book stand out? How will my book be different? What is my brand? You might be thinking, "Yeah, but, Bob—I just wanted to write a book. I don't know anything about branding."

Well, if you just want to write a book, don't read this chapter. Simply write your book, release it into the world, and hope it will find an audience that will cause it to climb the charts. Good luck with that. But if you *really* want a number one bestselling book, you need to understand this stuff.

The Keys to Building a Brand

Now, when my first book was published, I had no idea that *Nothing Down* would grow into a massive brand. It was way "above my pay grade." Perhaps, like you, I just wanted to write a book. Maybe I simply lucked into the number one spot.

But in hindsight, I've realized that I had stumbled upon the five keys to building a book into an enduring number one bestselling brand. It so happens that those five keys spell the word *brand*. (If you hang around me long enough, you'll notice that I love acronyms. ☺)

Make a Bold Promise

The first letter in *brand* stands for **Bold Promise**.

B old Promise
R
A
N
D

When my first book came out, the promise in the title was bold—almost shocking: *Nothing Down: How to Buy Real Estate with Little or No Money Down.*

My bold promise solved an urgent problem for hopeful buyers (no cash) and satisfied a burning passion at the same time (the American Dream of owning a home). The timing was perfect. The baby boomers were booming into the market in the early 1980s, and my book literally flew off the shelves.

> "If we would guide by the light of reason we must let our minds be bold."
> – Louis D. Brandeis

How does a nobody author from a nowhere town climb the big bad *New York Times* bestseller list to the number one spot? I made an unbelievable promise in my book title. I went from nobody to somebody in ninety days.

Then, to double down on that bold promise, I made an *outrageous* claim. In full-page ads in major newspapers nationwide, I boasted, "Send me to any city. Take away my wallet. Give me one hundred dollars for living expenses. And in seventy-two hours, I'll buy an excellent property using none of my own money."

The Los Angeles Times took the bait. They challenged me to put my lack of money where my mouth was. With an *LA Times* reporter by my side, they flew me to San Francisco, where I bought seven properties in fifty-seven hours and gave the reporter twenty dollars back in change. The front page of the *LA Times* financial section broadcasted the headline, "Buying Home without Cash: Boastful Investor Accepts *Times* Challenge—and Wins!"

Did this set me apart? Big time!

My following books used similar bold promises: *Creating Wealth*, *Multiple Streams of Income*, and *One Minute Millionaire*.

Here are some other bold brand promises you might recognize:

- "When you absolutely, positively have to have it overnight!" (FedEx)
- "Fifteen minutes or less can save you fifteen percent or more on car insurance." (Geico)
- "Your pizza in thirty minutes, or it's free!" (The early years at Domino's)

And in the book world, these titles crushed it:

- *Think and Grow Rich* by Napoleon Hill
- *The Four-Hour Workweek: Escape 9 to 5, Live Anywhere, and Join the New Rich* by Timothy Ferriss
- *The One Minute Manager* by Kenneth Blanchard and Spencer Johnson

When you and I work together, I'll help you craft a bold promise that will set *you* apart. Here is the bold promise I make with this book: "Become a number one bestselling author this year! When your book is done, it'll hit number one. You'll make a ton. Won't that be fun?"

Decide your outrageous promise, and reverse-engineer your book to deliver on your promise in the shortest time possible. I'll share more on this later.

Present a Revolutionary Concept

What is the second letter of our acronym? The *r* stands for **Revolutionary Concept**.

B old Promise
R evolutionary Concept
A
N
D

When a screenwriter tries to pitch a movie script to a studio, they need to show how their movie is different. There are hundreds of movies about love, but what makes a new movie on love burst through the crowd to become a classic? It needs a unique concept.

Think of classics like *Casablanca, Sleepless in Seattle, The Princess Bride,* and *Titanic*. They're just the same old love story but with a new twist or a memorable presentation that adds something fresh and exciting. How can your book do this? Here are some brilliant examples of books that revolutionized their topics:

- *Men Are from Mars, Women Are from Venus* by John Gray
- *Chicken Soup for the Soul* by Jack Canfield and Mark Victor Hansen
- *1000 Places to See Before You Die* by Patricia Shultz

When Patricia Shultz decided to write her book, there were already thousands of books on travel. The previous huge-branded bestseller had been written in 1957: *Europe on 5 Dollars a Day* by Arthur Frommer. (Notice the Bold Promise!) Frommer's book became *the* travel brand for decades afterward. But in 2001, Shultz came up with a revolutionary concept that leapfrogged over *all* of the previous bestsellers and became the brand of brands in the travel space.

> "The world accommodates you for fitting in but only rewards you for standing out."
> – Matshona Dhliwayo

At first, she wanted to call her book *100 Drop-Dead Places* but then changed it to *1000 Places to See Before You Die*. This was her reasoning: "When the first book came out in 2003, people told me, 'The book will never sell, you're crazy—you can't say "die" in the title.' It was so close to 9/11 then, and people were more fearful… I consciously chose the title to shock people—to get them to go somewhere other than the couch."[1]

The root verb of the word *revolutionary* is "to revolt." She was revolting against lazy people settling on the couch to die. And she shocked them into remembering their dreams and got them to start crossing off places they wanted to see before they kicked the bucket.

> "Innovation distinguishes between a leader and a follower."
> – Steve Jobs

In *Nothing Down*, I revolted against the real estate industry that sifted through their customers to find the strongest possible buyers and borrowers. If your "financials" were weak, you didn't qualify. And that pissed me off. (Please excuse the language.) When someone tells me, "It can't be done," I immediately try to prove them wrong. I had launched my real estate investing career right out of college with no job, no assets, no down

---

1. Syme, Rachel. "*1,000 Place to See Before You Die*: Traveling to Stay Alive" *Time*, Dec 13, 2011. https://entertainment.time.com/2011/12/13/1000-places-to-see-before-you-die-traveling-to-stay-alive/

payment, and no credit. I was the worst type of buyer, according to the bankers and realtors. Yet, starting with myself, I showed ordinary people how to revolt against the big players and buy even if they had "no money down."

Steven Pressfield shares this powerful insight in his revoltingly titled book, *Nobody Wants to Read Your Sh*t*:

> *The first question you ask yourself at the start of any project is, "What's the concept?"... A concept takes a conventional claim and puts a spin on it... to behold the product with fresh eyes... A good concept makes the audience see your product from a very specific sympathetic point of view and by its logic (or faux logic) renders all other points of view and all competing products moot and impotent. One of the seminal concepts in advertising history is Avis Rent a Car's "We're #2, so we try harder."*[2]

Avis's campaign turned a negative (being the number two ranked car rental company) into a positive ("we try harder") and also enabled Avis to revolt against Hertz (the top rental company) in a nonthreatening way.

What does your book revolt against? What is your revolutionary concept?

Show Your Authentic Identity

The third letter of our acronym, *a*, stands for **Authentic Identity**.

B old Promise
R evolutionary Concept
A uthentic Identity
N
D

You can't be all things to all people. If you want to be number one, you need to be *real*. That means lots of people will love you, but others won't because you're so iconic.

> "Always remember that you're unique—just like everyone else."
> – Unknown

Think of the icons of our time such as Donald, Michael, Oprah, Sting, Bono, Tony, Cher, Madonna, and Elvis. They're so authentic, they're mononymous—you only need to say their one-word name, and everyone knows who you're talking about. Whether you love

---

2. Pressfield, Steven. *Nobody Want to Read Your Sh*t: and Other Tough-Love Truths to Make You a Better Writer* (Black Irish Books: Los Angeles, 2016).

'em or hate 'em, you know exactly who they are because there "ain't nobody like 'em." They are "the only."

Spend some time identifying what makes you and your book "the only."

In writing *Nothing Down*, I didn't just write a general book about real estate investing. I delved deep into the biggest problem for all buyers of real estate: not having enough money. My book was "the first and the only" book on "creative" financing. It still is, almost fifty years later. I'm still the only one in the field to have done something as crazy as the *LA Times* challenge. That's why there's a secret word hidden inside the word: ch**Allen**ge. ☺

Position Yourself In The Untapped Niche

What makes you and your book "the only"? What is your "wow factor"? What sets you apart? What do you stand for, and what *won't* you stand for? When you and your message are truly authentic, that authenticity will resonate with your ideal audience like a tuning fork. They love the things you love (your passions). They hate the things you hate (your enemies). They become part of your movement. They identify with you. They become a part of your tribe.

Create a New Look

What is the fourth letter of our acronym? The letter *n* stands for **New Look**.

> **B** old Promise
> **R** evolutionary Concept
> **A** uthentic Identity
> **N** ew Look
> **D**

As I discussed in chapter two, almost nothing published today presents any new ideas or discoveries. When people buy books, they tend to buy the same topics, themes, and genres repeatedly. People know what they like, and they consume those topics in predictable patterns. You don't need to create an entirely new idea that no one has ever discussed before to write a bestseller. You just need to give your subject a new look and present it from an angle that gives people a different perspective and catches their attention.

When Malcolm Gladwell wrote *The Tipping Point*, it was fresh and new. He went even deeper in his next books, *Blink* and *Outliers*. He used unique language—words that became part of the cultural zeitgeist: the Law of the Few, the Ten-Thousand-Hour Rule, Connectors, Mavens, Thin-slicing, the Stickiness Factor, and more.

> "Whatever you do, always give one hundred percent. Unless you're giving blood."
> – Bill Murray

He came up with new ways of describing the same old things. He has become—perhaps—the most famous nonfiction author in the world. His books are always number one bestsellers. I'm not saying that you need to write like Malcolm Gladwell, but you at least need to try to think like he thinks.

Make your content fresh! Make it look new. That's why social media influencers, TV series, and news programs have addicted followers. High achievers in each of these areas know how to sell their products and messages like they're revolutionary, and people are addicted to *new, fresh* stuff. So, if you want to stand out, don't look like *old, boring* stuff.

When Mark Victor Hansen and I brainstormed before we wrote the million-copy bestseller *The One Minute Millionaire*, we asked ourselves, "How can we make this book different and new?"

We decided to write two books in one. On the right-side pages, we tell the right-brained story of Michelle, who loses her husband in a tragic car accident. Her underhanded in-laws pull some legal shenanigans to steal her two children. To get her children back, she needs to earn a million dollars in ninety days, or she'll lose custody forever. On the left-side pages, we tell the left-brained system showing how anyone can make a million dollars relatively quickly if they absolutely need it. There's never been another book like this that teaches the same content in both a fiction and a nonfiction format. It's new. It's fresh. It's "the only."

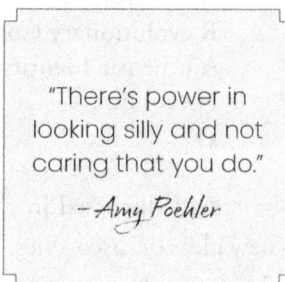

> "There's power in looking silly and not caring that you do."
> – Amy Poehler

When we work together, I'll teach you how to avoid being a cliché and stand apart from the rest of the crowd with a new look.

Cause a Disruptive Difference

The fifth letter of our acronym, *d*, stands for **Disruptive Difference**.

B old Promise
R evolutionary Concept
A uthentic Identity
N ew Look
D isruptive Difference

Study this next quote from Dave Chappelle for a few minutes. It's profound:

"The mark of greatness is when everything before you is obsolete, and everything after you bears your mark."

No matter the commodity you're selling, there will be competitors and rivals everywhere. You're trying to become "the only," and you don't want to be lumped in with everybody else. You need to "think different" like Apple so you can make a Disruptive Difference in your niche.

First, you need to do some basic competitor research. Search book titles on Amazon. Who are the biggest competitors in your space? What is the top selling book on your subject? Once you know who your rivals *are*, then you can identify who they *aren't*. As they say in baseball, "Hit the ball where they ain't."

Next, go deeper and continue to research your rivals. Look at each one carefully. What is their Big Promise? What is their Revolutionary Concept? What is their Authentic Identity? What is their New Look? What is their Disruptive Difference? Which part of the territory have they already "staked out," and which parts of the territory have they left undiscovered? What can you learn from them?

Sam Walton would drive hundreds of miles in the early days of Walmart to observe the innovations of a competitor. He adopted these ideas quickly and built the empire that now spans the globe—all from a nowhere town in Arkansas.

You might think you need to be famous to make money with your book. But when you create a unique brand, you attract the right buyers. Here's one of my favorite success stories:

"Hi, Bob. The first book you helped me write, Secrets of a Dealionaire, has made me a fortune. Thanks! My second book, Secrets Those Credit Doctors Don't Want You to Know, was just my gift to help people with their credit. I wasn't expecting to make any money on it. I posted it on Amazon. Then, Larry King began running infomercials about a credit repair program he was promoting, and my book was the beneficiary of the increased traffic. In February 2018, Amazon sent me a check for $60,025.55. I was shocked! For all of 2018, my total royalties were $144,930.19. Amazing. Thanks, Bob!"

– John Lee

You'll know how to become "the only" when you discover the parameters of "the everybody" in your category. But you don't only need to be different—you need to be disruptive. Isn't that exactly what Apple did? When the iPhone appeared in 2007, it put all flip phones out of business. Suddenly, all the competition needed to look like an iPhone to keep up. When you're disruptive, you make your competitors obsolete.

In 1962, Sam Walton opened the first Walmart. Over the next fifty years, Walmart put millions of small businesses out of business. Talk about disruptive!

When *Nothing Down* appeared in 1980, it put my seminar competitors out of business. Soon, my competitors needed to copy me.

Be disruptively different.

> "The only power that has any real meaning is the power to better the world."
>
> – Gregory David Roberts

When a Book Becomes a BRAND

So, let's review. Most bestselling authors don't do the kind of advanced planning that I've shared here. They simply publish their books and hope for the best. But, when you look at the history of the major number one bestsellers, you'll identify how they capitalized on at least a few of these characteristics outlined in the BRAND acronym. Study the following list and graph containing some of the top selling books in the past one hundred years:

• *Think and Grow Rich*	Napolean Hill	100 Million	1937
• *Men Are from Mars, Women Are from Venus*	John Gray	50 Million	1992
• *Rich Dad Poor Dad*	Robert Kiyosaki	40 Million	1997
• *Your Erroneous Zones*	Wayne Dyer	35 million	1976
• *The Secret*	Rhonda Byrne	35 Million	2006
• *How to Win Friends & Influence People*	Dale Carnegie	30 Million	1936
• *Who Moved My Cheese?*	Spencer Johnson	30 Million	1998
• *7 Habits of Highly Effective People*	Stephen Covey	25 Million	1998

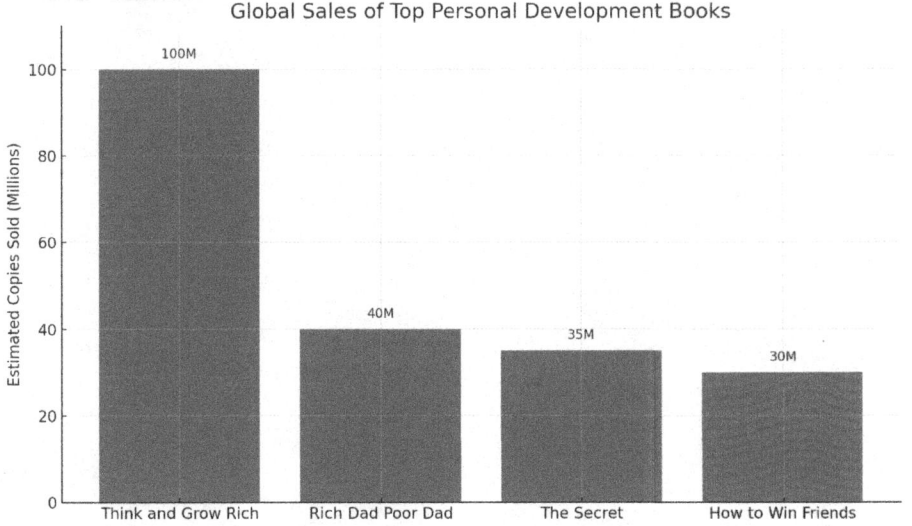

Ask yourself how these books set themselves apart and became "the only" in their categories. You'll soon see that they did so by making bold promises, presenting revolutionary concepts, showing authentic identity, creating a new look, and causing a disruptive difference. You don't need to check off every item in the BRAND list to become a number one bestseller, but I challenge you to check off as many as you can. Don't forget to ask yourself this question throughout the writing process: "How can I make this book bold, revolutionary, authentic, new, and disruptively different?"

Let's forge on to the next step. ☺

B — BOLD PROMISE
R — REVOLUTIONARY CONCEPT
A — AUTHENTIC IDENTITY
N — NEW LOOK
D — DISRUPTIVE DIFFERENCE

FREE GIFT: How to You-niquify – Bonus Training

Think your idea isn't original? I made a training that shows you how to build a brand so unique, you'll never compete on price again. Go to AuthorGifts.com or scan the QR code.

> "What a miracle it is that out of these small, flat, rigid squares of paper unfolds world after world after world, worlds that sing to you, comfort and quiet or excite you."
>
> – Anne Lamott

STEP 5: YOUR WORD FORGE

How to Make Your Words Irresistible

Words are vehicles of meaning: written words, spoken works, visual words, words you see, words you hear, and words you feel. A single word can sometimes be so awesome that the name of the Awesomeness Himself is *The Word*: "In the beginning was The Word, and the Word was with God, and the Word was God" (John 1:1). *Logos*—the Word. You could spend a lifetime pondering the power of that of that one single "Word."

They say that a picture is worth a thousand words. I say that the *right* word is also worth a thousand pictures. Because when the right words are delivered on the wings of spirit, the resulting pictures expand forever through multiple generations and rivers of time.

Just like blacksmiths forge iron into tools, you and I are wordsmiths. We forge words into the tools of transformation. As wordsmiths, we help people forge better lives. The leverage of our words can be immeasurable. Someone is waiting right now to experience your words. The transformation they need is just a few of your word-tools away. So, when you start writing, open your heart and seek to discover the words that will help and heal as they flow through you.

It All Boils Down to Words & Names

There are two terms that summarize the entire life of a bestselling author: *words* and *names*. A writer lays down "words," or ideas. Those words are delivered to "names," or people. If your words don't get read by enough names, then your bestseller dream is dead. You don't want to lay down the words and then have no names to read them.

Writers often assume that the publisher will do all the heavy lifting in finding the names to read their words. But here's what really happens—publishers don't sell books; they just distribute them to booksellers online and offline. And as soon as those books are published, printed, or posted online, they get lost in the vast stacks of published books. Your words wait silently for the right names to find them.

The largest bookstore in the world—Amazon—has tens of millions of titles in its online catalog, and they sell over 787 million printed books and eBooks per year.[1] Barnes and Noble reveals on its website that they sell over 190 million physical books per year.[2] If you're not careful, your words will get lost in a blizzard of titles and buried under the flood of books already being sold.

> "If you stacked the new books being published next to each other, at the present rate of production you would have to move at ninety miles an hour just to keep up with the end of the line."
> – Stephen Hawking

Sorry to break the news, but you can't delegate the selling of your book to the publishing industry. If you want to be a bestselling author, you need to learn how to find the names yourself. I'll show you how to do that in Steps 8 through 10.

But first, let's focus on your words.

How many words are there in an ordinary book?

Let's say an average book these days is about two hundred pages. Each page has an average of two hundred and fifty words, so an ordinary book would contain roughly fifty thousand words.

Imagine cutting out each of those two-hundred-plus pages from an ordinary book and pasting them, lined up in order, on a wall in a room where you live. Imagine seeing all two hundred pages—all fifty thousand of those words—displayed in front of you in one glance.

---

1. "2024 Amazon Book Sales Statistics: Insights & Trends You Should Follow" Automateed, Oct 9, 2024. https://automateed.com/amazon-book-sales-statistics/
2. "Quick Facts" Barnes and Noble. https://www.barnesandnobleinc.com/about-bn/quick-facts/

When I imagine this wall of words, I notice patterns that most new authors don't see because they are too close to the words to see the hidden ratios among them. I consider whether the author has taken some extra time to create a patina of Marketing Words. I also look for Transformative Words, Strong Words, Iconic Words, and Sticky Words. These are the five key word ratios that I use to determine a book's chance of becoming a bestseller:

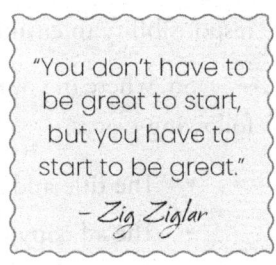

"You don't have to be great to start, but you have to start to be great."

– Zig Ziglar

Word Ratio #1
Message Words vs. Marketing Words

The bulk of the words inside your book are Message Words—the "how-to" information about your subject. They are the meat of your message and will likely make up ninety-eight percent of the words in your book. The other two percent of the words are what I call Marketing Words. Both types of words are important.

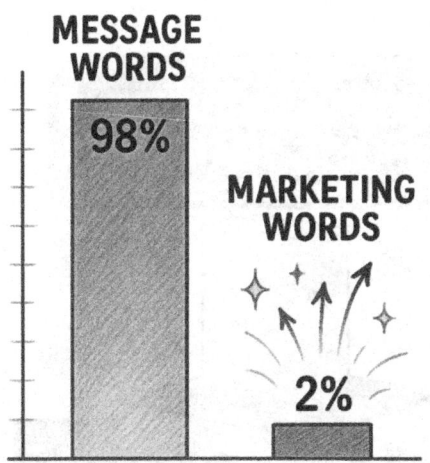

I've often said that a well-targeted message in a well-marketed book can ultimately generate up to one hundred dollars in revenue for every word inside. If your book has fifty thousand words, then we're talking up to five million dollars or more over the lifetime of the book. I'll show you how to discover those millions in "Step 9: Your Succession Stack."

Here's another way to think about the difference between these two types of words: Message Words are the steak or the meat of the text; Marketing Words are the sizzle and seasoning that enhance the message. Marketing words make up less than one thousand words in a fifty-thousand-word book. These words are designed to entice your potential reader to pick up your book and take a look. They are like the headline to a magazine article that captures your attention and gets you to read further. If you can't get a reader to look, then you'll influence *zero* names and earn *zero* dollars per word.

Message words teach. Marketing words entice. As I said earlier—it's *your* responsibility to ensure your Marketing Words are effective.

So, where in your book do you put Marketing Words? They are found in the following places:

- The title and subtitle on the cover of the book
- The ad copy on the back cover
- Your author bio
- The table of contents showing the chapter titles and subtitles
- The chapter titles and subtitles throughout the book
- The bolded headings and subheadings organizing your content within each chapter

According to *Forbes*, an intriguing cover can make all the difference in the success of a book.[3] As I just mentioned, the title, subtitle, and ad copy on the front and back of the cover are extremely important because their first job is to get someone to take a closer look. If no one looks, no one buys. We'll go into depth on how to further highlight these Marketing Words with a visually compelling cover in "Step 6: Your Bold Book Cover."

The next most important location for Marketing Words is the table of contents, or your list of chapter titles at the beginning of your book. When looking at a book in a bookstore or online, most people scan the table of contents to get an idea of what information the book contains. It should list the topic of each chapter in a persuasive and enticing way. These words sell the book.

---

3. Taylor, David. "The Art and Science of Book Cover Design in Book Publishing" *Forbes*, Mar 1, 2024. https://books.forbes.com/blog/book-cover-design

In this book's table of contents, there are about 160 words. When I craft a table of contents, I imagine that each word is a tiny salesperson encouraging a reader to buy the book. You must not have a boring title or table of contents! Here are some tips for incorporating Marketing Words into your table of contents.

How to Add Marketing Words to Your Table of Contents

Here is the basic pattern I followed when I created the table of contents for this book. As you organize your book, I encourage you to follow a similar pattern, and make sure to keep the Map you created in Step 3 in front of you as a guide to focus your efforts and keep you on track.

> "Build something 100 people love, not something one million people kind of like."
>
> – Brian Chesky

1. Identify the basic concepts you want to teach.

Before I began to write the words you're reading now, I asked myself, "What are the basic ideas I want to teach my reader about becoming a bestselling author? What do I want to include? What do I want to leave out?" As I mentally scanned through my past writing experiences, the ideas poured out in a jumble of basic ideas, or possible chunks of content. I wrote them down. You should already have some ideas about the content you'll include in your book after brainstorming to create your Map. Now is the time to build on those concepts, expand them, and think about other ideas you might include. Marketing words are about creating curiosity. They don't reveal the exact message. They entice you to take a closer look—to flip through a few pages.

2. Design the flow of steps to deliver the book's promise.

After expanding the preliminary list of basic steps from my Map and adding additional details, I reorganized the steps chronologically and refined them. (Remember that if you decide to reorder any of your steps, you'll need to update your Map as well.) Then, each concept became the topic for a chunk of content, and I designed each of these content chunks to build on a step I believe a reader should follow to become a bestselling author in one year.

> "We need to stop interrupting what people are interested in and be what people are interested in."
>
> – Craig Davis

3. Rename each step with a simple, interesting description.

Once I finalized the list of steps from my Map for my table of contents, it didn't look as appealing as it could. Here is my preliminary list of steps:

1. Refining your message
2. Targeting the correct reader
3. Choosing a compelling metaphor
4. Distinguishing a unique identity or presence
5. Completing the writing process
6. Creating an enticing book cover, title, and subtitle
7. Designing an interesting interior layout
8. Building an opt-in page
9. Implementing the marketing process
10. Using social media to your advantage
11. Launching the book to number one
12. Establishing a long-term presence

> "Good marketing makes the company look smart. Great marketing makes the customer feel smart."
> – Joe Chernov

To make this dry list more fun and interesting, I brainstormed a simple, memorable name for each step. You'll soon learn more about why making these terms iconic is important.

1. The Message
2. The Avatar
3. The Map
4. The Brand
5. The Word Forge
6. The Book Cover
7. The Layout
8. The Opt-in
9. The Succession Stack
10. The Buzz
11. The Launch
12. The Scalability

4. Add some marketing language to spice up each step & sub step.

After I found a compelling and memorable term for each step, I inserted marketing language to spice up each concept. I did this by adding sexy adjectives to catch the reader's attention and by creating a short description of each step to make it more persuasive and more unique. With some brainstorming, the steps became what you find in the table of contents at the front of this book. Flip there now.

Do you see the difference? This is marketing. Scan through the list of steps and notice a title that catches your eye. Not every title will grab you. Some might even turn you off. But one or two will pique your curiosity and send you to the checkout stand or shopping cart. Sometimes a reader might buy a book just to read a single chapter that grabs their interest.

Later, you'll learn how to use your author's bio and testimonials to include even more Marketing Words as you tell your reader all about your personal mission and how they can stay in touch, subscribe to your newsletter, or get involved in some other way.

As a potential book buyer is flipping through your book in the bookstore or scanning through your book online, they'll find the table of contents. A quick glance will show them that this book is different from other books. It seems to have some "personality." They'll flip through the pages and notice that each chapter is a step to help them accomplish something they've been wanting to do. They'll think, *Hmm, that's different*. As they skim the steps within the book, they'll notice bolded headings throughout—like the bolded headings in the step you're reading right now. They're eye-catching—curiosity generating.

They flip to the back cover and find testimonials from experts in the field who give credibility to the message. This creates trust and lowers barriers to buying. Look at the back cover of this book—you'll find tantalizing bullet points to remind potential buyers that the book's content is revolutionary, creative, fresh, or just plain different. These are all Marketing Words.

Most ordinary nonfiction authors don't do any of this marketing stuff. They just write Message Words—dry information about their content—one hundred percent Message Words with zero Marketing Words.

If you want your book to be a bestseller, you'll need to do both. About ninety-eight percent of your words will be Message Words, but it's the other two percent that provides the seasoning—the salt and savory spices—that help transform your book into a delicious meal of words. With the correct ratio of Marketing Words, the names you reach will start recommending your words like they

> "The aim of marketing is to know and understand the customer so well that the product or service fits him and sells itself."
> – *Peter Drucker*

would a new restaurant in town: "Have you read [insert your book's title here] yet? You've gotta get it!"

Many authors think that using these types of Marketing Words is unprofessional—that they're smarmy, pushy, salesy, or cutesy. But that's what all magazines and newspapers and online websites do to hook their readers. Your book is no different. You need to attract attention and entice readers to take a look. Why? Because the potential book buyer is skeptical. They'll ask questions like, "Who is this author? What do they have to teach me? Will this book be worth my time and money? Do I have the time to read this?"

> "Words can be like X-rays if you use them properly—they'll go through anything. You read and you're pierced."
>
> – Aldous Huxley

You need to find at least one reason to overcome their hesitation—something that is worth the hassle of clicking the "purchase" button. That's marketing. Let's discuss four more word ratios that are key to writing a bestselling book.

Word Ratio #2
Informative Words vs. Transformative Words

Ordinary writers organize their books into general areas of informational content distributed into chapters. They only use Informative Words. By the end of the ordinary book, the reader will have learned a lot of new stuff, but it's now the reader's job to extract the lessons and apply them to their lives.

But you're not an ordinary writer. You're a bestselling author. You need to use Transformative Words. You want your words to resonate so deeply that readers will use your word-ideas to improve their lives. When they've finished reading, you want them to say, "The writing was so simple that I can imagine myself doing it." And because they believe it, they'll follow through.

> "A blank piece of paper is God's way of telling us how hard it is to be God."
>
> – Sidney Sheldon

You don't want them to reach the end of your book and say, "Now, that was too complicated. I don't believe I can do it." If they set your book down and do nothing, you've failed as an author. Your words disappear as if they had never been written.

Informative Words Inform—Transformative Words Motivate

In my opinion, bestselling authors don't write to just inform. They write to inspire and empower the reader to act. They make bold promises that come with real results!

Here is my bold promise: If you get to the end of *this* book, and you don't get *your* book done and into the world *this* year, then I've failed as an author.

If your ratio of Informative Words to Transformative Words is one hundred percent to zero, you've got a problem. Do your words just inform, or do they motivate your reader to get something done? People don't really want more information. They want results! Educate them enough to generate results. You've got to increase the transformational content. The first step is to reorganize your information into a bold promise, like the bold promise in this book. I discuss bold promises in Step 4, so you likely remember why they're important. What is your bold promise? Focus on fulfilling that idea as you write your book.

"Read this book and you'll not only learn how to do _____, but you'll actually go and get _____ done in _____days! Finished! In the bank! In the rear-view mirror! Crossed off your to-do list! Done!"

The Diploma of Done

An ordinary how-to book describes the seed. Your bestselling book will get readers to plant the seed *and* enjoy the fruit. In the five-star reviews on Amazon, your readers will not only brag about what they learned but what they did and who they became because they read your words.

They did it! They lost the weight. They made the money. They found the love of their life. They moved into their dream home. They got organized. They graduated with honors. They raised extraordinarily obedient children. They learned a new language. They launched an online business. The lowered their diabetic A1C. They got pregnant.

Because of your words, they are not just smarter but healthier, richer, happier, lovelier. We don't have time in today's fast-paced world to just learn things. We need things to get *done*.

This is the diploma you offer—the Diploma of Done.

So rather than just fill your books with ordinary information, do some extra work for the reader. Ensure that the steps you've organized in your Map and table of contents will enable them to achieve your bold promise.

Don't just teach them— watch them win.

Ordinary writers don't dare take it this far. Bestselling authors make bold promises and then empower their readers to take the necessary steps. This is the reason that I generally don't have traditional chapters in my most recent books—like this one. Instead, I organize the content into steps. If your reader gets what you promise when you promise, their life is not just informed but transformed. Then the word of mouth starts. Your happy readers become superspreaders of your words because your words worked!

Word of mouth is the most powerful and least expensive form of advertising there is. The names read your words. The words inspire them to get results. The results cause the names to boast to other names who are then inspired to go buy more of your words. If they like the words in one of your books, they'll buy 'em all. They'll start by going back to buy your previous books and then wait anxiously until your new words hit the bookstores. They become fans.

> "Your intuition knows what to write, so get out of the way."
> — Ray Bradbury

I buy every book that Malcolm Gladwell writes. Why? They're interesting, fresh, and fun. But where is the bold promise? When you're finished reading, what to you get? How does your life improve? Yes, his books are huge bestsellers, but—in my opinion—they don't do enough to help you get stuff done. They're entertaining. They give you a new way to look at the world. But they don't change your life. They are informative and even imaginative, but I wouldn't call them transformative. For that reason, I don't use Gladwell as a model for the special kind of bestselling book that we're discussing now. Aspire to make your book transformative.

A retired financial advisor approached me about writing a book about the powerful financial principles found in the Bible. He had been sharing these ideas with family and friends, but now it was time to put them into a book. Here is what he says about forging his ideas into a manuscript:

> "Working with Bob has created accountability for me, kept me on track, and moved the project forward. Bob patiently taught me how to be a better writer and how to create a book that would capture my readers' attention—all to help me achieve the goal of creating a bestselling book. His guidance and assistance has been immeasurable."
>
> – Murray Lee, Financial Advisor

Word Ratio #3
Weak Words vs. Strong Words

When one of my students asks me to comment on their unpublished manuscript, I immediately scan the first few thousand words and notice a special word ratio. I call it the weak word/strong word ratio. It's the simplest ratio to spot. It's the ratio of "I" words to "you" words.

Beginning authors often make the classic mistake of telling their full story: "I did this, I did that, my success, my challenges," and so on. These books are ninety-five percent "I" words and about five percent "you" words.

> "Content marketing is really like a first date. If all you do is talk about yourself, there won't be a second date."
>
> – *David Beebe*

As we've discussed previously, nobody is really interested in your story unless you can show them how your story is integral to making *their* life story better. For example, I told parts of my story in my first book, *Nothing Down*, as an illustration of how my many *Nothing Down* techniques would help the reader buy their own property or create their own fortune starting with little or no money down. It's okay to tell a shorter version of your story—but only to illustrate your system.

If you've already written your manuscript, use the "find" function on your word processing program and count the number of these Weak Words: *I, me, my, mine*—as compared to these Strong Words—*you, your, yours, ours.*

If there are substantially more "I" words than "you" words, you've got a problem. There are some exceptions but very few. For now, check your ego at the door and write your autobiography after you're rich and famous. You need to flip the ratio, and at least eighty percent of your content needs to be composed of "you" words. A ratio of ten percent "I" words to ninety percent "you" words would be even better. This is another great way to "you"niquify your language.

Word Ratio #4
Simple Words vs. Iconic Words

Many how-to authors want to impress with their words to look intelligent. Readers these days don't need to be impressed. They want to absorb the information as quickly as possible and get down to business. Less is more.

Write as if you're speaking with a real person. Most authors write as if there is an audience in front of them, but don't use the plural "you." Write as if only one person is reading your words—use the singular "you." Picture delivering your message to one person at a time, and remember that ninety-five percent of your words should be simple and straightforward.

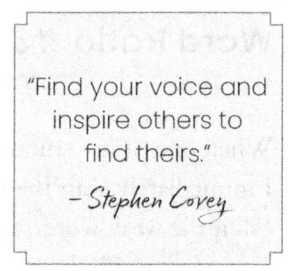

"Find your voice and inspire others to find theirs."
– Stephen Covey

However, five percent of your words should be iconic.

Bestselling authors find a way to put a memorable twist on a few of their words. For example, in my book on real estate investing, I discuss the importance of finding a highly motivated seller (Simple Words). But then I use a unique term to refer to these ordinary sellers. I call them "Don't Wanters." This term is not even grammatically correct, but it's a fresh way of describing the type of seller I want my readers to look for—people who don't want their property! When my readers read this, they are conditioned to remember and use my iconic, "you-nique" language and further spread my brand.

Therefore, I set myself apart. My vocabulary is branded. If anyone else copies the way I describe the *Nothing Down* process, then they are copying me, and I know it. When an author/leader creates new vocabulary that their fans begin to use, they elevate themselves from a mere author to an icon. Icons have different ways of speaking that is unique to them only. It's a fresh, new lexicon.

Entrepreneur and business coach icon Lisa Sasevich calls her high-paying fans her "Sassies." Bestselling fiction icon John Locke calls his fans the "OOUs," which stands for "one of us." Sports talk icon Jim Rome calls his fans "Clones," and a "drone" is a Clone in training. His listenership is called the "Jungle." His entire list of Iconic Words is found in his online "Smacktionary."[4] The business icon Gary Vaynachuk uses "Gary-speak." He tells his fans to "crush it" with multiple "side hustles."

> "Our chief want is someone who will inspire us to be what we know we could be."
> – Ralph Waldo Emerson

The iconic Donald Trump calls his raving fans the "MAGA faithful." *The Washington Times* declares that "Donald never met a superlative he didn't like."[5] He has a unique way of talking. Everything is either the best of all time ("yuge," "winning," "great," "incredible," "MAGA"). Or it's the worst in history ("stupid," "loser," "fake news," "deep state," "drain the swamp"). These words are not just iconic, they're emotional! No wonder Trump has created a movement. His vocabulary gets people to *move*. They either move strongly toward him or strongly away from him, but they *move*.

Create a Bestselling Movement!

You also want to create a movement, so think like an Iconeer. You want your readers to *move* their finger and click that purchase button! You want them to *move* toward your book in a bookstore so your book *moves* up the bestseller lists. You want your readers to *move* their mouths and *move* other people to read your book.

I'm not asking you to come up with a complete dictionary of your own made-up words (most of us are not that creative), but I am asking you to start thinking about a few unique ways to describe the distinct basics of your content. The more you teach the content of your book, the more new iconic terms will

---

4. "Jim Rome Smacktionary" StuckNut. https://www.stucknut.com/jimrome/smacktionary.php
5. Pruden, Wesley. "Donald Trump's Speech Features Superlatives," Feb 23, 2017. https://www.washingtontimes.com/news/2017/feb/23/donald-trumps-speech-features-superlatives/

bubble out of the conversation. Capture those words! I challenge you to come up with ten unique words in your subject lexicon and write them below:

1. _____
2. _____
3. _____
4. _____
5. _____
6. _____
7. _____
8. _____
9. _____
10. _____

Brand your content with your own words like a rancher brands cows. You-niquify your words. Enticify your words. Sexify your words. Iconify your words.

Authors earn royalties. I love that word: *royalty*. Think kings and queens. You join an exclusive club when you earn your first royalty check. They'll refer to you as "Your Highness" when your book hits a bestseller list. When you hit a million views on your social media platforms, you'll be a "millioneer."

Play with the words. Come up with your special language.

Word Ratio #5
Slippery Words vs. Sticky words.

Slippery Words are so ordinary that they slip right through your mind with little impact or emotion. They're closely related to Informative Words in that they educate, instruct, and tell—usually in a somewhat forgettable way. In contrast, Sticky Words activate the imagination. They inspire, arouse, excite, emote, motivate, transform, and sell.

> "Fill your paper with the breathings of your heart."
> – *William Wordsworth*

Here are some ways to make a few of your words stick.

Stickiness Factor #1: "You" Is the Stickiest Word

I realize we've already discussed that *you* is a strong word, but this concept is vital. There is no word more attractive and compelling to readers than the word *you*. People are more interested in your message when you show them how to get what they want and achieve their dreams or how to avoid what they *don't* want, such as their fears. When you address your reader directly, they won't want to miss a single word, and they won't be able to stop reading. Use the word *you* a lot.

Stickiness Factor #2: Engaging Imagination

Sticky words get people to imagine. The word *imagine* means to form a mental image of something that is not actually present to the senses.

When you can get your reader to imagine a concept, it will be far more likely to stick because it will form a picture in their minds. What percentage of your words are visual?

The picture superiority effect is a scientific theory that proves how pictures are more memorable than mere words.[6] So turn your words into pictures, and your readers will remember them. They'll grasp your ideas more quickly and have more "aha" moments.

> "To bring anything into your life, imagine that it's already there."
>
> – Richard Bach

Frank Kern said, "If you want to create money, you create desire. You build desire by showing the end result." So, get your reader to imagine the end result. To make their desire for the end result even stickier, get them to imagine how they'll feel when they have achieved their dream or accomplished their goal. You need to lift them above their invisible walls of fear so they can look off into a future where they have blown through all of their excuses and are living a new successful life. What would that look like? What would that feel like?

I've asked you several times throughout this book to imagine what reaching *your* goal will feel like, and now, I'm going to ask you again: What will it feel like to see your book hit number one on Amazon? Can you imagine yourself telling a

---

6. Defeyter, Margaret Anne; Riccardo Russo; Pamela Louise McPartlin. "The Picture Superiority Effect in Recognition Memory: A Developmental Study Using the Response Signal Procedure," *Cognitive Development*, Volume 24, Issue 3, 2009.

group of people that you just became a bestselling author? Notice their impressed smiles and their genuine approval. How will that feel? Do you want that?

Conjure those kinds of images in the words you write.

Stickiness Factor #3: The Secret Power of Storytelling

Facts tell, stories sell. It's a cliché, but it's true. Read it again—and again. Most nonfiction books tell. The head is a doubtful place. Too much left-brain content directs people into their minds and puts them into thinking mode. Thinking is the antitheses to action. The critical voice is always trying to talk you out of something. It questions everything. You need to get your reader out of their analytical heads and into their believing hearts.

> "Confidence is the most important single factor in this game, and no matter how great your natural talent, there is only one way to obtain and sustain it: work."
> – Jack Nicklaus

How? Do it with a story.

A story is the shortest distance to your reader's heart. It gets your reader to feel, and emotion prods people into motion. It's subliminal. A story slips the message right past the reader's critical mind and into their heart. The heart is a truster—a believer—because of the picture superiority effect. That's why Christ taught mostly in parables. Parables are short, memorable, and easy to picture.

How to Turn a Bio into a "Buy-o"

One of the simplest stories you can include in your book is your bio. Almost all books include a picture of the author and a brief bio. It's your writer's resume, and it lists the reasons why you've earned the right to write the book.

Don't write an ordinary bio that brags about all the great stuff you've done in your life. Write a "buy-o" instead. Use it to tell the reader why they should "buy" you and your information. As I've taught you, the weakest word you can use is "I." Use your buy-o to briefly share the highlights of your resume and build your credibility. Then shift into "you" language.

Be authentic. Tell how you struggled personally and then "discovered" the system you reveal in your book that has helped your students succeed and will help your reader succeed. For an example, look at my buy-o at the beginning of this book and model that.

How to Massage a Testimonial into a "Bestimonial"

The next type of stories to include in your book are testimonials, which are short stories sharing peoples' success in using your material. The best testimonials, or "bestimonials," are not just a recounting of success but a description of how your information helped someone overcome one of the many excuses your future readers might use for not acting. Some of these excuses might include not enough time, not enough support, not enough money, not enough information, or not enough courage.

Coach people on how to give a bestimonial. Help them come up with short, simple, one-sentence stories. One good bestimonial can subtly destroy a reader's excuses for not taking action and get them to buy your book and move forward. Notice the excuse killers in these testimonials:

> *"My boss asked me to speak during a company meeting. But I was terrified of speaking in public. Janice's book showed me how to overcome my fear of public speaking. I got a standing ovation!"* – Tanya

> *"I lacked the down payment that my real estate broker told me I would need. But Robert's book showed me where to find the money I needed that was hidden right under my nose. It took me less than three months for me to buy my dream home using very little of my own money."* – Tim

> *"We were so busy raising our kids that we thought we'd never find the time to implement (the author's) Brilliant Kids strategy. But it only took fifteen minutes a day. Our kids were making their own beds and cleaning their own rooms within the first week. We were amazed!"* – Ted and Tricia

Stickiness Factor #4: Include Questions

Questions are sticky, and they will engage your readers' minds. How many questions do you think you should include in your steps? What is the most powerful type of question? Should you ask the question and then immediately answer it? Or should you let the reader "stew" on the question to discover their own answers? What is this method of teaching called?

> "If there are no stupid questions, then what kind of questions do stupid people ask? Do they get smart just in time to ask questions?"
>
> – *Scott Adams*

It's called the Socratic method, and it's been around for over twenty-five hundred years because it works.[7] Why does it work? Because your brain loves questions! Questions ignite the mind *and* activate the heart. Include questions to get your reader thinking whenever you can.

Stickiness Factor #5: Use Short Metaphors & Similes

Word pictures are metaphorical. A metaphor or a simile is just a one-sentence story. When you include them, it's like your book provides the last number of a combination lock. It's a magician's sleight of hand. It's an insider's secret. It's the hidden passageway into the pharaoh's tomb. It like your message slips right under the radar. It pulls back the curtain to reveal a valuable secret. It's the… you get the idea.

> "Metaphors have a way of holding the most truth in the least space."
> – *Orson Scott Card*

Metaphors add an exclamation mark to summarize the lesson and engage the reader's imagination. When I wrote each of my multiple bestsellers, do you think I sat down beforehand and learned how to write visually? Not once. It's only in hindsight that I began to recognize how many of these tactics I had employed naturally. I love to teach, so I just used my teacher's toolbox and unconsciously applied it to my writing.

There's so much more to teach you about this magical, "sticky" way of writing, but this chapter is already getting too long. I'll share more with you in my Authors Accelerator Program. Check it out.

Can you write a bestseller without using any of the above strategies? Probably, but the purpose of this step is to stretch your mind to embrace a new way of thinking. At first, you'll have to do these things consciously, and it will take significant effort to implement them. But eventually, you'll find yourself writing and speaking using these sticky methods naturally.

It's Time to Write!

Now that you're equipped with the vital writing tools you'll need to take on your bestseller journey, it's time to begin. First, you'll need to create a detailed outline.

---

7. Conor, Peter. "The Socratic Method: Fostering Critical Thinking" The Institute for Learning and Teaching: Colorado State University. https://tilt.colostate.edu/the-socratic-method/

Craft Your Bestselling Outline

Begin the outline of your book by placing your Map from Step 3 and your new table of contents in front of you. Once again, list each step that the reader should follow to achieve the promise of your book. Underneath each step, list at least three ideas for chunks of content that will flesh out and explain how the reader will accomplish that step effectively. Refine and revise the chunks of content until they fit on one or two pages, and be careful not to duplicate material ideas and topics.

As you create this outline, imagine the metaphor you've chosen and look for places within the outline that you can draw connections between your metaphor and the sections you've designated. Imagine your reader following your Map, taking each step, overcoming each obstacle, and finally achieving the result you've promised.

With your outline in hand, the writing process will be much easier. Rather than stewing for hours about what to write, you can simply describe the journey in the order you've already outlined using words and word pictures. Keeping in mind the five word ratios I've just revealed, it's time to begin writing.

Create a Personalized Writing Routine

Every author has their own unique way of accomplishing their task. Some "bite on the nail" like Hemingway every day from six in the morning to noon, no matter what they were doing the night before. Some procrastinate until a deadline looms and write early and late until the book is done. Choose a routine that works best for you.

But just because you're an author doesn't mean you need to personally write every single word. Most successful books are collaborative efforts. You could hire a ghostwriter. You could transcribe the text by speaking it into your Word processor or another transcription program. You could teach each step of your process in a

Your writing ritual is your forge. Just show up and pound the keys.

zoom class and use a copy of the transcription as your preliminary draft. You could even have an AI program write it for you. However you do it, you've gotta hammer out the work—that's why I call it the "Word Forge." You're a wordsmith, pounding out the message until it's shaped and sharpened and ready for work.

If you choose to keep a daily route, try to lay down five hundred to one thousand words a day. The next day, revise what you wrote the day before and forge another five hundred to one thousand words. Whatever you choose to do, be consistent, and don't quit! If you keep forging ahead, you'll be able to pound out that fifty-thousand-word book in fifty to one hundred days. Then, you'll be ready to move on to the next step: creating a visually appealing cover for your masterpiece.

> "Work every day. No matter what has happened the day or night before, get up and bite on the nail."
> – *Ernest Hemingway*

FREE GIFT: AI for Authors Masterclass + Prompt Sheet

If you're stuck on what to say or how to say it, ethically steal my 1,000 AI writing prompts—plus a video masterclass on how to use them to write faster. Access everything at AuthorGifts.com or scan the code.

> "We put our money in banks, we put our food in the pantry, we put our clothes in the clothes closet, but God and great people have put their wisdom and counsel, their caution and best thoughts in books."
>
> – Jeffrey R. Holland

STEP 6: YOUR BOLD BOOK COVER

The Hook of Hooks

Topping the most influential bestseller list in the world—*The New York Times*—is the dream of every author. I hate to tell you this, but it's highly unlikely your book is ever going to land there. It's not impossible—but nearly. I've been lucky enough to land there four times, with my books spending one hundred weeks on this, most prestigious of all lists. The *New York Times* list is the Mount Everest of publishing.

However, if I were writing a book today, I would take a different approach to publishing it. I wouldn't try to find a major publisher—yet. I wouldn't aim to climb the *New York Times* list—yet. I would aim to build an audience first. And I would probably self-publish.

You can still be a number one bestselling author if you go this route instead. You might not top the list of the one hundred bestselling books out of the tens of millions of books on Amazon, but you can certainly reach the one hundred bestsellers in your niche topic. And, who knows? You might even hit the top spot. If you do, you'll be able to say you're a number one bestseller on Amazon. You'll be able to print this achievement on the cover of your book. To be number one on the largest bookstore on the planet would be a good start, wouldn't it? That's the minimal goal of your book launch, which you'll learn more about in Step 11.

But if you don't set up your book for success, it won't climb *any* lists. You won't even top your *neighborhood* bestseller list. Pallets of your books will sit in your garage gathering dust. Worse yet, your message will go unheard. The people's lives you were destined to change will remain unchanged. That's unacceptable, isn't it?

> "People say, 'Don't judge a book by its cover.' But if you want to sell copies, make sure your cover is dressed to kill."
> – *Unknown*

Well, the unacceptable happens every day as thousands of newbie authors release their cherished messages in forgettable books that only a few will ever read. Don't make that mistake. Your bestsellerdom depends upon it. Now that you've finished writing your book, make sure you prepare it to catch all of the attention it deserves with a winning cover design.

Can You Judge a Book by Its Cover?

They say you can't judge a book by its cover, but that's nonsense! All books are instantly judged by their covers. As we discussed in Step 5, some of the most important Marketing Words you'll ever write are the words on the cover of your book. If most of your book's success will depend on the appearance of and wording on the cover, then deciding on the best design, color, title, and subtitle is vital. Your cover is prime real estate. Don't make it look like a slum! That's just plain stupid.

Which one would you visit first?

A beautiful cover won't happen by accident. Effective book covers combine an eye-catching focal point, colors that fit your theme, and attractive fonts into one cohesive and memorable design. To gather ideas, take a look at what's currently selling well in your niche. Think about how you can appeal to the same audience while still setting yourself apart.

Unless you're already an experienced and qualified graphic designer, spend a little money on the cover. Find an expert online at Fiverr or 99designs to help you craft a professional looking cover. But it doesn't stop there—you'll need a winning title too.

The Importance of a Great Title

Many "would-be" authors seem to come up with the *lamest* titles. No wonder their books never go anywhere! I can't tell you how many first-time authors proudly show me copies of their books and want my feedback. I always cut right to the chase: "How is it selling?"

"Not as well as I hoped," they admit sheepishly.

"How much did you spend to get your name on that cover?"

There's usually a long pause here. They're embarrassed to admit the number: "Too much."

"Did you test the title of your book before you launched it?"

> The most valuable of all talents is that of never using two words when one will do."
>
> —Thomas Jefferson

Sadly, the answer is almost always "no."

I wish they had met me *before* the book was written and published, and I would have taught them my (almost) foolproof six-step Bestselling Title Test. It's how you create a title with the greatest probability of becoming a bestseller. I've developed this process from over forty-five years of painful experience. Some of my own book titles were million copy blockbusters, but a few of my titles were absolute busts. Trust me, I know the pain of working for two years on a book that doesn't go anywhere.

Creating a fresh, exciting, eye-catching title, subtitle, and book cover is IMPORTANT! You've *got* to get these things right! Period. *End* of story.

Do you want to slave late nights and early mornings for months on the message inside of your book, just to have people dismiss that message based on the *outside* of your book? Don't shut the door to your future without people reading a single word! Don't choose to have a cheap, self-published looking cover! This decision makes or break a book, sending it toward the bestseller lists or to the bargain bins.

That's why I spend so much effort in my Authors Accelerator program guiding my participants through a revolutionary process to discover the perfect bestselling titles. I'll share that process with you here. This doesn't guarantee you'll reach the bestseller list, but I can almost guarantee that if your book title sucks, your message will disappear into darkness.

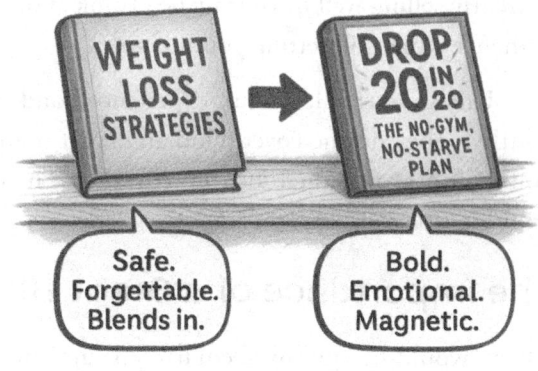

Numbers Trump Your Personal Opinion

Let's take a look at four of my million-copy bestselling titles and subtitles:

- *Nothing Down: A Proven Program That Shows You How to Buy Real Estate with Little or No Money Down* – This book sold a million copies, and it's still selling after forty-five years!
- *Creating Wealth* – This book has no subtitle, but the promise is so clear to wealth seekers that a million of them (and counting) have added this book to their home libraries.
- *Multiple Streams of Income: How to Generate a Lifetime of Unlimited Wealth* – This title has become iconic, and the phrase "multiple streams of income" can be heard on the lips of entrepreneurs worldwide. It resonates. I hated the subtitle, but when we tested this subtitle with my students, it was the overwhelming favorite. Numbers should always trump your personal opinion. The book became a *New York Times* bestseller and is still selling after twenty-five years. It's closing in on a million sales. It will likely sell for another hundred years. It's an iconic brand.

> "The greatest deception men suffer is from their own opinions."
> – Leonardo da Vinci

- *The One Minute Millionaire: The Enlightened Way to Wealth* – The promise for this book is in the main title. It's a head turner. It raises eyebrows.

The subtitle seems like an oxymoron—how can money be enlightened? Most people think money is dark and dirty. Not so! And in the book, we prove it. Another million sales!

But several of my titles have bombed. ☹ For example, my third book—arguably my best book that took two years of my life to write—is called *The Challenge*. What's enticing about this title? What urgent problem does this title claim to solve? What burning passion does this title satisfy? Nada! When you go to a bookstore, are you hoping to find a challenge? It's a stupid title.

And the subtitle is even worse: "Send me to any unemployment line. Let me select someone who is broke, out of work, discouraged. Let me teach him in two days' time the secrets of wealth. And in ninety days he'll be back on his feet, with $5,000 cash in the bank, never to set foot in an unemployment line again."

Broke, out of work, discouraged people don't usually frequent bookstores. I thought it was a wonderful title. And so did the publisher who gave me a $500,000 advance to write it. But we didn't test that title. We just published it and thought the weight of my bestselling reputation would carry it on to great success. Dumb and dumber.

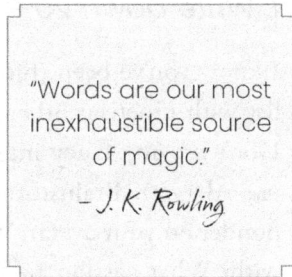

"Words are our most inexhaustible source of magic."
– J. K. Rowling

What's tragic is that this bad title not only cost me a bestseller status, but the message reached dramatically fewer readers. My royalties dried up, and so did the dreams of a million people who could have benefited from the message. My publisher was so bummed that they reverted the publishing rights back to me, essentially saying, "Have your manuscript back. We can't sell it." Don't worry—there was gold in this disaster. In "Step 8: Your Opt-in to Wealth," I'll show you how I turned this catastrophe into a Cash Cow.

But first, there is an art to creating a bestselling cover. When I'm teaching my Authors Accelerator class, I have each member design their own cover showing their title and subtitle using free tools on Canva.com. Then, we display the covers to the group on Zoom. Everyone gets five seconds to vote on each cover by giving it a score from one (bad) to ten (great). If a cover doesn't score at least eight, nine, or ten, it's not good enough. In a group that includes twenty-five covers, typically only one or two will score above eight. Most score lower than five.

I ask my students to tell me why the winners won. What principles emerge in the patterns of great titles? They learn, by experience, how a few titles are winners, but most are losers. Then, I have them re-engineer their losing titles by using this Bestselling Title Test.

The 6-Step, Stoopid-Proof Bestselling Title Test

Remember—your ideal customer has an urgent problem and/or a burning passion that they need to resolve. They are googling *right now* to find a book with solutions. Google processes one hundred thousand searches a second. You want some of these searches to find you and your book, so your title must point to your message as the solution. To make sure your title is effective, you'll need to test it. Here's how:

1. Write Down 20 Possible Titles & Subtitles

I know you've been thinking of a title for your book already. Put that title on a list with nineteen other brainstormed titles for a total of twenty possible titles. Don't use any fancy internet search algorithms. Don't use AI (yet). Brainstorm by yourself. Let your mind ponder on your avatar. What problem are they dealing with? What passion are they trying to satisfy? Imagine you only have five seconds to shout out one specific twenty-word message to someone who is anxiously, earnestly, desperately, hungrily, addictively, enthusiastically, passionately searching. They are not just curious

> "The last thing we discover in composing a work is what to put down first."
> – *Blaise Pascal*

or interested or absentmindedly glancing. They are on a mission—obsessed, even. They don't just *want* the information, they *need* it. You only have five seconds to get their attention. With this goal in mind, come up with twenty titles and subtitles consisting of twenty words or less.

2. Discard Any & All Clichés

How can you tell if your title contains a cliché? *Merriam-Webster* defines a cliché as a "trite phrase or expression" that is "overly familiar or commonplace."[1] If you need examples, Go to clichelist.net, and you'll find thousands of clichés starting with every letter in the alphabet: "**A**s good as gold. **B**et the farm. **C**lear as a bell.

---

1. "Cliché," Merriam-Webster Online Dictionary. https://www.merriam-webster.com/dictionary/cliche

Deer in the headlights. **E**asy as Pie. **F**lat as a pancake. **G**ood as Gold. **H**alf-baked idea. **I**cing on the Cake. **J**ump the Gun. **K**eep it Simple Stupid. **L**ight at the end of the tunnel. **M**aking money hand over fist…"

Do I need to go on?

Stay away from clichés. Why? Because someone has probably already snagged that cliché, bought the domain, and written a book about it. You don't want to waste money advertising a boring, ordinary, clichéd title to drive customers to a bookstore only to find a dozen other books with that same title. Don't confuse your avatar. Don't send people to buy a competitor's book!

> "Either write something worth reading or do something worth writing."
> – Benjamin Franklin

Besides, clichés are so commonplace that they slip through our awareness unnoticed. You want your book to be noticed!

3. Expand Your Brainstorm

When you're done de-cliché-ifying your list of possible titles, bring in a handful or two of friends, customers, or family members. Show them your twenty titles and share with them the following list of descriptive adjectives frequently used in bestselling titles: specific, unique, radical, simple, revolutionary, outrageous, different, crazy, interesting, fresh, new, cutting edge, bold, provocative, shocking, silly.

Show them a list of bestselling titles that fit the desired mold. The following list contains examples. Ask them to pick out the bold promise in each of these titles:

- *The Four-Hour Workweek: Escape 9–5, Live Anywhere, and Join the New Rich*, by Timothy Ferris
- *Eat that Frog: 21 Great Ways to Stop Procrastinating and Get More Done in Less Time*, by Brian Tracy
- *7 Habits of Highly Effective People: Powerful Lessons in Personal Change*, by Stephen Covey

- *Rich Dad Poor Dad: What the Rich Teach Their Kids about Money That the Poor and Middle Class Do Not*, by Robert Kiyosaki
- *The Subtle Art of Not Give a F*ck: A Counterintuitive Approach to Living a Good Life*, by Mark Manson
- *Think and Grow Rich: For Men and Women Who Resent Poverty*, by Napoleon Hill
- *The Purpose Driven Life: What on Earth Am I Here For?* by Rick Warren
- *Men Are from Mars. Women Are from Venus: A Practical Guide for Improving Communication and Getting What you Want in Your Relationships*, by John Gray, PhD
- *Chicken Soup for the Soul: 101 Stories to Open the Heart and Rekindle the Spirit*, by Jack Canfield and Mark Victor Hansen
- *Atomic Habits: Tiny Changes. Remarkable Results. An Easy & Proven Way to Build Good Habits and Break Bad Ones*, by James Clear

Now, start brainstorming with your small group and see if they can come up with anything better. Don't immediately judge any title as good or bad. Eventually, discard the titles that the group doesn't like. Add some new ones. Reduce the list of twenty down to only ten. Then, have a final vote to reduce the list to the best five titles and subtitles. Now you have a list to test.

4. Start Testing

Bounce the list of five possible titles off of at least one hundred people. Where will you find these one hundred people? You can select names of friends and family right from your cell phone contact list. If you have a database of contacts/customers, survey them. If you're active on social media, then ask those audiences. If you have a podcast, test your title there, too.

> All writers know how important a good title is. It's the first thing readers see, along with a knock-your-socks-off cover – a seductive 'come hither' for the story within.
>
> – Caroline Leavitt

If you still don't have one hundred people, you can survey random people you meet in the elevator or on the street or at the mall.

Show each person your list of titles, and say something like this: "Excuse me, can you help me decide the title for my next book? Is there a title here that would make you want to buy it?" If there's extra time, ask them if they can think of a better title. Record each vote and take note of the final tally. Which title got the most votes? Which was number two?

This process is not very scientific. It's a random survey of uninterested people. Still, you'll start to see patterns. Generally, one or two titles will top the popular vote. Some titles will get zero votes. Keep the top two

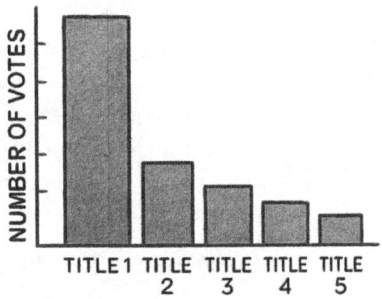

Your best title should win by a landslide.

or three winning titles, delete the losers, and replace them with two or three new titles. Then, test the new list again with the same databases. Eventually, one title will win against all the others. And, if tested with enough people, the winning title will be twice as good as the second-place title and three times as good as the third-place title.

Zipf's Law: The Amazing Hidden Ratio

My bestselling author friend Marshall Thurber introduced me to Zipf's law. This a scientific law named after a linguist from Harvard called George Zipf who noticed in the 1940s that the most-used word in the English language, *the*, occurred about twice as frequently as the second most-used word, *of*, and three times as frequently as the third most used word, *and*.[2]

From this observation, he created Zipf's law, which states that when given a large sample of words used, the frequency of any word is inversely proportional to its rank in the frequency table. So, nth word has a frequency proportional to $1/n$.

Confusing, huh?

Zipf wondered if this pattern existed in other areas besides linguistics. He found that in many areas of life, this ratio held true. The most populated city in America (New York—with about eight million residents) was twice as large as the second most populated city (Los Angeles, with a population of about four million) and about three times as large as the third largest city (Chicago—about three million). Or to put it in a ratio, the third largest city is one third the size of New York. This ratio also holds true for the most visited websites or company sizes within an industry.

---
2. Zipf's Law, Britannica. https://www.britannica.com/topic/Zipfs-law

> "Productivity is never an accident. It is always the result of a commitment to excellence, intelligent planning, and focused effort."
>
> – Paul J. Meyer

So, why not use Zipf's law to find the best title for your book?

For example, I gave an assignment to an Authors Accelerator class to come up with twenty possible titles for their book. Bill Barnett had a hard time coming up with twenty titles. He could only think of nineteen. Out of desperation to think of the twentieth item, a strange title popped into his mind. He thought it was crazy—even stupid. Still, he went to a local mall to conduct his survey with total strangers. He was shocked when the twentieth title on the list was more than twice as popular as the second-place title. Bill had tapped into Zipf's law. Here is his winning title: *Are You Dumb Enough to Be Rich? The Amazingly Simple Way to Make Millions in Real Estate*, by G. William Barnett II with a foreword by Robert G. Allen.

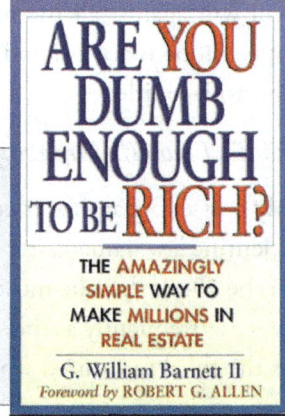

> "Thanks, Bob. With your guidance, I created a bestselling book that has sold tens of thousands copies and has generated hundreds of thousands of dollars of profit."
>
> – William "Bill" Barnett

If you survey a list of five possible titles, the winning title will usually get twice as many votes as the second-place title and three times as many votes as the third-place title. Sometimes just changing *one* word in a title can a have dramatic effect.

I encourage you to continue testing your group of titles until one title seems to be chosen about twice as much as the second title, and so on.

After you've conducted general testing within your circle of influence or in your community, expand out to larger databases. Then, expand out to ChatGPT. See if AI can suggest a few titles to add to your title test. As always, narrow down to a list of five for testing.

5. Get Serious about Your Testing

If you want a more professional testing option, go to PickFu.com and set up a title testing survey for about one dollar per response. It's kind of cool to see total strangers weigh in on your chosen titles.

For example, I recently ran a test on PickFu.com to discover which of the following two titles I should choose for *this* book:

- *Number One! How to Write a Bestselling Book*
- *#1 Bestseller! How to Become a Bestselling Author*

Here are the results: *#1 Bestseller!* Got thirty-two votes. *Number One!* got eighteen votes. Each response came with an explanation of why the voter made their choice, so the survey also provided me with constructive feedback. Before I posted this survey, I had already chosen my favorite title: *Number One! How to Write a Bestselling Book*. I was so confident that I had already bought the domain name. But the survey showed me I was totally wrong.

> "Employ your time in improving yourself by other men's writings, so that you shall gain easily what others have labored hard for."
> – Socrates

It took about an hour and cost me seventy dollars. With this information and through additional testing since, I learned I needed to emphasize the word *author* instead of the word *book*.

Do you see how just one word can make a difference?

Why Testing a Few Different Titles Makes a Massive Difference

Without a lot of testing, Stevens Anderson, the creator of a book called *The Compact Classics* was hoping the title of his book would catch on. His book was based on a brilliant concept. He'd spent tens of thousands of dollars selecting, reading, editing, and summarizing the greatest classic books on success, business, and literature. He thought it would be valuable for someone to read a summary of *War and Peace* or *7 Habits of Highly Effective People* or the biography of Walt Disney in just two pages. But, when he published *Compact Classics*, the sales were disappointing. Then someone had the brilliant idea to test a totally different title. This is the rather embarrassing new title: *The Great American Bathroom Book: Summaries of All-Time Great Books*

Imagine reading the greatest books in history in just one sitting! ☺ His sales skyrocketed! The book has now sold over a million copies, with three volumes published in the United States and two volumes in the United Kingdom. By the way, the UK title is, *Passing Time in the Loo: Summaries of All-Time Great Books*

This story is a warning to pre-test your titles, and I've only shown you the tip of the iceberg on title testing. I go into more detail in my Authors Accelerator program. With millions of titles to compete with, your book needs all the help it can get. It had better stand out, or it will be overlooked!

6. Ask a Higher Power to Weigh In on Your Title

This should probably be the first step in deciding a title, but I've listed it last because I realize you may not believe in a Higher Power. Obviously, I do.

I have some personal experience with the subtle nudges that come from the Universe. (I refer to Him as my Father in Heaven, but I'll use a more generic term in this discussion.)

I was given a heavenly "hint" about the title of my first book on a drive between Salt Lake City and Provo, Utah, after receiving the spiritual impression, *It's time to write your book now.*

I pondered, *What should I call it?*

I felt the answer: *Nothing Down.*

I did no testing. I just knew it was the title. I *knew* it. A few days later, I drove to the office of my real estate broker and quit my career as a real estate investment advisor. I declared, "I quit. It's time to write my book now. I will never collect another real estate sales commission."

To use some clichés: I burned my bridges, I sank my boats, I crossed the Rubicon, I passed the point of no return, and I jumped in with both feet.

> "Trusting our intuition often saves us from disaster."
> — Anne Wilson Schaef

Within a few short weeks, I was writing my book. It turns out that the title and the timing could not have been more perfect. The long recession was over. Ronald Reagan was the new president. Baby boomers were seeking to make their way in the world with new families and burning to buy their first homes. But many of them did not have enough money to afford it. My book was the perfect solution. *Nothing Down* hit the *New York Times* list within ninety days. For a time, I thought I was just lucky or savvy or smart. In hindsight, I believe that the Universe knew all of this. I was blessed with the right title at the right time.

The Bestselling Title of All Time

My co-author of *The One Minute Millionaire* is Mark Victor Hansen, who authored *Chicken Soup for the Soul*. He shared with me how he and his co-author—Jack Canfield—struggled for months to find the ideal title for their new book of short stories. Mark would go to bed each night while saying a hundred times under his breath, "Mega bestselling title! Mega bestselling title!" Jack Canfield shared the story of how the title finally appeared. After brainstorming hundreds of titles, he woke up in the middle of the night, and the title whispered in his mind: *Chicken Soup for the Soul*. He just *knew* this was the title of titles.

> "Faith is taking the first step even when you don't see the whole staircase."
> – Martin Luther King, Jr.

In my opinion, that title was "downloaded" from a higher source. Higher Power knew this would eventually become the all-time bestselling series of books in the history of the world. And the *Chicken Soup* family of books has generated thousands of life changing testimonials.

There are hundreds of Higher Power title stories like this. So be open to those gentle nudges.

If you believe in a Higher Power, ask yourself the following questions:

- Does the Universe know the best title for my book right now?
- Does the Universe know who needs the solution that my book offers, right now?

If you answered "yes," then why wouldn't you at least petition the Universe for a little guidance? Saying something like this might be appropriate: "I want to be part of the solution to the problems of the world." Or, "Please help me reach the right people with the right title at the right time."

And then be open to impressions from above.

The perfect title for your unforgettable book cover is out there—it just takes a little time and effort to find it. Once you do, you'll be ready to design your book's interior. Let's move on to Step 7.

FREE GIFT: AI Title Generator

A strong cover grabs attention—but your title closes the deal. I built a tool that helps you brainstorm faster by generating title ideas in seconds. Try it at AuthorGifts.com or scan the code.

> "Start writing, no matter what. The water does not flow until the faucet is turned on."
>
> – Louis L'Amour

STEP 7: YOUR IMPRESSIVE LAYOUT

Making Your Book Interior "Sticky"

Let me tell you a dirty little secret: there are lots of so-called "experts" out there who will brag that they can help get your book on a bestseller list. Here's how they do it. Most people don't know that Amazon's bestseller list changes *every hour*. These "experts" show you how to organize a marketing "push" to drive a lot of sales to Amazon during one specific hour on one specific day. With a rush of hourly sales, your book hits the top ten in one narrow niche on the site. But in the *very next hour*, your book falls off the list, often never to return.

Sure, you can tell people that you're a bestselling author, but let's be real—it's a racket. You don't want to just *say* you're a bestselling author. What you *really* want is a *perennial* bestseller—a book that brings you steady streams of income for decades, not days. Look at any of the bestseller lists on Amazon. You'll see a few books that have remained on the list of one hundred top sellers in their niche for years! They're perennial!

I'm still earning royalties on books I wrote decades ago. That's where *you* want to be. The best way to do that is to create an online marketing machine for your books. You'll create a successful platform for finding new readers. These readers become the customers for your online businesses—which is where the serious money is made.

Rather than making small money from book royalties, I'll show you how to earn big money by giving your book away for free! I'll share more on this in

Step 9, but trust me—you'll never get tired of seeing money show up in your bank account twenty-four hours a day—NEVER.

Once your platform is established and your self-published book is selling consistently online, *then* you will be much more attractive to a traditional publisher. *Then*, you can negotiate a much more advantageous publishing contract where you retain more rights and more control. *Then*, using your own growing database of potential readers, you can make every book you write a number one bestseller.

> "It took me fifteen years to discover I had no talent for writing, but I couldn't give it up because by that time I was too famous."
> – Robert Benchley

Would you like that? Fabulous steams of income *plus* the credibility of becoming a bestselling author with a bestselling book published by a major traditional publisher? Why not!?

Just to whet your appetite, this chart shows four of the largest selling books in history that were first self-published and *then* became traditionally published bestsellers:

Title	Author	Copies Sold
Your Erroneous Zones	Wayne Dyer	100 million
The Celestine Prophecy	James Redfield	23 million
Rich Dad, Poor Dad	Robert Kiyosaki	40 million
What Color is your Parachute?	Richard Nelson Bolles	10 million

But as exciting as it is to sell millions of books, nothing compares to the thrill of learning that your influence has improved someone's life. Because when you change *one* life, you influence a generation of lives. You only earn a royalty once for each book you sell, but the power of the information in your book can live on forever. That's heady stuff.

I can't go anywhere in the world it seems, without someone spotting me and saying, "Are you Robert Allen? Your book changed my life!"

Would you like to hear those words from your readers?

"Robert, Because of your help, my second book, *How to Turn Your Knowledge into Income*, which included your endorsement, was a big success for me—a bestseller! It sold almost forty thousand copies! My publisher asked me to write a third book. I really want to say, THANK YOU VERY MUCH!"

– *Tetsuya Inamura*

I don't know about you, but that's the reason I write. How sad, then, when you've got a message to share, and your message gets lost because you're missing just a few numbers of the combination lock to the Bestselling Author Vault.

You already know that this book shares the twelve numbers (or steps) to open that vault. The biggest myth in publishing is that your job is to write the book, and the publisher will get your book "out there." As I've explained, after the first thirty days, the publisher is on to the next dozen books in their pipeline, and you'll be left with the job of marketing. So, let's start with the correct assumption: You're in charge of marketing whether you self-publish or publish traditionally. If you want to be a bestselling author, you need to become an author who knows how to sell.

"I am so clever that sometimes I don't understand a single word of what I am saying."

– *Oscar Wilde*

One of the best ways to support that goal is to give your book a professional-looking interior that will draw your readers in and maintain their interest in your message.

Avoid the Look & Feel of a Self-Published Book

Your book might be self-published, but make sure the inside of your book doesn't *look* "self-published." Maybe this is my personal pet-peeve, but I can a spot a self-published book with one glance.

When you open a self-published book, you can usually tell it's not a "real" book. It just doesn't feel right. The layout is haphazard, the font looks cheap, and the spacing is off. The illustrations often appear subpar and generic, and the style is inconsistent. It's as if someone didn't care enough to do it right. It's like fingers scratching on a chalkboard to me.

There is a *flood* of bad self-published books pouring into the world—millions this year alone! I'm not railing against *all* self-published books. Some of the biggest titles, like the list I shared earlier in this chapter, were first launched as self-published books. But they looked professional, they had great titles, and they were backed by smart marketing!

Here are a few common interior book design pitfalls you should avoid falling prey to:

Formatting Your Book Without Learning How First

Similar to cover design, there's an art to interior book design that follows certain rules. These rules are designed to invite your reader into your message and lead them from page to page and chapter to chapter with text that is easy to read comfortably.

Text that's too small and dense will overwhelm your reader's eyes and cause mental exhaustion. Too many words on one page can look as unappealing as a traffic jam on the freeway at rush hour. That's *not* the experience you want to give your reader.

In addition, a good book design incorporates both variety and consistency by using attractive display fonts (typefaces used for titles and headings) and appealing body fonts (typefaces used for your actual text). An effective book design will create a consistent theme with these elements and then stick to that theme in a logical and harmonious way.

> "The idea is to write it so that people hear it, and it slides through the brain and goes straight to the heart."
>
> – Maya Angelou

While book design isn't inherently difficult, it does require some training and a good eye for visual detail and composition. If you'd like to try and design your book's interior yourself, find an online training program with a good reputation or ask someone knowledgeable to teach you. You can format a book using a basic word processing program, but keep in mind that your ability to customize and control the formatting will be limited. If you're working on a full-length book and you don't know how to use the available formatting tools to your advantage, your task may quickly become frustrating and overwhelming.

Hiring the Cheapest Typesetter You Can Find

You usually get what you pay for, and book design is no different. There are several websites that can connect you with book designers, but don't choose someone to typeset your book based solely on price or how quickly they can accomplish the task. These designers will likely spend a little time cleaning up your manuscript, slap it into a PDF file format, and send it back to you looking like a glorified high school project—not like a professionally published book.

> "There are two doors in life: The door marked Security and the door marked Freedom. If you choose the door marked Security, You lose both."
>
> – Robert G. Allen

Ask potential book designers for samples of their work or request referrals from other authors who have done well with their own book interiors. Have a little dignity—this is your legacy. Don't be afraid to spend a little money to achieve an excellent result.

In addition, make sure you understand what's included in the price you've agreed to pay. Will the designer provide you with the original design files in case you'd like to make changes in the future? Will they help you with text revisions within the design should you find typos? It may be tempting to negotiate one low, set fee to complete the design, but this will likely limit the designer's ability to make your book's interior exactly how you want it. Ensure that you have a clear agreement that's fair for both of you *and* meets your book's needs.

Draw Your Reader's Attention with Images

As I said in Step 5, a single word can be worth a thousand pictures. I shared how to empower your words by making them stickier—or more imaginatively visual with metaphors and questions and stories.

When designing your book, don't just use visual *language*—add *actual* images to your interior. Once again, a picture is worth a thousand words because sixty-five percent of us are visual learners.

Go to your own library and select any book at random. Notice the ratio of verbal content to visual content. Most books are ninety-nine percent verbal (words) and one percent visual (images, charts, graphs, etc.).

Many people don't read beyond the first chapter of any book they buy because sixty-five percent of people are visual learners. Perhaps the title grabbed their attention, but then they got lost in the forest of words.

Why do you think that more and more books are "audibled" or "YouTubed" today instead of physically read? Is it because listening to books is an efficient use of time that allows readers to multitask? Or is it because we're conditioned by our television, movies, and social media to consume visual content? That's part of the answer. But primarily it's because it's faster and easier to learn visually or auditorily. Your book *must* include visual material.

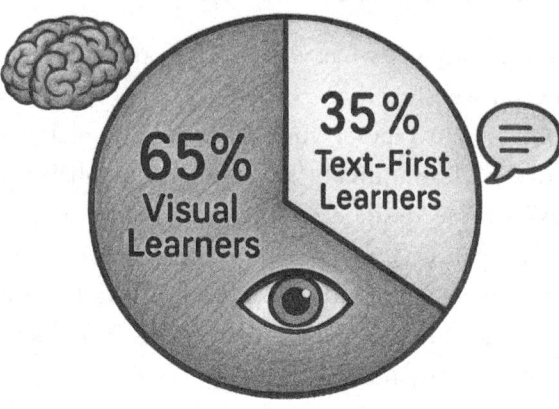

Words tell. Pictures sell.

Strive to increase the ratio of words to images in your chapters. I challenge you to include at least one or two images or visual elements for every page in your book. If each of those images is worth a thousand words, that's thousands of words of learning accomplished in a fraction of the time!

**A Wall of Words
=
Visual Fatigue**

**Sticky Visuals
=
Reader Engagement**

When you open my book *Multiple Streams of Income*, I dare you to find a single page with only words. You'll find at least one of the following on every page:

- chart
- graph
- illustration
- comic
- photograph
- quote
- humorous thought
- bulleted list
- numbered list
- sidebar
- table
- diagram
- outline
- logo
- map
- stylized text

Why should you go to this trouble? Because it makes your book look sticky. People will quickly flip through your book and get stuck on an image. They will immediately grasp the image without reading the ten thousand words around it. If they find an image or two that speaks to them visually, they'll want to buy the book just to capture that image.

So, as you finish writing the words in your book, scan back through the text to find places where an image could summarize the thought. Do some googling to find a quote that illustrates the ideas you're trying to share like the quotes found in this book.

Or add a humorous thought about your subject that will put a smile on your reader's face, like the quote about Moses on this page.

> "If Moses were alive today, he'd come down from the mountain with the Ten Commandments and spend the next five years trying to get them published."
>
> – Amit Tiwari

Put the thoughts and quotes in a unique visual template that sets them apart from the text as an eye grabber—a visual distraction.

To illustrate, let me share with you one of the most important chapters from *Multiple Streams of Income*. Go to www.authorsummits.com/MSI to download the chapter. The ideas in this chapter share how I generated over a billion dollars from books and information in my career. You need to read it. It's called "Your Eight Stream: Infopreneuring—How to Turn a Tiny Classified Ad into a Fortune."

Notice the charts and other visual content in this thirty-two-page chapter. What can I say? It's sticky. These images call out to the sixty-five percent of us who are visual. People like us will want to get the book so they can view the images.

Now, could a book be a bestseller without a lot of images? Well, thirty-five percent of your audience is more left brained. Words and numbers are the language of left-brained people. So, yes—it's possible. But I have a philosophy: when I decide to succeed at something, I go *all* in. You can't get an airplane off the runway at half throttle. I want to use every possible advantage to help myself into the air. I want to speak to the right brainers *and* the left brainers. That's why *The One Minute Millionaire* includes both a fictional story (the Story Side) and a detailed plan for achieving it (the System Side.)

The Pareto Principle of Steps

You may have heard of the Pareto Principle, or the 80/20 rule, which observes that our efforts and the resulting outcomes are not evenly distributed.[1] Often, eighty percent

---

1. "Understanding the Pareto Principle (The 80/20 Rule)" *Better Explained*, https://betterexplained.com/articles/understanding-the-pareto-principle-the-8020-rule/

of our output results directly from only twenty percent of our input. This means that taking the right actions at the right time in any activity is vital to our goal. Similarly, some of the twelve steps in this book are *absolutely* vital to *your* success. It's highly improbable that you'll become a bestselling author without a great title (words—which you read about in Step 5) or a Succession Stack (names—which you'll learn more about in Step 9). At least get those two steps right.

You can't skip steps and expect sweet results.

Some of the steps may not be as essential as others, but even these smaller steps, like creating visual hooks for the inside of your book, can tip a hesitant buyer off the fence and result in a sale. So, I recommend that you accept my challenge to include at least one graphic element or image per page in the visual layout of your book. You'll be glad you did!

FREE GIFT: Self-Publishing Layout Toolkit

Want your book to look traditionally published? I put together a toolkit with formatting templates and layout guides. Download it at AuthorGifts.com or scan the QR code.

"Everything you want is on the other side of 'no.'"

– Robert G. Allen

STEP 8: YOUR OPT-IN TO WEALTH

A License to Print Money

Remember the two key bestseller concepts: words and names. In the first few steps of this book, I shared with you how to organize and massage the words of your message. Now, let's go deeper on the importance of names—the names of real people, real customers who are searching for answers to their real problems. Ninety percent of the names who opt-in to your database will never buy anything from you. They'll consume your free information. They'll become mildly interested observers. They'll "lurk" on your webinars and peruse your emailed lessons.

Ten percent of the names who opt in will become fans. After a few weeks or months, they might pick up a copy of your book on Amazon. They might buy your next level info-product, investing the minimal money to level-up their learning experience.

But one-to-five percent of your names will become your superfans. They'll buy everything you offer. They'll become addicted to you and your message because it resonates deeply with them. Here's the path that they'll follow:

Disinterested → Curious → Interested → Intrigued → Fan → Superfan

Think about your own consumption of information over the years with various experts and info-providers. Where do you fit along this continuum? It depends on what the information is and who is marketing it. All business is about building lists of potential and actual customers.

I learned this lesson the hard way.

As I explained in "Step 6: Your Bold Book Cover," my first two books were million copy bestsellers, but my third book—*The Challenge*—was my "worstselling" book because of its terrible title and subtitle. However, I had already learned an expensive lesson by not building a database of readers with my first two books. So, embedded in the text of *The Challenge*, I offered various free gifts to the readers.

> "There is nothing to writing. All you do is sit down at a typewriter and bleed."
> – Ernest Hemingway

In eighteen places throughout the book, I offered free supportive information to enhance the information in the book. On page thirty-six, I offered a free audio cassette of a powerful motivating story called *The Blue Vase*. At the back of the book, I offered a free poster of the twelve secrets of wealth contained in the book. The reader just needed to call a toll-free number and give their contact information, and my team sent all the bonuses and gifts by mail. Only sixty thousand people bought the book, but twenty thousand of those readers called the toll-free number. This was a highly qualified, highly motivated database.

Plant gifts inside your book to build your list.

The Challenge tells the true story of how I selected people from the unemployment line and showed them how to get back on their feet to earn at least five thousand dollars in ninety days. The twenty thousand people on *The Challenge* database were offered a five-day training in San Diego, California, to recreate the experience. It was called the Wealth Retreat. The tuition was five thousand dollars, and five thousand people eventually attended! Multiply those numbers:

5,000 students × $5,000 tuition = $25,000,000

This is how I learned the power of building a database.

All of this happened before the internet exploded into the world. When the internet arrived, we had to learn new ways of building databases.

> "The Internet is becoming the town square for the global village of tomorrow."
> – Bill Gates

What does it mean to opt in? The verb *to opt* means to decide, to choose, to select. In the internet world, when you "opt in" you are choosing to share your contact information, such as your name and email address, with another person or entity in exchange for access to something. In layman's terms, "Give me your email address, and I'll send you some free stuff."

Because of CAN-SPAM laws, you can't send unsolicited marketing offers to someone unless they have opted in and given their consent to receive your marketing messages.[1] So, when you visit someone's website, you'll often see a place to enter your email address in exchange for free bonus information. To be squeaky clean, internet marketers sometimes ask you to double opt in. Once you opt in at their website, you receive an email from them to verify that you really want the information requested.

Your database is the most valuable asset you own.

So as a potential bestselling author, why do you need to jump through all of these hoops to build an opt-in page? Because possessing a list of potential customers is like having the power to print money. You can use it to push your book up the bestseller lists. In fact, with a large enough database, you can propel every book your write to the top of the bestseller list.

Before the internet, it cost a minimum of one dollar to send a single piece of direct mail through the post office, so

---

1. "CAN-SPAM Act: A Compliance Guide for Business," Federal Trade Commission. "https://www.ftc.gov/business-guidance/resources/can-spam-act-compliance-guide-business

sending ten thousand letters through the mail was a ten-thousand-dollar decision. Then, it would sometimes take weeks for the resulting sales to materialize. A decent response rate was about 0.5 percent, or fifty people. If you received responses from fewer than fifty people, your ten-thousand-dollar investment went up in smoke. Very risky.

But then along came the internet. An email blast to ten thousand people could be sent out in one minute at a cost of close to zero. Responses could show up in seconds, not weeks. It was revolutionary.

I remember the first time someone demonstrated this to me. It was 1998. David, one of my students, called me and asked, "Hi, Bob. Have you figured out this internet thing yet?"

"No," I confessed.

He said, "Well, I've figured it out. Do you want me to show you?"

When I hesitated, he said, "Let me come to your house and sit at your computer. I'll send one email. And I'll make money for you in minutes, not months."

> "Dreams are illustrations from the book your soul is writing about you."
> – Marsha Norman

He had me. A short time later, he was sitting in my home in front of my computer. He told me that he'd built a list of subscribers to his internet newsletter. His list had grown to 1,500 email addresses. While I watched, he typed a message to his subscribers—just one email—and said something like this:

> *"Hi, it's David. I'm in Robert Allen's house. You know Robert as the author of the #1* New York Times *bestselling books,* Nothing Down *and* Creating Wealth. *Well, he has a new 6-CD program called* Multiple Streams of Income *that talks about 10 ways of making money. I've twisted his arm for you. The retail price is about $100. He's willing to sell to my subscribers for HALF PRICE! But only today. In fact, only for the next HOUR. So, if you're interested, send me your name, address, and credit card number, and I'll get him to send it to you. Thanks, David"*

When he finished typing, David turned to me and said, "Look at your watch. Let's see how long this takes." Back then, it was radical to share sensitive credit card information over the internet. But David had built up a level of trust with his subscribers, and they followed his advice. Then he clicked the "send" button, and one email went to each of his 1,500 subscribers. The first order came back in sixty-one seconds! In the next few minutes, dozens of orders flowed in.

I was agog, floored, stunned!

I asked him, "What's your fee? Mentor me on how to do that!"

Without blinking he said, "Six thousand dollars." I took out my checkbook and wrote him a six-thousand-dollar check on the spot.

Because of my busy schedule, it took nine months for David to coach me and my staff to build a website with opt-in features. Over those months, I offered free information to my own growing list of subscribers. I never sold them anything. I just provided valuable, free information week after week. My list eventually grew to 11,516 names.

> "Writing a bestseller is easy.
> Step one: write the book.
> Step two: convince 10,000 strangers you're a genius.
> Step three: take a nap."
>
> – Unknown

Nine months later, it was time to test out David's theory. My business partner, Tom Painter, had organized a camera crew to witness and record my first attempt at selling my own information using the internet.

I realized that to create interest, I needed to make a bold promise. A message is nice, but a promise moves people to action. As I've shared earlier, you need to decide on your outrageous promise and reverse-engineer your offer to deliver on your promise in the shortest time possible. It'll make you stand out.

To my TV viewers that day, this was my promise: "Sit me at the computer with access to the internet, and in twenty-four hours, I'll generate at least $24,000 in cash."

Had I ever done this? No. I actually had *no clue* how much money would roll in that day. But because of what David had shown me, I felt fairly confident that somebody would want to buy. I had "warmed up" my database with a series of emails to test their level of interest. I announced that on one day *only*—May 24, 2000—I would offer huge bargain prices on a select group of my information products—books, audio programs, and an exclusive seminar in my home with me personally.

That day, at 12:36 p.m., I sat at my computer and sent a final email to 11,516 names. The next day, just twenty-four hours later, I was amazed that $94,500 had flooded in overnight! What? My six-thousand-dollar investment had grown to almost a hundred thousand dollars! That six grand was one of the best investments I've ever made because with that knowledge, over the following twenty-five years, my companies have brought in millions of dollars.

(By the way, if you'd like a copy of the exact email sequence that produced these amazing results, go to www.authorsummits.com. I'll send you several powerful chapters of my book *Multiple Streams of Internet Income* that share specific details on how I earned almost $100,000 in twenty-four hours.)

Of course, in the ensuing years, many details have changed, but the strategy remains basically the same:

Free Information → Opt-in → More Free Information → Offer to Sell

It seems simple, but each step of the process requires a *lot* of fine tuning, so keep reading.

Why You Should Build & Maintain a Database

Now that you've heard my story, you're probably saying, "Yeah, I can offer free gifts, but I'm not Robert Allen! Why would they want something from me?" Well, if you build a database of your own loyal customers, they'll look to you as their advisor. To them, *you* are the guru. They are *your* fans—*your* avatars.

This why it's so important to build and nurture your database. It's a gold mine, yielding golden nuggets whenever you dig. It's an oil well in your backyard, pumping out liquid cash.

The ultimate goal is to build a list of at least ten thousand interested names. As this list churns through names—adding some, losing some—you'll eventually find a thousand or more superfans. They'll be with you through thick and thin. They'll notice when you come out with a new book and will be first in line. They'll attend all your webinars and seminars. They'll become superspreaders and fans for life. You need to give them reasons to stay.

> "The need for connection and community is primal, as fundamental as the need for air, water, and food."
> – Dean Ornish

With ten thousand names and one thousand superfans, you control your destiny. Whenever you launch a new book on Amazon, inform your superfans of the exact release date and time. Even one hundred sales of a specific book during a specific hour on Amazon will propel your book up the bestseller lists in your chosen category. Every time you release a book, it can become a number one bestseller. I share these insider secrets during my Bestselling Author Summit to guarantee a number one bestselling book almost every time, and I also show you the exact process in Step 11.

With a dedicated database, every time you need a surge of cash, you can send a new promotion to your database of ten thousand. If just one percent of them take advantage of your promotion, you have one hundred potential buyers. As the chapter subtitle says, it's like a license to print money. Size matters—the bigger your list, the more immediate cash!

So how do you build this database of ten thousand names? Follow these ten steps, and I'll show you:

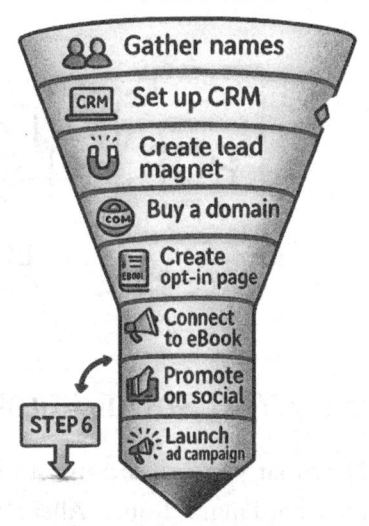

Build your database, one step at a time.

1. Gather Your Existing Names

Collect any existing names from you cell phone contact information, address lists, or wherever else you've stored them. Add your family and friends to your database list. If you have a company, decide which customers would want to know that you are writing a book, and add them as well.

2. Start a Digital Online Database

Gather all of the names you have into an online database. We call this a CRM—a customer relationship manager. There are many free online companies that offer to store your names. My favorite free tool is MailChimp, where you can store up to five hundred names for free.

For the beginning businessperson, I particularly recommend MonetizePro.ai, which includes all the necessary software to run an online business, including an excellent CRM. When we work together in my Authors Accelerator group, I'll tutor you on using MonetizePro, and you'll have ninety days to test it out for free.

3. Create a Lead Magnet

On the internet, free valuable information is often called a lead magnet. An interested party might want a free eBook, a free webinar, a free video (often called a VSL—video sales letter), a free consultation, free online access to a vault of information, or even a free dinner. My favorite lead magnet is a well-designed eBook. Summarize the hottest points of your future book into an eBook.

Advertisers have been using this tactic for centuries. It acts as a sample of the information you offer, like how a free bite of a hot, aromatic cookie at the local bakery can entice you to take home a dozen.

While you're in the process of writing your big book—what I call your magnum opus—plan to release a smaller version of your book in a digital format. Your magnum opus will be fifty thousand to one hundred thousand words. Your summary eBook will have a fraction of that information—no more than fifteen thousand words.

> "It only takes one person to mobilize a community and inspire change. Even if you don't feel like you have it in you, it's in you. You have to believe in yourself. People will see your vision and passion and follow you."
>
> —Teyonah Parris

4. Buy a Domain Name

You can buy a domain name using an online domain name marketplace, such as GoDaddy or SquareSpace. Think it through carefully, and choose something unique, short, and memorable that relates to your business.

5. Create a Website

There are plenty of free tools for building a website, such as Canva, Wix, and Google Sites. Explore the options and choose the platform that best fits your business, needs, and style. If you buy your domain and design your site using the same online service, your domain name will link to your site automatically. But if you buy a domain name somewhere else, you'll need to link it to your site using a hosting service. Then, when someone visits your domain, they will land on your opt-in page.

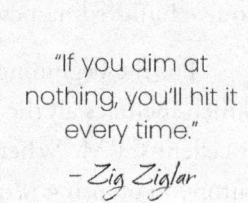

"If you aim at nothing, you'll hit it every time."

— Zig Ziglar

6. Link Your eBook to an Opt-in Page

Format your site so that anyone who opts-in with their email address will have immediate access to your free eBook. Your eBook is designed to introduce your information to new customers in a fun, enticing way and open the door to your more advanced levels of training.

Just like popular membership warehouse stores offer food samples to curious shoppers, your eBook offers a free taste—an appetizer—of your various info-products and prepares your followers for the release of your full-length book. The eBook has to be appetizing, or your upsell will be a "no-sell"!

7. Alert Your Followers

Once your eBook is available to download, announce your free eBook release on social media and to your website subscribers. Invite everyone you can through all of your social media channels to opt in and receive a free copy.

8. Announce Your Book

Once your message has built a following, inform your database about your future book and keep them updated on your progress to build excitement for its release. You can also use your database as your sample group to test your possible list of titles using the process that I shared with you in Step 6.

9. Create a Paid Ad Campaign

Eventually, you'll create a campaign to run paid ads on Facebook, Instagram and YouTube to drive traffic to your opt-in page and further build your database. This sort of advertising is serious marketing, and I strongly recommend that you consult with an expert marketing company. My favorite is Monetize Media. In the next step, I've partnered with Aaron Watson and Lyndsey Merriman of Monetize Media (the co-authors of this book) to share greater detail on building a profitable marketing funnel, or Succession Stack. There are a lot of questions to answer, such as,

- How do you drive visitors to your opt-in page? (sometimes called a squeeze page)
- How do you increase the percentage of people who actually opt in?
- How do you rapidly build a database?
- Where do you host your database?
- How often do you communicate with your database?
- How do you turn an interested name into a superfan?
- Once they opt in, how do you encourage visitors to eventually buy?

If one detail is off, the whole Succession Stack goes dry. It's a very, very tricky process, but if you partner with the right people, you'll be set for victory.

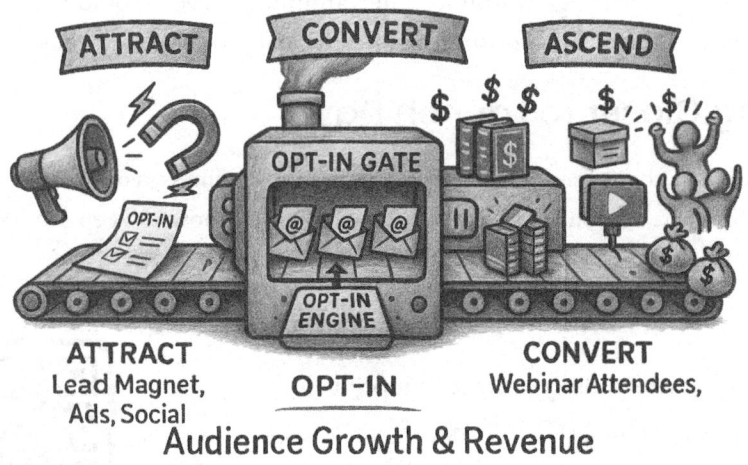

10. Plant "Seeds" to Continue Building

Next, plant seeds in your book to invite readers to join your database, check-out your additional courses or products, and stay in touch. If you've been paying attention, you've likely noticed a few invitations to join my database in *this* book.

The following letter demonstrates the power of using a book to create quality leads for a business. I received this letter from a student named Jesse Cannone in 2007. Jesse has been marketing his book as a way to find customers for over twenty years:

> "It's hard sometimes—to shake yourself off, say out loud the things you dream of—but taking that chance, that leap of faith, that bravery, will always pay off."
>
> – Angela Scanlon

> Bob,
>
> I have been a Protégé of yours since August 2001. I was a broke personal trainer making $20,000 a year looking to fulfill a dream and in debt up to my eyeballs. Can you imagine the horror I felt putting $4,000 on my credit card to join your program only one month before 9/11? My bad situation went to worse. But life goes on, and my thick skin prevented me from giving up, and in 2003, I created the Lose the Back Pain System. I then self-published The 7-Day Back Pain Cure, and it's rapidly becoming an international bestseller. Today we are doing $200,000 per month. There are over a million copies of my book in print.
>
> – Jesse Cannone

As they say, "What goes around comes around." I have become a customer of my student's company and consume his nutritional products every day.

Moving Closer to Launch Day

When you use these ten steps to build your info business, you're opting in to wealth! But there's far more to learn. Let me show you how to keep that database growing and more in "Step 9: Your Succession Stack."

FREE GIFT: List-Building Secrets Blueprint

Your book should grow your list. This blueprint shows you how to turn one chapter into a lead magnet that builds subscribers automatically. Get it at AuthorGifts.com or scan the code.

"You can have everything in life you want, if you will just help enough other people get what they want."

– Zig Ziglar

STEP 9: YOUR SUCCESSION STACK

Earn $100 for Every Word You Write

Congratulations! You've finished writing your book, and you've started building a database of fans and superfans. This is an enormous accomplishment—a milestone many never reach. So take a moment to celebrate! But you're not done yet. You should fully understand by now that your book is only the beginning. Rather than viewing it as the finish line, treat it as the gateway to something bigger—a structured path that takes readers from a single purchase to deep, life-changing experiences. In this chapter, I'll call that journey your Succession Stack.

In previous steps, you've learned how to refine your goals, pinpoint your audience, write a compelling message, create a professional-looking product, and grow your database. Now it's time to harness that momentum and create an ecosystem of products and services that build on each other, fueling your readers' transformation while significantly boosting your revenue.

Providing "Multiple Streams of Income" & Increasing Your Impact

As I've mentioned several times, much of my legacy is built on the principle of multiple streams of income, famously detailed in my number one bestselling book by the same name, which has sold over one million copies worldwide. The core idea is simple yet powerful: instead of depending on a single source of revenue—like a standard job or just one product—you create multiple channels, each contributing to a more stable, diversified flow of income.

That's exactly what a Succession Stack does. You start with a lower-cost offer (your book) and gradually guide people to higher-priced solutions—often called "high-ticket" offers. These offers might be things like one-on-one coaching, small-group masterminds, or premium consulting packages that can cost thousands of dollars. By building a ladder of value—from an entry-level product up to an in-depth, premium service—you can do the following:

THE 4 STREAMS

YOUR BOOK

IMPACT

REVENUE

EVENTS & SPEAKING GIGS   DIGITAL PRODUCTS   COACHING & CONSULTING   PHYSICAL PRODUCTS

1. **Diversify Your Earnings:** Each tier in your Stack becomes its own "stream," so you're never dependent on just one product or price point.
2. **Boost Consistency:** If one offer experiences slow sales, others can pick up the slack.
3. **Amplify Impact:** Different readers have different needs—and budgets. Some want a quick win at a lower price, and others crave a deeper transformation and are willing to invest more.

> "It is literally true that you can succeed best and quickest by helping others to succeed."
> – Napoleon Hill

In short, every step of your Succession Stack acts as a dedicated revenue channel, boosting your financial stability while helping your readers at increasingly deeper levels. You're no longer reliant on a single product for income or impact—you're offering *multiple paths* for people to engage with your expertise, each one building on the trust you first established in your book. It's a win for your audience, who gets the precise level of support they need, and it's a win for you as you create a thriving, sustainable author business. Here are three reasons you need a Succession Stack to reach your greatest potential:

1. Increased Income, Deeper Impact

Let's be real: even if your book hits bestseller lists priced at twenty or thirty dollars, it's not likely to fund your dream lifestyle on its own. But when you add layers—like group programs, coaching courses, and higher-tier consulting—you widen your impact *and* your revenue streams. Instead of a single product, you've got multiple gateways for readers to dive deeper into your message. It's like turning a single note into a full orchestra—more dimension, more volume, more life.

Beyond the boost to your bank account, this expanded lineup ensures you're delivering different levels of transformation. A short, self-paced course might offer a quick win, but a high-touch mastermind (or a course that offers personal feedback and instruction) could drive someone to a total life or business overhaul. In other words, you're not just selling more—you're helping more.

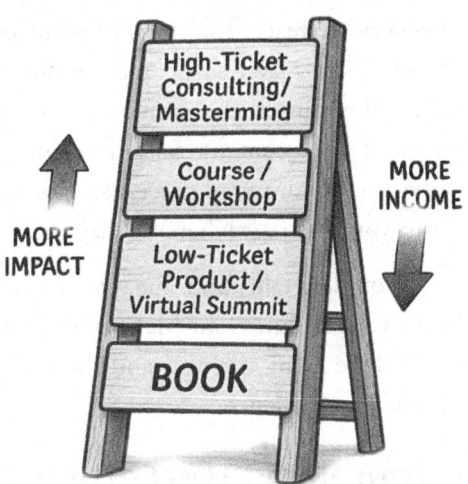

Stack your offers to scale your message and income.

2. Credibility & Authority

Picture this scenario: a reader finishes your book with a burst of enthusiasm—now they want to progress further. If you don't have a "next step" available, that excitement cools. Worse, they might find a competing expert who *does* have a program ready.

By structuring a clear Succession Stack, you're the one guiding their ongoing journey. Each tier confirms your expertise, establishing you as a trusted mentor, not just a passing author. Think of it as building a ladder: each rung your readers climb cements your authority. They begin to see you less as a distant name on a cover and more as their go-to strategist or coach. And there's no better way to earn industry respect than by consistently over-delivering on solutions people genuinely need.

3. Lasting Community & Relationships

Reading is often a solitary pursuit—the activity itself involves your reader, your words, and some quiet reflection. But a well-planned Succession Stack can evolve into something far more communal. Imagine an online forum where members discuss your techniques, celebrate milestones, and support each other's questions.

Maybe you launch a membership site offering monthly calls or even host real-world retreats. The sense of connection multiplies loyalty and sparks word-of-mouth buzz. When people see tangible growth in each other—shifting bad habits, doubling their revenue, dropping the last ten pounds—it reinforces the power of your content. Soon enough, your readers aren't just "fans"—they're a thriving community of success stories, spreading the word about your message wherever they go.

Now, let's talk about the four stages of your Stack and how each will function. Make note of each "golden nugget" I share along the way, and think about how it might benefit *your* audience.

> "Timidity does not inspire bold acts."
> – Mae Jemison

1. Your Book: The Entry Point

Your book is more than ink on paper—it's the handshake that invites readers into your world. Sure, you're sharing your ideas or story, but also think of it as a gateway: you want to naturally guide them to the next step in their journey with you.

Sprinkle Freebies into Your Chapters

Rather than burying all your offers at the end of the book, consider including mini "free bonuses" right in the chapters themselves. For example, halfway through a chapter on budgeting tips, you might say, "Grab my three-part Budgeting Road Map at [YourSite.com/Budget], then join me for a free webinar where I walk you through it." This small nudge moves them from passive reading to active participation—without feeling pushy.

Explain Your Calls to Action (CTAs)

A "call to action" (or "CTA") is simply an invitation for your reader to do something—like download a worksheet, sign up for an online event, or join your email list. Since your audience might be new to all this, make the benefit crystal clear: "Want to put Chapter 2 into action? Get my free workbook and watch a short tutorial." Suddenly, they'll see exactly what they'll gain—and won't be able to resist checking it out.

> "I'm writing a book. I've got the page numbers done."
>
> – Steven Wright

Use a Dedicated "Next Steps" Page

At the end of the book, or even at the end of each major section, dedicate a page to discuss "what's next?" This could include direct links or QR codes that the reader can scan with their phone to lead them to a free webinar, a virtual summit, or the next level of your Succession Stack. If your main message solves Problem A, give them a hint that Problem B is tackled in your online class or group program—and show them exactly how to sign up.

Offer a Seamless Path

Once a reader downloads your free bonus, don't leave them hanging. After they grab that workbook or watch the tutorial, point them toward your upcoming live workshop or membership site. Think of it as providing gentle guidance: "Now that you have the workbook, why not join our live Q&A webinar next week to see it in action?" Every step is designed to help them get even more value while building trust and momentum.

Golden Nugget

If you're releasing a printed version of your book, consider adding a QR code right in the chapter margin or at the end. When readers scan it, they're whisked straight to your next offer—like a short video or a sign-up page for your event. You'll be surprised how many people love this easy, modern shortcut.

> "Do not take life too seriously. You will never get out of it alive."
>
> – Elbert Hubbard

2. Low-Ticket Offers: Quick Wins

By the time someone finishes your book—especially if they've taken advantage of your in-chapter freebies or "next steps" invitations—they've already begun to trust your approach. A low-ticket offer is the perfect way to keep that momentum rolling. Generally priced between $27 and $97, it's an easy, low-risk "yes" for readers who want to see faster or more tangible results.

Possible Products

- **A Short Video Course:** If you've written a book about personal finances, your title and topic might be something like this: "Jumpstart Your Budget in 7 Days."
- **Workbooks or Toolkits:** These might include short booklets or downloadable templates such as investor toolkits, meal plans, habit trackers, or scheduling templates that complement the information in your book.
- **Live Micro-Workshops:** This might be something like a one-time Zoom event priced at $47, focusing on a single skill or outcome.

Implementation Tips

- **Focus on Immediate Action**: Avoid drowning your avatar in theory. If you promise to "Set Up a Budget in 24 Hours," deliver exactly that—simple steps, straightforward how-to videos, and an easy checklist they can follow.
- **Show Social Proof**: Even if only a handful of people tested your method and achieved great results, share those mini-success stories. Real wins spark excitement in new buyers, reassuring them that your methods actually work.

Golden Nugget

Consider making your low-ticket offer time sensitive. For instance, "Grab fifty percent off this mini course in the next seventy-two hours!" By doing so, you'll ride the wave of excitement they feel after finishing your book and translate interest into action before they get distracted by something else.

> "I write because talking to myself in public raises eyebrows. On paper, it raises royalties."
>
> – *Unknown*

Remember, you don't have to implement all the tiers or build out a complete Succession Stack right from day one. Start with your book, and then add a single low-ticket product. As you gather feedback and gain confidence, layer on the mid-tier and high-ticket levels.

Real-World Example: From Book Buyer to Big Success

One of our clients, an investing expert, demonstrates this concept masterfully. After someone buys his bestselling investing book, they're invited to download a "New Investor Toolkit" for free. That toolkit then points them to a $27 virtual summit, which offers a VIP upgrade for $197. By the time they've completed the summit and VIP experience, readers are primed for deeper transformation—so he offers them a $1,997 full course, and ultimately, some choose to join his $12,000 yearlong Investing Mastermind.

> "Most people work just hard enough not to get fired and get paid just enough money not to quit."
>
> – George Carlin

Here's the kicker: he's made *over $10 million* from this exact funnel—starting with a simple, free toolkit (the "easy yes") and guiding the most dedicated clients up the ladder. Each tier is designed as a logical next step for someone who is serious about accelerating their investing knowledge.

It's a shining example of how a low-ticket entry point doesn't just boost immediate revenue; it sets the stage for long-term engagement. Readers don't feel "sold to"—they feel supported. Each offer builds on what they've already learned, giving them bigger wins at every turn.

3. Mid-Tier Offers: Deeper Transformation

You've already sparked a relationship with your readers through lower-priced offers—they trust your insights, and they're eager for bigger results. Mid-tier offers, generally priced between $297 and $997, aren't just about delivering deeper value—they're about amplifying your authority and revenue at the same time. These programs or courses allow you to showcase your expertise on a grander scale, evolving from simply "someone who wrote a book" to a recognized leader in your niche.

Possible Products

- **Online Courses**: By crafting a structured, multi-lesson curriculum with videos, exercises, and group Q&A, you become both a teacher and guide. This is your chance to dig into the nuances that a book simply can't cover, establishing yourself as the definitive source on your topic.

> "I tried writing a serious how-to book once. It seriously didn't sell."
> – *Unknown*

- **Group Coaching or Masterclasses**: Scheduling weekly or monthly sessions—live or recorded—lets you connect face-to-face with your audience. You deliver hands-on guidance, yes, but you also demonstrate your adaptability and skill in handling real-world challenges.

- **Membership Communities**: Rolling out fresh content regularly (articles, short videos, templates) to your paying subscribers keeps people engaged, while a private forum or Slack channel fosters community. For you, this creates a reliable, recurring revenue stream—money that lands in your account month after month.

How This Benefits You

Mid-tier offers aren't just good for your audience and your bottom-line. They can benefit you in other important ways. Here are three valuable goals that mid-tier offers will help you accomplish:

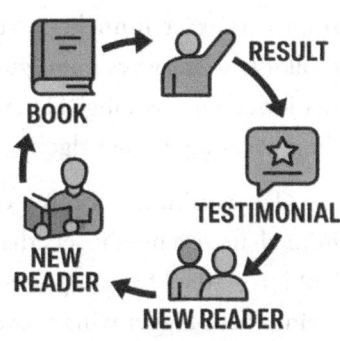

Transformation drives referrals.

- **Deepening your expertise**: Teaching at this level forces you to refine your ideas, tackle fresh questions, and respond in real time. The more you teach, the sharper your expertise becomes, which can then act as fuel for future books, talks, or even higher-ticket programs.

- **Forging real connections**: In a book, you're a distant expert. In a mid-tier environment—like live Q&As or group sessions—you become a trusted mentor. These personal touches often translate into glowing testimonials, referrals, and a vibrant community that rallies behind your brand.

- **Establishing a lucrative middle ground**: Not everyone is ready or able to jump straight into premium, four-figure coaching. A mid-tier offer becomes the sweet spot where many people opt in, scaling up your income and your reputation without demanding the full one-on-one commitment you might reserve for high-ticket engagements.

Golden Nugget

Poll the buyers of your lower-ticket items for their toughest challenges or biggest gaps in knowledge. Build your mid-tier program to solve those exact needs—no guesswork required. Not only do you get authoritative content that resonates, but you also create a stepping stone that naturally leads to even higher-tier opportunities down the line.

4. High-Ticket Offers: The Ultimate Experience

When you step into the realm of high-ticket offers—typically priced at $5,000 and above—you're no longer just delivering insights; you're creating powerful, one-on-one (or small-group) transformations. These elite programs aren't for everyone, but the participants who do enroll bring a level of commitment—and investment—that can take both their results and your reputation to new heights.

Possible Products

- **One-on-One Coaching:** This might be a deep, bespoke mentorship that tackles individual challenges head-on. Imagine guiding a business owner personally through weekly calls and check-ins, tailoring every step to their unique circumstances.

> "When you believe in your dream and your vision, then it begins to attract its own resources. No one was born to be a failure."
>
> – *Myles Munroe*

- **Mastermind Groups:** These groups are small, curated cohorts who meet regularly (either online or in person) to push each other toward bigger goals. You, as the facilitator, not only share your expertise but also harness the collective wisdom of the group.
- **Done-for-You Services:** If you're an expert in, say, copywriting, event planning, or digital marketing, you can handle the heavy lifting for

clients—at a premium price. This concierge-level service saves them time and ensures a professional finish.

Why You Want One

- **Client Success Stories:** High-ticket clients are deeply invested—both financially and mentally. They're the most likely to achieve remarkable breakthroughs, become your case studies, and spread the word about their experience with you.
- **High-Level Networking:** Whether it's a mastermind or a VIP coaching package, these settings attract serious go-getters. Their drive and connections can amplify your brand's reputation, leading to even more opportunities down the road.

Golden Nugget

Remember, charging more doesn't mean you're being greedy. If your program truly delivers transformation—be it health, wealth, or personal growth—you deserve to be compensated. It's an exchange of value: they invest financially in themselves, and you invest your time and expertise in guiding them. That's how real impact happens.

> "Love, friendship, networking—these are all critical connections and the foundation of a healthy, happy life."
> – Whitney Wolfe Herd

Dip your toe in the high-ticket waters with an exclusive ninety-day pilot program for just a few clients. Charge a premium, gather powerhouse testimonials, and refine your approach before scaling to a larger audience or a year-long offering. This ensures you deliver maximum transformation without feeling overwhelmed and primes you for future, full-scale success.

Crafting a Seamless Journey
CRM & Funnel Basics

Having a complete suite of offers—your book, low-ticket, mid-tier, and high-ticket—is one thing. But if you can't easily guide people from one stage to the next, you'll leave them lost or stuck. That's where two key concepts come into play: CRMs (Customer Relationship Managers) and funnels. Think of them as the digital infrastructure that makes your Succession Stack run like clockwork.

Part 1: Using a CRM (Your Backstage Coordinator)

A CRM—or Customer Relationship Manager—is like a personal assistant that remembers every detail about your readers. It organizes who's bought what, which freebies they downloaded, and what emails they should receive next.

1. Why a CRM Matters

- **Elimination of Guesswork**: No more spreadsheets, no more manual sends. The CRM knows who purchased your $47 workbook and can automatically follow up with them about your $497 course.
- **Targeted Follow-Ups**: If someone only grabbed your free checklist, your CRM will nudge them toward the $47 workbook first—while those who already purchased the workbook might see a $497 or $997 offer instead.
- **Hands-Off Automation**: You set the rules once ("Day 1: send welcome, Day 3: send success story, Day 7: present next offer"), and the CRM handles it from there.

Your CRM keeps the show running behind the scenes.

2. How to Use Key Automation Tactics

- **Tagging and Segmentation**: Label readers based on their actions—buying your book, attending a webinar, etc. This ensures nobody receives irrelevant pitches or misses out on valuable next steps.
- **Timed Email Sequences**: Schedule a welcome email the moment someone buys, followed by carefully spaced messages that move them toward higher tiers without feeling pushy.

Golden Nugget

Always frame your follow-ups around the *reader's* bigger why. Instead of merely pitching a course, show them how it fills the gap they identified in themselves, like this: "You've mastered a; now let's tackle b."

I'll tell you more about my favorite CRM platform, MonetizePro.ai, in Step 10. It's an all-in-one solution that automates your funnels, upsells, and sends follow-ups so you can focus on delivering real transformation.

Part 2: Websites Versus Funnels

A typical website might have a homepage, an "about" page, a blog, and a product listing—all of which are great for general browsing but are often overwhelming for newcomers who aren't sure where to start. They may get lost in the sea of links or simply click away to a different site. A funnel, on the other hand, is *streamlined*. Each page has one specific action (opt-in, purchase, etc.) that guides people step by step. That singular focus is especially crucial if you have multiple tiers in your Succession Stack because a funnel highlights only one offer at a time—keeping visitors on the exact path you want them to follow.

At its core, a funnel is just a specialized set of web pages that guide someone from a starting point—like a free download or a $7 mini-offer—to progressively higher-value products. Each page in the funnel highlights *one* product or action step, so there's no confusion about what to do next. Think of it as the online road map for your Succession Stack: your reader starts at the beginning of your journey, and each page in the funnel leads them further along, product by product.

Why a Funnel Is Different from a Regular Website

- **Single Focus**: Traditional websites might have multiple tabs and distracting menus. A funnel page keeps it simple, focusing on just one choice: "Ready to buy?" "Sign up here!" or "No, thanks!"
- **Logical Progression**: After a visitor to your site takes that first action, the funnel automatically shows them the second step. It feels like a conversation: "You enjoyed the $47 workshop—would you like my $497 course?" There's no hunting around for links—the path is laid out clearly.

A Quick Example Funnel

Are you feeling confused? Here's an example funnel built for a hypothetical investment business to illustrate:

1. **Opt-In Page:** This offers a free "Investor Cheat Sheet." Readers enter their email, and the funnel captures this new lead.
2. **Thank-You/Low-Ticket Offer**: Right after they opt in, the page says, "Hey, want my $47 Quick-Start Investor Toolkit?" (They can either say "Yes" or "No, thanks.")
3. **Upsell Page**: If they buy the $47 toolkit, the funnel can immediately present a $197 VIP upgrade or a $497 in-depth investment course.
4. **Confirmation/Next Steps**: Once they choose to buy (or pass) on the upsell offer, they get a confirmation page that will link to the business's membership area, where they'll be invited to mingle with and learn from other investors for a monthly fee.

> "Unless your advertising contains a big idea, it will pass like a ship in the night. I doubt if more than one campaign in a hundred contains a big idea."
>
> – David Ogilvy

Notice how each page only promotes *one* thing at a time, in a sequence that matches your Succession Stack.

Making Funnel Creation Newbie-Friendly

If the thought of creating multiple web pages and upsell paths sounds daunting, don't worry—this is exactly where platforms like MonetizePro.ai step in. Here are some of the great features they offer:

- **Over 1,000 Templates**: Select a design you like, swap in your text and images, and you're basically set.
- **Automated Upsells**: The moment someone buys your low-ticket product, MonetizePro can show them the mid-tier option. No coding, no complicated integrations are required—just a few clicks.
- **Membership Areas**: If you plan to deliver online courses or premium content, MonetizePro can also host all of your lessons. Once someone buys, they gain immediate access—no extra steps.

Golden Nugget

By focusing each funnel page on a single offer, you help your readers see *exactly* why they should move forward. It's not a cluttered "shop" with twenty different items—it's a coherent invitation to take the next, logical step in their transformation.

What If I'm Still Overwhelmed by the Tech?

Even with user-friendly platforms, it's understandable if you'd rather focus on crafting valuable content than tinker under the hood. In that case, here are several additional options you might enjoy:

1. **Hire a Freelance Funnel Builder**: You can find skilled tech experts on platforms like Upwork or Fiverr who specialize in MonetizePro (or your preferred tool). They'll set it up to your specifications—saving you hours (if not days) of trial and error.
2. **Tap Into These Recommended Resources**: Head to Authorgifts.com for a curated list of services and professionals who can handle everything from funnel design to course setup. This way, you can keep your energy focused on writing, coaching, or crafting your next offer—while the behind-the-scenes tech is handled by an expert.

> "The bestseller list: where self-help gurus, celebrities, and one guy with a really good marketing funnel all become equals."
> – *Unknown*

Bringing It All Together

Let's review what I've shared so far:

- **Succession Stack**: Your product map that moves readers from your book to your low-ticket, mid-tier, and high-ticket offers.

- **CRM**: The backstage brain that tracks purchases, sends targeted emails, and ensures each reader sees the right offers at the right time.
- **Funnels**: A streamlined, page-by-page experience that sells each product from your Succession Stack in a logical order.

When these three elements work together, your audience isn't just "shopping around"—they're guided along a well-lit path. Each funnel page, each email, and each product tier feels like the natural next step, providing more value while simultaneously increasing your revenue. And that's the ultimate win-win: you grow your business sustainably, and your readers get the deeper help they've been craving.

Real-World Examples

Below are six additional examples to show how a Succession Stack can work across various niches and specialties. Notice how each one follows the same structure—book, low-ticket, mid-tier, and high-ticket—while adding a unique twist that resonates with the author's expertise and audience needs.

Fitness Author – "Body & Mind Transformation"

- **Book**: *30 Days to a Healthier You* ($20)
- **Low-Ticket**: $49 two-week meal prep plan and gym routine videos
- **Mid-Tier**: $597 twelve-week online boot camp (weekly group calls, progress tracking, community forum)
- **High-Ticket**: $5,000 one-on-one coaching (custom workouts, nutritional analysis, monthly check-ins)

Added Bonus: A certificate for completing the twelve-week boot camp. It might seem minor, but people love tangible proof of their achievements.

Business Consultant – "Startup-to-CEO Road Map"

- **Book**: *Start Small, Scale Fast* ($19.95)

- **Low-Ticket**: $27 "Business Model Canvas" workshop (recorded)
- **Mid-Tier**: $997 eight-week group coaching (live Zoom calls, peer accountability, bonus checklists)
- **High-Ticket**: $10,000 mastermind (in-person retreat, VIP Slack channel, direct feedback on business plans)

Added Bonus: Each new mastermind cohort begins with a "Vision Casting Call," a one-hour session to set big goals. This personal touch fosters loyalty and jump-starts serious progress.

Relationship Coach – "From Conflict to Connection"

- **Book:** *From Conflict to Connection in 30 Days* ($16.95)
- **Low-Ticket:** $47 "Date Night Blueprint" (a two-part video series and printable worksheets for couples)
- **Mid-Tier:** $497 "6-Week Relationship Reboot" (weekly group Zoom calls, guided exercises, and a private forum for peer support)
- **High-Ticket:** $5,000 one-on-one couples coaching (custom conflict resolution strategies, monthly check-ins, and optional weekend retreats)

Added Bonus: Each couple is provided with a "Couples Success Journal," to use throughout the program. It not only tracks progress but also becomes a sentimental keepsake that reminds them of how far they've come.

Mindset Mentor – "Limitless Mind, Limitless Life"

- **Book:** *The 7-Day Mental Reset* ($14.99)
- **Low-Ticket:** $39 "Morning Affirmations and Visualization" audio bundle (short daily recordings and a printable journal)
- **Mid-Tier:** $599 "Mindset Mastery" course (eight-week online curriculum, weekly group coaching calls, and deep-dive exercises to break limiting beliefs)
- **High-Ticket:** $8,000 "VIP Intensive" (an exclusive ninety-day coaching package with personalized meditations, direct text support, and a two-day live workshop)

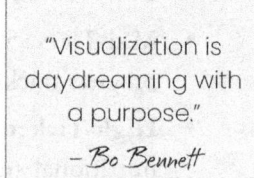

"Visualization is daydreaming with a purpose."
– Bo Bennett

Added Bonus: VIP Intensive clients get a "Mindset Road Map" poster with custom affirmations tailored to their life goals. It's a small detail that makes the premium experience feel even more personal.

Tech Educator – "Code from Scratch to CEO"

- **Book:** *Code in 10 Days: The Beginner's Road Map* ($19.95)
- **Low-Ticket:** $49 "HTML/CSS Essentials" mini course (video tutorials, project templates, and a private Slack channel)
- **Mid-Tier:** $997 twelve-week coding boot camp (live Zoom sessions, group challenges, and personal code reviews)
- **High-Ticket:** $7,500 "Startup Launchpad" (a six-month mastermind helping graduates turn their coding skills into a tech startup; includes pitch-deck reviews, investor connections, and advanced coding mentorship)

> "Success is not the key to happiness. Happiness is the key to success. If you love what you are doing, you will be successful."
> – *Albert Schweitzer*

Added Bonus: Coding boot camp students can showcase their projects to peers and potential employers during a virtual "Demo Day" at the end of the course. This public celebration boosts their confidence and often leads to first clients—or even job offers.

Nutritionist – "Holistic Harmony"

- **Book:** *Holistic Harmony: Balancing Your Nutrition, Mind, and Soul* ($18.95)
- **Low-Ticket:** $37 "3-Day Detox and Meal Planner" (digital recipes, shopping list, and a daily detox checklist)
- **Mid-Tier:** $497 "Nourish & Thrive" eight-week program (weekly webinars, personalized meal feedback, and a supportive Facebook group)
- **High-Ticket:** $6,000 six-month wellness mentorship (private consults, functional lab reviews, custom meal planning, and optional in-person retreat)

Added Bonus: Every mid-tier participant receives a welcome kit with measuring cups, a branded water bottle, and a weekly habit tracker. This tangible starter pack doesn't just bridge the gap between digital and real-world coaching—it also taps into the law of reciprocity. When you give someone a meaningful freebie, they often feel a subconscious drive to reciprocate—whether that's deeper engagement, a glowing testimonial, or an eagerness to invest in your *higher*-ticket offers.

By the time they've put those measuring cups and tracker to use, they're far more inclined to see the value of premium $5,000 one-on-one coaching. It's a small gesture that forges a strong emotional connection *and* sets the stage for greater impact—and greater income—down the line.

A Quick Note on Regulated Fields

If you work in a regulated industry—such as financial services, law, or healthcare—you'll likely need to include specific disclaimers or follow particular guidelines. For instance,

- **Financial advisors** may need to state that "past performance is not indicative of future results" and clarify they are not offering individualized investment advice.
- **Legal consultants** often need to specify that any content is for educational purposes only and does not form an attorney-client relationship.
- **Health and wellness coaches** might add disclaimers about consulting a doctor to ensure readers understand they're not a medical professional (unless they are).

> "Writing is like a 'lust,' or like 'scratching when you itch.' Writing comes as a result of a very strong impulse, and when it does come, I, for one, must get it out."
> – C. S. Lewis

In other words, *always* check the regulations in your field before publishing high-level claims or offering personalized coaching. Complying with industry rules not only keeps you on the right side of the law, but it also builds trust with your audience because they'll see you take your responsibilities seriously. If you're unsure about the regulations in your field, consider hiring legal counsel or an experienced professional in your industry to review your materials.

Overcoming Common Pitfalls

Pitfall #1: Overwhelming Your Audience

Don't flood new readers with everything all at once. If someone has just discovered your book, wait before pitching them the $5,000 coaching program. A step-by-step approach (book → low-ticket → mid-tier → high-ticket) keeps them engaged without scaring them off.

Pitfall #2: Underpricing

If you're charging a fraction of what your expertise is worth, not only do you earn less, you also risk sending the message that your offer might be "cheap" in quality. Price your offerings according to real value and outcomes. When you solve a big problem, it's okay to charge accordingly.

Pitfall #3: Lack of Testimonials

Social proof propels sales at every level—whether it's a $27 workshop or a $10,000 mastermind. Even a handful of positive reviews or short success stories can reassure a hesitant buyer. Make it easy for satisfied clients to share feedback: send them a quick follow-up email or a short survey, and then highlight their results on your sales pages.

Pitfall #4: Stagnation

Your funnel and content shouldn't be something you "set and forget." As you learn more from each group of students or coaching clients, refine your material. Add fresh lessons, tweak your methods, and stay up to date with industry trends. This keeps returning customers interested and shows new leads that your system is alive and evolving.

> "The future belongs to those who believe in the beauty of their dreams."
> – *Eleanor Roosevelt*

Golden Nugget

Consider launching your Succession Stack in "beta" mode with a small group—say, five to ten people—who get early access at a discounted price. Their feedback will help you refine your offers, and their success stories can become raving testimonials. It's a double win: you improve your products and build instant social proof that draws in your next wave of clients.

Tracking Numbers: Keep It Simple

Even if you've never touched an analytics dashboard before, here's a quick way to see if your Succession Stack is actually working. Think of it like checking the speedometer and gas gauge in a car—you don't need to be a mechanic, but you do need to know when to fill up or slow down. Here are four numbers you should keep a close eye on:

> "Becoming an author is easy. You just have to wrestle self-doubt, imposter syndrome, procrastination, caffeine addiction, and a blinking cursor—and win."
>
> – Unknown

1. Opt-in Rate

How many people visit your freebie page—and how many sign up? If one hundred visitors show up and twenty-five enter their email, you have a twenty-five percent opt-in rate. It's a good sign that your freebie offer is interesting enough.

2. Conversion Rate

After someone watches your webinar or lands on your sales page, do they buy? Let's say ten out of one hundred buy your $47 workshop—that's a ten percent conversion. If you notice only one or two buyers, it might be time to tweak your copy, price, or even your offer itself.

3. Average Order Value

Are people taking you up on upsells? If someone buys your $47 product and also grabs the $197 VIP upgrade, your average order goes up. This tells you how much revenue you're making per customer, on average.

4. Drop-off Points

Keep an eye on where people "disappear." For example, if they're buying your low-ticket workshop but not moving to your mid-tier course, that's a clue. Maybe the upsell page isn't clear, or the offer isn't compelling enough.

> "The world is full of people who have never, since childhood, met an open doorway with an open mind."
>
> – E. B. White

Golden Nugget

You don't have to be a data wizard. Just glance at these few key numbers once a week. If something is way off (like a one percent opt-in rate or zero sales at mid-tier), that's your signal to adjust your messaging, price, or even your product. It's a simple loop: test, learn, and tweak until you see better results.

Start Building Your Succession Stack Today

Let's review what you've learned about Succession Stacks formatted as six simple steps you can use to get started on your Stack right now:

1. Identify Your Value Ladder

Sit down and list every major challenge your audience faces, from the simplest fix ("I just need a quick strategy now") to a big, long-term transformation ("I want a six-month road map"). Assign each problem to a corresponding offer—from a low-priced "starter" solution to an immersive, high-touch experience. This sorted list becomes the backbone of your Succession Stack.

> If you could kick the person in the pants responsible for most of your trouble, you wouldn't sit for a month.
>
> —Theodore Roosevelt

2. Optimize Your Book for Lead Capture

Think of your book not as the end product but the doorway to something bigger. Add short calls-to-action near the beginning, middle, and end. You might include a QR code that sends readers to a free workbook or a bonus video. Each time someone downloads that free resource, capture their email address to guide them to the next step.

3. Create Your Low-Ticket Offer

Brainstorm a quick-win product—like a seven-day mini-course, a live micro-workshop, or a simple digital workbook. Price it low enough that buyers say "yes!" without overthinking, but still high enough that it conveys genuine value. This is where trust in your system really starts to form.

4. Build a Mid-Tier Product for True Transformation

Once you've established credibility, some of your audience will crave more depth. Survey your low-ticket buyers or book readers. Ask, "What else do you still struggle with?" or "Where do you feel stuck?" Then craft an online course or membership site that tackles those exact hurdles. Deliver step-by-step content, inject live elements like Q&As, and ensure each lesson feels like a milestone on a well-defined journey.

5. Design a High-Ticket Program

When you're ready to help people at an even higher level—and, yes, charge accordingly—offer a more intimate experience. Maybe that's one-on-one coaching or a small mastermind group. Provide exclusive perks (like direct email access, personalized critiques,

> "Writing the book is the easy part. It's believing anyone will read it that takes guts."
> – *Unknown*

To show you the power of building a Success Stack, read the story of one of my book readers, Lance Edwards, who bought a copy of my book *Multiple Streams of Income* while vacationing in Hawaii. He was a stressed-out employee in a corporate job and was looking for more freedom and a new opportunity. The real estate chapter fascinated him, and after attending one of my seminars, he soon began buying small apartment buildings in Texas. Then, he decided to share his success with other people (Avatars) in his own seminars. He writes,

"I bought your book, *Multiple Streams of Income* in 2001 and became a Protégé of your trainings. In three short years, I retired from my corporate job. My first book became a number one bestseller on Amazon and has sold tens of thousands of books. Through my seminars and books, we've impacted thousands of students. My book is called *How to Make BIG MONEY in Small Apartment Buidlings. How to Finally Earn the Money You Deserve in Real Estate Investing*. Thanks a million, Bob."

– *Lance Edwards*

or in-person retreats) that justify the premium price. Start small—maybe a ninety-day pilot with a handful of people—and refine it as you go.

6. Automate & Scale

It's tough to handle all these steps manually. That's why tools like MonetizePro come in handy. Configure your upsells, tags, and email sequences so each purchase triggers the next logical offer. Then monitor your data: Which offers resonate most? Where do people drop off? This feedback loop helps you continually tweak your Succession Stack—so it stays profitable and keeps delivering deeper transformations.

Remember that your Succession Stack isn't just about more products—it's about building a structured path that respects your readers' time and aspirations. Start small, polish each offer, and let genuine results speak for themselves. Over time, you'll have a fine-tuned ecosystem that serves your audience's needs at every level—and grows your business while doing it.

If your reader asks "what's next?"—you're doing it right.

Your Book Is a Beginning, Not an End

When someone closes the final page of your book and whispers, "What's next?" you need a clear, compelling answer. A thoughtfully built Succession Stack makes sure every reader—from the casually curious to the deeply committed—has a place to go. By expanding your reach and offering progressively deeper levels of transformation, you're not just growing your revenue streams; you're changing lives in more profound ways.

Embrace this mindset: your book isn't the end of your contribution—it's merely the gateway. Each step that follows—whether it's a low-ticket workshop, a mid-tier course, or a high-end coaching program—carries readers further on a journey of personal growth and real results. That's how you transition from "author" to "architect of transformation," building a suite of products and services that genuinely impacts people. If that isn't a clear measure of success, what is?

Ready for an Audience? Here's What Comes Next

You've laid out your Succession Stack—your book, low-ticket offers, mid-tier programs, and even a high-ticket experience. You've got the funnels and CRM basics down, and you're equipped to guide readers from entry-level interest to transformative results. But *how* do you actually get people into that funnel? How do you attract those first curious readers, turn them into buyers, and ultimately lead them to the deeper levels of your Succession Stack?

> "If you want to write a bestseller, remember: readers don't care how smart you are. They care how much you can make them feel like *they* are."
> – Unknown

That's where the Bestselling Buzz comes in. In the next chapter, we'll explore the simplest, most effective ways to broadcast your message—everything from free social media tactics to paid advertising and influencer collaborations. If you've been shy about posting online or feel uncertain about "putting yourself out there," don't worry. We'll break down exactly how to drum up excitement without feeling pushy or fake.

You now have the ecosystem that converts casual browsers into high-value clients. Next, it's time to fill that ecosystem with eager fans by creating the kind of buzz that propels your book—and your entire Succession Stack—to number one. So turn the page, and let's unleash the power of strategic promotion.

FREE GIFT: Book Funnel Formulas

Need to monetize beyond the book? I created twelve funnel blueprints you can swipe to sell courses, coaching, or digital offers off your book. Grab them at AuthorGifts.com or scan the code.

> "Courage is resistance to fear, mastery of fear—
> not absence of fear."
>
> – *Mark Twain*

STEP 10: YOUR BESTSELLING BUZZ

Free & Paid Ways to Get the Word Out

Are you nervous about posting on social media? Do you worry about launching a podcast, running ads, or speaking at an event? Are you fearful people might judge you? Get over it! Don't be afraid to make a fool of yourself. Remember, the two key bestseller concepts: words and names.

Look into the near future and imagine that you've just published your book. It's packed with life-changing stories and priceless advice—yet *nobody* knows it exists. Why? Because you're so afraid of sounding silly on social media—or messing up on camera—that you *never* post about it in the first place.

If you want to be a number one bestselling author, you'll need to learn how to make a little noise—okay, maybe a *lot* of noise. You can't climb a mountain quietly. You need to broadcast your message from every peak and valley—online and offline.

This chapter focuses on why creating buzz matters and how to do it successfully. In the next chapter—"Step 11: Your Guaranteed Launch"—I'll discuss how and when to use these strategies to boost your book to the top of the bestseller lists. But for now, absorb the information in this chapter to the best of your ability, explore the tactics you're learning, and get comfortable with the idea of making a little noise!

Why Fear Holds You Back

Many aspiring authors think, "I'm not ready," or "I'm going to look ridiculous if my post bombs or if my live video is awkward." But here are a few key secrets:

1. **Mistakes are the fastest way to learn.** If you never risk flubbing your words or shooting a less-than-perfect video, you'll never discover which stories or soundbites truly resonate with your future readers.
2. **A small audience equals minimal risks.** Social media often feels huge—but in reality, your initial posts may only reach a few dozen people. That's the ideal "practice arena." If you goof, they'll scroll on to the next post—no big deal.
3. **Authenticity is more important than polish.** Sometimes, the posts you think are subpar can go viral, and the ones you carefully plan can flop. It's unpredictable—*so just start sharing*.

Here's the truth: You could write the most amazing book in history, but if no one knows about it, no one will buy it. Let's fix that by igniting "buzz"—the free and paid ways to get your book into as many hands (and hearts) as possible.

> "Content builds relationships. Relationships are built on trust. Trust builds revenue."
> —Andrew Davis.

The Buzz Mindset

Becoming a number one bestselling author is about letting the world know your book exists. That requires buzz—people talking about you, posting about you, and telling their friends.

- **Buzz = Visibility.** The more often people see your name and your book's promise, the more likely they are to click "buy now."
- **Visibility = Opportunity.** Each post or video is another chance to land a podcast interview, a speaking gig, or a joint venture that skyrockets your sales.

I often share how one of my protégés started posting random tips on TikTok. Some were polished and others were blatant stumbles—yet the videos he considered "mistakes" ended up racking up millions of views. Why? Authenticity. People respond to genuine content, even if it's messy.

Action Step: Post Something Today

Before I dig into free versus paid marketing channels, here's a three-part challenge:

1. **Pick a platform** that you're already familiar with such as Instagram, Facebook, TikTok, or LinkedIn.
2. **Share one small thing** about your book: a single tip, a behind-the-scenes anecdote, or even your biggest writing struggle.
3. **Invite a response** by asking, "Do you like this title?" or "What's your biggest question about [topic]?"

It won't be perfect—and that's the point. Every post is a tiny test that tells you something about your potential readers. Embrace any awkward moments as tuition in the school of real-world buzz-building.

Free Buzz vs. Paid Buzz

There are two major ways to get the word out and build "buzz" around your book.

1. **Free Buzz** – Posting on social media, blogging, or collaborating at zero cost.
2. **Paid Buzz** – Spending money on ads or sponsored content to amplify reach.

Both can be incredibly powerful, and often they're at their best when you use them together—like a one-two punch that first warms up your audience and then multiplies your reach. Let's talk about how each approach works.

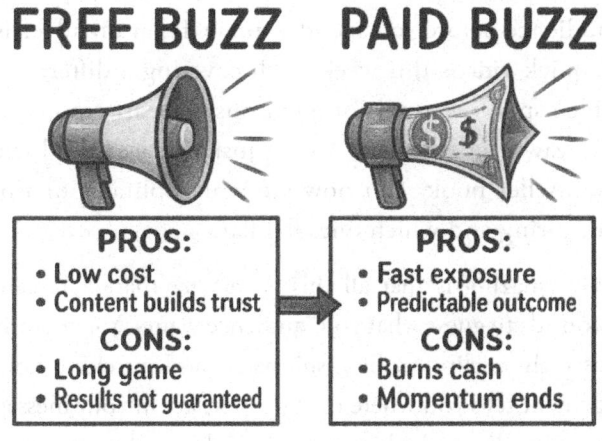

Free Buzz: Test & Tweak Without Breaking the Bank

Free buzz includes all the methods that only cost you time, creativity, or relationships—no credit card required. Free buzz is perfect for new authors with limited resources or for those who simply want to warm up the market before launching paid ads. If you want to dip your toe in the water before going all-in on advertising, this is your ideal starting place. Here are a few ideas!

Social Media Posts

Maybe you only have a handful of followers at first—great! That means you can experiment fearlessly. Shoot a quick video from your phone to share a snippet of your upcoming chapter. Hit "Go Live" on Instagram or Facebook to show a behind-the-scenes look at your writing day. Notice where people perk up and comment or ask questions.

Have you ever posted a quick video or a social media update and felt disappointed when it only racked up three "likes" or a single comment? Let me tell you something—that lone comment can be *pure gold*. It's a real person telling you exactly what resonates with them. Maybe they say, "I'm stuck on Chapter Four—how do I keep going?" Or, "I love your tip about morning writing routines!" That passing remark isn't just chatter—it's a tiny clue, guiding you toward the topics and angles people genuinely care about.

> "Mentoring is a brain to pick, an ear to listen, and a push in the right direction."
> – John C. Crosby

Every small response, even if it's just a thumbs-up, helps you measure the pulse of your audience before you spend a single dollar on advertising. Suppose you post three quick videos this week, each covering a different angle of your book. If one video sparks a couple of questions or heart emojis, and the others barely register a yawn, guess what? You've just discovered which angle might become your bestseller hook. You now see which phrases or tips people find interesting or inspiring and which ones fall flat.

What's truly amazing is that all this is *cost-free* market research. You're not burning money on ads to guess what your audience wants. You're simply putting out feelers—free posts, short clips, or blog snippets—and watching how people react. This early engagement tells you where the hot spots are in your message, where your avatar's real pain points lie, and where readers might need extra encouragement. By the time you're ready to invest in, say, a Facebook or Amazon ad, you already know which "headline" or "promise" turns heads.

Think of it as a dress rehearsal before the big opening night. You get to try out different lines or angles, see what draws applause (or polite silence), and fine-tune your performance. By the time you step into the spotlight and pay for ads that reach thousands more eyes, you'll have a proven script in hand. You'll know precisely what to say to catch that spark of recognition in your readers because you've already tested it on a smaller stage. And that, my friend, is the power of using every drop of feedback—no matter how small— to sharpen your message and pave the way for a truly successful launch.

> "Effective networking isn't a result of luck—it requires hard work and persistence."
> – Lewis Howes

Podcast Guesting & Interviews

Think about it—podcast hosts are always hunting for fresh stories and insights to keep their audience engaged. You bring your expertise, and they share their microphone. No fee, no fuss—yet you could reach thousands of listeners who already trust that host. A thirty-minute chat might lead to a hundred new followers who say, "I like how this author thinks," or "I need that book!" It's one of the simplest and most cost-effective ways to build authority fast.

Blogging & Writing Platforms

If you enjoy writing, consider posting articles on popular sites like Medium. You might write an article called "Top 10 Ways to Overcome Writer's Block" or share an inspiring story from your own journey. At the end of every post, gently invite readers to grab a free chapter or checklist from your website.

Dr. Benjamin Hardy did exactly this and published hundreds of articles that eventually attracted a three-hundred-thousand-person email list, which empowered him to land a six-figure deal for his first major book, *Willpower Doesn't Work*. This success gave him the opportunity to co-author with even more influential experts such as Dan Sullivan in *10X is Easier than 2X* and *Who Not How*. It didn't happen

> "Why don't escaped convicts make good writers? Because they never finish their sentences."
> – Unknown

overnight, but his steady stream of content built a powerful audience, beginning with a free media avenue.

Buddy Marketing & Joint Ventures

Some of the best opportunities for growth come through collaboration. Think of it as building bridges between your audience and someone else's. Do you have a friend or colleague who caters to a similar audience? Why not cross-promote each other's content? If your book is about fitness, team up with a meal-planning influencer to create an offer together: "Grab my book, get her seven-day meal plan free!"

Start with influencers in your niche—not the mega-stars who are out of reach, but the micro-influencers who speak directly to your audience. Reach out with genuine interest, offering them a free copy of your book and asking for their honest feedback. Many will share their experience if it resonates with their followers.

> "It takes collaboration across a community to develop better skills for better lives."
> – Jose Angel Gurria

For example, if your book is about wellness, partner with a fitness influencer to host a joint Instagram Live. If you've written about business, collaborate with a popular LinkedIn creator to co-author an article or webinar. These collaborations introduce you to their audience and lend credibility to your message.

Authors in complementary niches are also fantastic allies. If you've written a book about mindset, team up with someone who's focused on productivity. By combining forces—co-hosting an event, sharing each other's newsletters, or simply endorsing one another—you both gain credibility and access to new readers.

Local Meetups & Speaking Gigs

Never underestimate the impact of in-person connections. Look for community events, business luncheons, or local meetups. Offer a short talk or Q&A about your book's theme—whether it's personal finance, health, relationships, or spiritual growth. Often, the folks who hear you speak in person are your most dedicated buyers and your biggest evangelists. One fifteen-minute talk could lead to future invitations or even a wave of online testimonials saying, "I just met this author—go check out their book!"

Paid Buzz: Amplifying What Already Works

Some authors shy away from advertising, thinking it's either too expensive or too "salesy." But let's be clear: when they're done right, paid ads can rocket your book into the awareness of thousands of potential readers. It'll never replace the fundamentals—great content, social proof, and a strong author-reader relationship—but it can multiply your reach on Launch Day. The trick is combining these tactics with your proven free buzz so you know what angle or hook resonates before you spend a dime.

Amazon Ads

Why Amazon? Because that's where people go to buy books. It's one thing to catch casual scrollers on social media, but it's another to catch shoppers in the very act of hunting for a new book. When you pop up in their search results or appear under "also bought" titles, you're knocking on the door of someone already eager to read. Here are three keys to getting it right:

> "Marketing is a very good thing, but it shouldn't control everything. It should be the tool, not that which dictates."
>
> – Nicolas Roeg

1. **Keywords, Keywords, Keywords:** Picture your reader typing "self-help for new moms" or "weight loss on a budget." Your job is to guess (or research) the exact words they'll use so that your book appears at the perfect moment.
2. **Sponsored Products vs. Sponsored Brands:** If this is your first rodeo, start with sponsored product ads. Test a variety of keywords, watch which ones convert to actual sales, and shift your budget accordingly. Keep a close eye on your ACOS (Advertising Cost of Sales)—it tells you whether you're making money or just spending it.
3. **Little Tweaks = Big Wins:** If you see a keyword is burning money without driving sales, pause it. If another keyword is converting well, give it more budget. Small, regular adjustments can make the difference between losing your shirt and becoming a top category seller.

Pro Tip: If you spot a winning keyword—one that consistently drives cheap clicks and steady sales—add variations of that keyword too. Sometimes a simple tweak like "best weight loss book for seniors" (instead of just "weight loss book") can unlock a whole new cluster of buyers.

Facebook & Instagram Ads

If your book is about real estate investing, picture being able to narrow your audience to people in that exact niche. Or if you've written a book about time management, how about focusing on busy parents? With platforms like Facebook and Instagram, you can do exactly that—laser-target the folks most likely to say, "Yes, I need this book now." Start small with five or ten dollars a day, test different headlines or images, and see which ones spark clicks and comments. Then, scale up.

While Amazon ads grab readers who already have their credit card out, Facebook and Instagram catch folks who might not know they need your book yet. Maybe they've got ten spare minutes to scroll for something interesting at lunch. Enter your ad with a captivating promise, a striking image, or a short video that piques curiosity. If you choose to try these, here's a three-phase approach you can implement during your Soft Launch and Hard Launch, which you'll learn more about in Step 11:

1. **Warm-Up (2 Weeks Before Launch):** Show ads with short, engaging posts—perhaps a quick "sneak peek" video or a personal story from your book. You're not shouting, "BUY NOW!" yet; you're laying breadcrumbs that lead back to Launch Day.

    > "The difference between a good book and a bestselling book? About $10,000 in Facebook ads—and a miracle."
    > – *Unknown*

2. **Launch-Day Blitz:** Once your book is live, shift gears. Run ads with a direct call-to-action: "Grab it now for just one dollar!" or "Limited-time bonus if you buy today!" Keep the ad's text clear, urgent, and consistent with your overall brand message.

3. **Retargeting (After Launch):** Did someone click your ad, visit your book page, and then disappear? Hit them with a retargeting ad: "Still on the fence? Here's what early readers are saying…" Show off those early five-star reviews or a short excerpt that sparks a fresh wave of interest.

Pro Tip: Video ads often deliver better engagement if they're real and relatable. Don't worry about shooting in a fancy studio—an honest, heartfelt thirty-second snippet from your living room can be far more convincing than a glossy, overproduced video.

YouTube Pre-roll Ads

You've likely seen those fifteen-second clips that appear before the main YouTube video loads. Annoying? Sometimes. Effective? Definitely—if your book aligns with the channel's content. Imagine someone clicking on a "How to Start a Business" video. Before it plays, they see your fifteen-second mini-commercial that says, "Ever wonder how to launch your dream idea without going broke? My new book shows you the way." If you can hook someone in those first five seconds, you've just found a new reader. Done right, this kind of marketing can be a powerful match.

> "If uncovering the truth is the greatest challenge of nonfiction writing, it is also the greatest reward."
> – Candice Millard

Google Search Ads

For nonfiction authors tackling big problems—like financial freedom, nutrition, or personal development—Google search ads can be gold. When someone searches, "Best book on getting out of debt," your ad pops up. If your pitch resonates, they're one click away from your Amazon page.

Sponsored Email Blasts

What if someone else has a massive newsletter audience that perfectly fits your niche? Some influencers or websites let you pay to feature your book or a special announcement in their next email. A single send could reach tens of thousands of potential readers. Negotiating how you're introduced is key—a personal endorsement from an influencer can far outperform a generic, "Here's a new book—check it out" ad.

Book Promotion Sites

Want a direct shot of pure reading traffic? Try specialized book deal newsletters or websites like BookBub, Bargain Booksy, and Ereader News Today. While some require an application and can be competitive, a single feature can land you in front of thousands of dedicated readers in your exact genre—sometimes enough to vault you into the top spots on Amazon overnight.

> "Good marketers see consumers as complete human beings with all the dimensions real people have."
> – Jonah Sachs

Striking the Balance

The beauty of free versus paid buzz is that it isn't an either/or situation. Many successful authors start by posting and networking for free, refining their message until they see what truly resonates. Then, they *amplify* that winning angle with paid ads. It's about moving from the small stage to the big stage once your script is already honed.

Are you short on funds or wanting to practice before you leap? Start with free. Do you have a hot angle that's proven to catch fire? Go with paid, and watch your audience multiply. Use both sides of this coin, and you'll see how quickly your author platform can grow.

Choosing Your Platform: Where to Start & Why

At this point, you may be thinking, *But which social media channel deserves my time?* Should you be everywhere—Facebook, Instagram, YouTube, TikTok, X—or *just* focus on the one you like best?

If you're brand-new or feeling overwhelmed, pick one platform and go deep. Master its quirks (whether that's hashtags on TikTok or consistent posting on YouTube), build a small community, and then expand to other channels. On the next page, you'll find a simple table comparing the top five networks along with their pros, cons, and best uses—so you can choose wisely.

Master one platform before you expand.

The best plan is the one you can stick to. If you can only manage one channel while writing your book, do that. If you have more bandwidth, dabble in two. You can always repurpose your best content once you figure out *what* that is and *where* it resonates.

The One-Platform Strategy

If you're feeling overwhelmed by the sheer number of social media channels—Facebook, Instagram, YouTube, TikTok, X—you're not alone. Many authors think they must be *everywhere* at once, posting nonstop. But let me save you a headache: *start with just one*. Choose the platform that speaks to you most naturally. Maybe you love scrolling Instagram for visual inspiration; maybe you're drawn to the spontaneity of TikTok. Wherever you already feel comfortable is often the best place to begin.

Where Different Demographics Hang Out on Social Media

Avatar	Demographic Profile	Social Media Platforms	Example Behaviors
	Gen Z High Schoolers 13-18, High School Students, Digital Natives	TikTok, YouTube, Instagram	Viral trends, memes, music, pop culture content
	Gen Z College Students 18-24, College-Age, Social And Career-Focused	LinkedIn, YouTube, TikTok, Instagram	Campus life updates, entertainment, career prep
	Young Professionals 25-34, Urban Early-Career Millennials	LinkedIn, YouTube, TikTok, Instagram, Facebook	Career milestones, lifestyle posts, self-education
	Aspiring Entrepreneurs 25-40, Side-Hustlers And Startup-Minded	LinkedIn, YouTube, TikTok, Instagram, Facebook	Business education, content marketing, brand building
	Young Mothers 25-35, New Parents	YouTube, TikTok, Instagram, Facebook	Parenting groups, family milestones, humor, tips
	Busy Parents (Gen X) 35-50, Working Parents With School-Aged Kids	LinkedIn, YouTube, TikTok, Instagram, Facebook	Family coordination, lifestyle tips, parenting hacks
	DIY Homeowners 28-45, Home Renovators	YouTube, TikTok, Instagram, Facebook	DIY tutorials, home projects, inspiration boards
	Fitness & Wellness Fans 20-40, Health-Focused Individuals	YouTube, TikTok, Instagram, Facebook	Workout routines, health tips, personal progress
	Social Foodies 25-40, Recipe Lovers	YouTube, TikTok, Instagram, Facebook	Cooking videos, food hacks, restaurant content
	Retired Hobbyists 65+, Retirees With Time For Hobbies	YouTube, Facebook	Hobby groups, nostalgic content, how-to videos

A Quick Platform Analysis

Platform	Typical Audience & Tone	Pros	Cons	Growth Speed	Best For
Facebook	Broad demographic (30+), community and family-oriented	- Has groups for niche interests - Familiar and comfortable for many	- Organic reach is often low without paid ads - Feed is crowded	**Slow to Moderate**	Authors who want close-knit "book club" communities, family-life topics, or can afford FB ads
Instagram	Wide age range, very visual and curated vibe	- Great for photos/videos/Reels - Reel algorithm can spark quick discovery	- Highly visual; camera-shy folks may struggle - Consistency is key	**Fast** (Reels can go big quickly)	Authors with photogenic content (cooking, travel, behind-the-scenes visuals)
YouTube	Broad demographic, from teens to retirees; suits deeper, longer-form content	- Perfect for in-depth tutorials and Q&As - Content has a long "shelf life"	- Production and editing can be time-consuming - Slower to build if starting fresh	**Steady to Fast** (niche-dependent)	Authors who enjoy teaching and talking on camera, creating how-to or interview-style content
TikTok	Younger-leaning (though expanding), loves short-form, "fun" video content	- Huge viral potential for raw, authentic clips - Even new accounts can explode fast	- Requires frequent short videos - User base skews younger (though broadening)	**Fast** (one viral clip can explode)	Authors comfortable with quick, casual videos and "showing personality"
X	News-oriented, thought-driven, short-form text with real-time interactions	- Great for quick takes, witty insights, and trending topics - Can build loyal followings via threads	- Character limit demands brevity - High "noise" level; tough to stand out	**Moderate** (depends on your niche and posting frequency)	Authors who excel at punchy writing, hot takes, or want real-time convos on industry topics

Why? Because every network has its little quirks, from hashtags and video length to the most fruitful times of day to post. By pouring your energy into mastering one platform, you learn these ropes faster, spot audience reactions more clearly, and start building momentum in a single, fertile corner of the internet. You'll also get to know your followers on a more personal level. That sense of community can be lost when you spread yourself too thin across five different apps.

When you do find a winning angle—perhaps a behind-the-scenes clip of your writing process, or a lively Q&A about your book's topic—you can later repurpose it across other platforms. At that point, you already know the piece resonates because you tested it where you're most active. This approach isn't just more efficient—it's more fulfilling. Instead of chasing scattered "likes" in a dozen places, you'll see genuine engagement grow in one place you truly enjoy.

Which Platform Fits Your Book?

If you're still torn on which platform to pick, take a moment to think about your book's core audience. Are they in their thirties or forties, juggling kids and careers? If so, you might lean toward Facebook, where close-knit groups discuss parenting, life hacks, or personal growth. Maybe your book is more visual—a travel guide or cooking lessons—so Instagram could become your canvas, showcasing vibrant Reels and snapshots of your creative process.

If you have a knack for talking at length (and you love teaching or explaining concepts), a YouTube channel could be your ideal domain. Long-form content thrives there, where you can record deeper "mini seminars" or host guest conversations that mirror your book's subject matter. Meanwhile, TikTok rewards quick, casual authenticity for those who enjoy shorter, spontaneous clips. And if you live for witty comebacks or punchy quotes, X might be your playground, where you can engage real-time with trending topics or craft short, impactful threads.

> "The need for connection and community is primal, as fundamental as the need for air, water, and food."
> – Dean Ornish

No matter which you choose, the question to ask yourself is, "Where does my message flow most naturally? Where are *my* people likely to hang out?" That intersection—of your comfort and their presence—is usually where the magic happens.

Fast Growth vs. Steady Growth

While choosing a channel, it's also wise to consider the kind of growth you want. Are you hungry for rapid visibility, willing to post more frequently, and comfortable on video? TikTok and Instagram Reels can catapult unknown creators to viral status overnight with the perfect spark. One short clip could rack up thousands or even millions of views if it hits the right nerve.

> "Communication leads to community, that is, to understanding, intimacy and mutual valuing."
> – Rollo May

On the other hand, if you enjoy steady, thoughtful engagement, or you prefer more substantial discussions, Facebook groups and YouTube channels build strong followings over time. People on these platforms often crave deeper content, which means more time spent crafting your posts or videos—but also a more loyal base that genuinely connects with your material. X falls somewhere in between. It's suitable for quick commentary and "thread" essays that can blow up if you strike a chord in the social zeitgeist. There's no right or wrong approach—just the one that fits your personality and writing style.

Questions to Ask Yourself

To summarize what you've just learned and guide you in choosing the most appropriate platform, ask yourself these questions:

- **Where do my ideal readers spend their free time?** A younger crowd might prefer TikTok or IG Reels; a family-oriented audience might scroll Facebook groups.
- **What kind of content am I naturally drawn to?** Quick 30-second clips? Long-form tutorials? Punchy text posts?
- **How much time do I have for filming, editing, or writing?** If you can't film daily, maybe YouTube's weekly schedule suits you better. If you can't resist daily, real-time comments, X might feel like home.

Answer honestly, and you'll have a clearer sense of which platform deserves your focus. Remember, overcommitting often leads to burnout. Choose one place, serve it well, and watch your audience grow.

Repurposing: The Expansion Plan

Some authors worry that if they pick just one channel, they'll miss out on all those other audiences. But that's the beauty of repurposing. Once you've refined a piece of content—let's say a short video that demonstrates three writing tips—you can slice it up or rework it for different platforms. Here's how:

- Take that five-minute YouTube tutorial and convert it into three micro-clips for TikTok or Instagram Reels.
- Turn a thoughtful X thread into an eye-catching quote graphic on Instagram or a short reflection on Facebook.

The key is to do it one step at a time. Master your chosen channel, gather feedback, and only then should you "bolt on" additional platforms. This approach prevents overwhelm and ensures that whenever you do expand, you're expanding with proven content that resonates. Before you know it, you'll have a presence on multiple channels without feeling like you've waded into quicksand.

Create once. Repurpose everywhere.

Becoming a Content Machine

Have you ever wondered how some authors and influencers manage to flood every social media platform with fresh, engaging content—and still have time to write their next book? You might think they possess superhuman stamina or bottomless resources. In most cases, it's neither. Instead, they've learned the art of batching their content and systematizing the process.

What if you could produce a week's worth of videos, posts, and updates in just one focused day? That's the secret behind becoming a true "content machine." Let me show you how it works.

Set Aside One Day a Week

Picture this: You wake up on a Tuesday (or whichever day you choose) knowing it's your "content creation day." Instead of stressing daily about what to post, you use this day to give yourself a few hours to brainstorm, film, and organize all the content you'll release over the next seven days.

Why does this help? Because you only need to "gear up" creatively once a week. No more scattered attempts at filming a reel in the middle of a hectic Wednesday. No more late-night, last-minute scrambles to post something—anything—to keep your feed active. Instead, you only need one day and one burst of energy for a week of consistent exposure.

> "It is not in the stars to hold our destiny but in ourselves."
> – William Shakespeare

Plan Before You Film

Don't just wake up on your chosen social media day and start talking to the camera. First, decide the themes you want to cover for the week. Maybe you'll highlight three key insights from your upcoming book or show behind-the-scenes details of your writing process. Next, jot down short outlines or scripts—it can be as simple as a few talking points scribbled on a notepad. If you're feeling stuck, you could even ask an AI tool for ten new angles on your subject.

Keep track of these ideas in a simple spreadsheet or doc. It might sound too mundane or "corporate" for a creative mind, but it's a lifesaver. You'll always know what you'll be filming and when it'll go live.

Batch-Film Everything in One Sitting

On filming day, gather your smartphone or camera, set up decent lighting, and get ready to roll. Start with the first topic on your spreadsheet. Maybe it's a sixty-second tip on how to break through writer's block or a thirty-second clip showing your favorite productivity hack.

Here's another trick: change your background or shirt between videos. Spend thirty seconds moving your tripod to the other side of the room. Swap out your jacket or throw on a ball cap. Suddenly, each segment looks like it was filmed on a different day—keeping viewers visually engaged. If you're camera-shy, use a teleprompter app or create a simple list of points to guide you.

Don't worry about editing yet. Just talk, share your enthusiasm, and let the camera run. When you're done, you'll have a handful of raw clips ready for the next stage.

Delegate the Editing & Scheduling

The smartest authors realize they don't have to handle every detail. If you can afford it, hire a virtual assistant or an editor who can clean up your clips, add subtitles or captions, and format them for different platforms. They'll also take charge of scheduling each post at optimal times across TikTok, Instagram, Facebook, YouTube—wherever your audience lives.

And if you don't have a helper yet, try using simple editing apps on your phone or free tools online. Once you see the benefits of consistent content, you might decide it's worth bringing in extra help.

Consistency Matters—Aim for Three Posts a Day.

Be as consistent as the sunrise. If you really want traction, post up to three times a day, every single day. That number might sound overwhelming, but remember that you're capturing it all on that single content-creation day. If you're filming, you could make twenty to thirty short videos—enough to sprinkle throughout the week on multiple platforms.

Why so many posts? Because every piece of content is like a tiny salesman working for you 24/7. Each snippet introduces new followers to your message, warms up existing fans to your ideas, and eventually funnels them toward buying your book, joining your email list, or attending your webinar. Frequent posting also pleases the algorithms, giving you a better shot at landing on someone's "for you" page or feed.

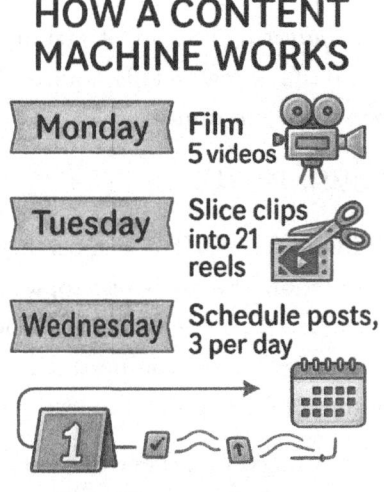

HOW A CONTENT MACHINE WORKS

Monday — Film 5 videos
Tuesday — Slice clips into 21 reels
Wednesday — Schedule posts, 3 per day

One focused day fuels your whole week.

It's Easier Than You Think

You might worry about running out of topics or feeling silly changing shirts three times in an afternoon to keep the content looking fresh. Let me assure you: once you experience the relief of having your entire week's content "done and dusted," you'll never want to go back to daily guesswork. It frees up your mind to focus on deeper creativity—like finishing that book you've been dreaming about.

Imagine this: Sunday night rolls around, and all your posts for the coming week are already scheduled. You've filmed your best tips, shared teasers of your new chapter, and revealed a behind-the-scenes writing blooper that shows your human side. Now you can relax and engage with comments as they come, rather than scramble to make new content on the fly.

> "I love deadlines. I love the whooshing noise they make as they go by."
> – *Douglas Adams*

Using AI to Plan Your Entire Week of Content in Seconds

Have you heard the buzz about AI but aren't sure how it fits into your weekly content routine? Let me introduce you to ChatGPT, a free (yes—free!) tool that acts like a personal assistant for your ideas. It doesn't replace your creativity—it *amplifies* it. Instead of racking your brain for fresh angles, you simply give ChatGPT a few details, and it fires back a ready-made content plan you can personalize in minutes.

How It Works

Think of ChatGPT as a supercharged brainstorming buddy. You type in a quick description of your book's topic, your audience, and the main benefit you offer. Then, ask for a week's worth of social media prompts, or a batch of short TikTok scripts—whatever you need. ChatGPT reads your request and responds with an outline you can tweak to match your voice.

For a complete newbie, here's the simple process:

1. **Go to ChatGPT.** You can find it by searching "ChatGPT OpenAI" in your browser.

2. **Type or paste in your prompt.** See the sample below for ideas.
3. **Wait a few seconds**—and voilà! You'll see a structured list of ideas and scripts.

Content Creation Sample Prompt

Type the following sample prompt into ChatGPT and customize it to your needs: "Act as my marketing strategist. I'm writing a book about [topic] for [target audience] who struggle with [pain point] and want [desired outcome]."

"Please create a one-week schedule of short social media posts (three per day, twenty-one total) featuring quick tips, insights, or behind-the-scenes glimpses. Keep each post under fifty words, and end with a question or call-to-action."

When ChatGPT delivers its ideas, *don't* just copy and paste—add your personal touches, stories, or examples so your readers hear *your* passion. Then, schedule them using whichever platform you prefer. (And yes, you can even feed these scripts into your MonetizePro scheduling if you like. I'll share more on this later.)

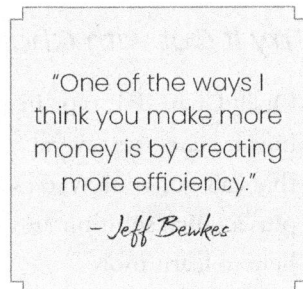

"One of the ways I think you make more money is by creating more efficiency."

– *Jeff Bewkes*

Why It's Worth Trying

- **Saves Time**: Instead of manually brainstorming twenty-one post ideas, ChatGPT knocks it out in seconds.
- **Sparks Creativity**: Seeing AI-generated prompts can trigger new angles you might never have considered.
- **Doesn't Require a Tech PhD**: If you can type into a chat box, you can use ChatGPT. It's that simple.

Use this approach whenever you feel stuck or pressed for time, and let ChatGPT be your digital "co-writer" to keep your social media channels buzzing all week long.

Using AI to Craft High-Performing Ad Scripts

So you've got a book (or product) to promote, and you're thinking about running paid ads—maybe on Facebook, Instagram, or even YouTube. You're excited, but you're also a bit unsure how to write those compelling ad scripts that make people stop scrolling and say, "I need this!" That's where ChatGPT comes in. Think of it as your friendly co-pilot, ready to help you turn your ideas into short, punchy ads—even if you're brand-new to all this.

First, Know Your Avatar

By now, you understand that your avatar is your ideal customer—the person you most want to reach. Picture this avatar when you craft your ads. Give them a name, imagine their routine, pinpoint their pain points (the urgent problems or frustrations they face). Maybe they're a busy mom who wants more time with her kids or a twenty-something struggling to land a dream job. The better you know this avatar, the more specific your ads can be. And specific *sells*.

Try It Out with ChatGPT

Open ChatGPT, type in a few details about your avatar and your offer, and watch how it generates several ad versions within seconds. You'll see short, snappy hooks that call out your avatar's biggest issue—like "Too little time, too many tasks?"—plus a quick solution and a call to action telling them what to do next, like "Click here to learn more."

Ad Copy Sample Prompt

Below is a beginner-friendly prompt you can type into ChatGPT. Just plug in your own details:

"Act as my advertising copywriter. My book helps [avatar name] (who is [description]) solve [big problem]. They struggle with [pain point 1] and [pain point 2], but dream of [their goal]. Please write three short Facebook (or Instagram) ad scripts (one hundred words or less each). Each ad should:

> "Writing a bestseller is 5% talent, 15% hustle, and 80% Googling 'how to write a bestseller.'"
> – *Unknown*

1. Grab their attention by mentioning their pain points.
2. Briefly show how my solution/book helps them.
3. End with a strong call to action. ("Click here," "Buy now," etc.)"

Press "enter," and ChatGPT will give you three ad variations right away. You can adjust the tone, add your personal anecdotes, or fine-tune the wording to sound more like you. If any particular line really resonates, keep it. If not, ask ChatGPT for revisions or more examples.

Learn Why This Approach Works

1. **Instant Inspiration:** No more staring at a blank page. ChatGPT handles the heavy lifting, so you can focus on what you truly want to say.
2. **Pain Points First:** By calling out your avatar's top frustration in each ad, you show readers you "get" them—a trust-builder right off the bat.
3. **Strong CTA:** AI can help you craft that final line telling people exactly what to do next— "Click here to learn more," "Sign up now," etc.—which is crucial for actual conversions.

> "It's important to find what really suits who you are, because style isn't only what you wear, it's what you project."
> – Carolina Herrera

By knowing your avatar's pain points and letting ChatGPT shape your message, you'll create ads that feel personal and get results. It's a fast, beginner-friendly way to launch effective paid advertising—without having to learn complicated marketing lingo or advanced copywriting formulas. So give it a try, refine the ads to sound like you, and get your book (or product) in front of the right people—fast!

Using AI to Write in Any Theme or Voice

One of the most thrilling parts of using AI—like ChatGPT—is how it can instantly shift into any style, persona, or mood. Feeling festive? Tell it to draft your ad or social post in a holiday theme, laced with snowflakes, jingles, or Valentine hearts. Craving a high-energy boost? Ask the AI to channel its "inner Tony Robbins," sprinkling in motivational lines and bold calls to action. Want a sprinkle of childhood magic? Tell it to write with the "charming wonder of a Disney movie script."

Sample Prompt Ideas

- **Holiday Vibes:** "Write a short social media post about my new book, but in a cozy Christmas theme—mention snow, hot cocoa, and family gatherings."
- **Motivational Tone:** "Create an Instagram Reel script about conquering fear, as if Tony Robbins himself were giving the speech."

- **Disney-Style Magic:** "Draft a whimsical, fairy-tale–inspired ad for my upcoming webinar, complete with a 'once upon a time' opening."

Why This Matters

Using this tool is helpful because it will,

1. **Captivate Your Audience.** People love content that resonates with the season or taps into a nostalgic style.
2. **Allow Instant Personalization.** You don't have to master every tone yourself; ChatGPT "wears the costume" for you.
3. **Keep Your Content Fresh.** Even if you're always marketing the same product, AI-generated themes keep your message new and exciting.

So, if you want to spice up your next promotion, remember: AI can do more than just churn out bullet points—it can sing your message in any key you ask for, from holiday cheer to Tony Robbins–level motivation. Just *ask*—and let the magic happen!

Train AI to Match Your Unique Voice

Here's another fantastic trick—you can even use AI to match your unique voice. Simply upload samples of your existing writing—maybe a few paragraphs from your blog or a snippet of your book. When ChatGPT sees how you phrase things, it can spin new content that sounds just like you—complete with your quirks, your humor, and your brand's style.

All you need to do is paste your chosen writing sample into ChatGPT. Then say something like, "Please write a new Facebook ad that uses this tone and style." Suddenly, you're not just getting generic AI responses—you're getting AI that channels your unique flavor.

Whether you want to craft something in a custom tone, a fairytale vibe, or your own personal voice, ChatGPT can help. That's how you keep your brand consistent and instantly familiar to your readers, no matter what wild theme or style you decide to run with next!

> "Failure is simply the opportunity to begin again, this time more intelligently."
> — *Henry Ford*

Putting It All Together

Now that I've shared some winning strategies for easy and efficient content creation, let's review and put it all together. Follow these five action steps to get started today:

1. **Mark a "content day" on your calendar.** Don't leave it to chance. If you can't spare a whole day, at least block out a four-hour window.
2. **Prepare a spreadsheet.** List the topics or angles you'll cover. Jot down short talking points.
3. **Hit record.** Film your batches in one go, remembering to switch up your look or location.
4. **Outsource the editing (if you can).** Otherwise, use simple apps yourself.
5. **Schedule your posts.** Load up your posts, and let them run.

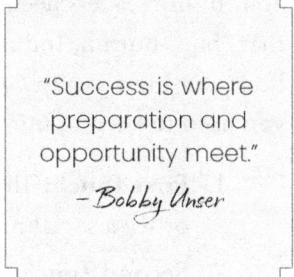

"Success is where preparation and opportunity meet."
— Bobby Unser

That's it. By adopting this single-day content creation method, you'll become a consistent, reliable voice in your niche—without letting social media take over your life. The only thing left is to keep writing your book. Because the moment your audience starts buzzing, they'll want to dive deeper into your world.

Try Our Favorite Social Media Scheduling Tool FREE

You already know the power of batching your social media posts in one day. Now imagine a single platform that not only schedules those posts for you but also brainstorms fresh ideas the moment you feel stuck. That's why I lean on MonetizePro.

Here's how it works: pick your "content day," film your videos in one big burst, and then upload them into MonetizePro. The system's built-in AI can help you polish captions, generate hashtags, and even give you quick tips on what to say. Once you approve each post, you schedule it—all in a single dashboard—so you can step away knowing your feed is set for the whole week.

That's it—no more juggling half a dozen tools, and no more missing posting deadlines. MonetizePro helps you keep the "content machine" well-oiled, giving you more time to write, rest, or dream up the next big idea. If you want to free your mind from day-to-day social media stress, I can't recommend it enough. If you're still not sure it's for you, just see for yourself with a free trial! Visit authorgifts.com/trial to learn more.

The "Buzz-to-Buy" Journey

Your future readers need to hear about your book *multiple* times before they click that "buy" button. Industry experts say that on average, someone needs to see or hear your message *seven times* before they act. Here are the seven stages of interest you need to keep in mind:

1. **First Touch:** They hear a podcast mention or see a social media post.
2. **Second Touch:** They come across your ad or a friend's Facebook share.
3. **Third Touch:** They visit your website or Amazon page but don't buy yet.
4. **Fourth Touch:** They encounter another piece of free content—maybe your blog or an interview.
5. **Fifth Touch:** They sign up for your freebie (such as a printable checklist or short eBook) and opt-in to your newsletter.
6. **Sixth Touch:** They receive your email newsletter.
7. **Seventh Touch:** They see a final post or email, then say, "Yes, I'm in!"

> "Every moment is an organizing opportunity, every person a potential activist, every minute a chance to change the world."
> – Dolores Huerta

It takes a long time to reel in a customer. Be patient and keep the momentum going. Consistency is your best friend.

3 Must-Haves to Make Your Buzz Stick

1. A Clear, Bold Promise

Reiterate the main benefit or transformation your reader will get from your book. Don't hold back—be bold.

Example: "Lose ten pounds in thirty days—without starving yourself."

2. A Memorable Hook

Use the same short tagline or phrase everywhere so people automatically connect it to you.

Example: "When your book hits number one, you'll make a ton. Won't that be fun?"

3. A Simple "Next Step"

Whether it's "Buy now on Amazon," "Get my free bonus," or "Comment below if you want x,y,z," ensure it's one main action. If you confuse them with too many different links or instructions, they do nothing. Always remember that a confused mind does not buy.

Remember To Be Where They Are

The key to connecting with your readers is to show up in the spaces they frequent. We call this omni-presence, because you want to be everywhere your avatar looks! Picture your audience scrolling through their favorite social media platforms, engaging in online communities, or attending events. You need to plant yourself squarely in their line of sight—not by barging in, but by becoming a valuable presence.

Take social media, for example. Imagine your ideal reader relaxing after a long day, scrolling through Instagram or TikTok. Your post appears: an eye-catching graphic or an authentic video sharing a story from your book. It's not just content—it's a conversation starter. You're showing them that you understand their world and have something to offer.

Offline spaces matter too. Perhaps your reader is sipping coffee in their favorite bookstore, attending a local meetup, or exploring a hobby that aligns with your book's theme. These are places where you can make an impact with strategic partnerships, personal appearances, or even thoughtful promotional materials.

Speak Their Language

Once you've found your audience, the next step is resonating with them. It's not enough to know where they are; you need to understand how they think. What keeps them up at night? What questions are they asking? Your content should answer those questions and provide solutions they didn't know they needed.

Start by crafting messages that address their pain points. If your book teaches financial independence, speak to the frustrations of living paycheck to paycheck and the dreams of a more secure future. If it's about self-discovery, share your own moments of struggle and growth, showing them that transformation is within reach.

Your tone should match your readers' preferences. Are they formal and professional or casual and conversational? Let their style guide yours, ensuring you come across as relatable and trustworthy.

Provide Value Before You Ask for Anything

In the world of modern marketing, generosity wins. Before you ask your audience to buy your book, give them something that shows you're invested in their success. Consider this as your way of earning their trust.

Start by sharing your own journey—challenges, breakthroughs, and hard-won lessons—so people sense your authenticity. Then, entice them with a free resource like a downloadable checklist, a short quiz, or a "bonus chapter" that speaks directly to their pain points. If your book focuses on financial freedom, for instance, give a quick budgeting hack you use yourself—enough so they think, *If this is the free stuff, the book must be gold.*

> "Buzz and the right publicist are not only important but crucial."
> – Roy Halston

Next, turn these teasers into lead magnets by placing them behind a simple opt-in page. If you're writing about productivity, put together a PDF called "5 Tools I Use to Save 10 Hours a Week." Post it everywhere—social media, your website, even at the end of a blog article—so people trade their email address for immediate access to real value. That way, you're not just collecting names; you're building trust. By the time you announce your launch, they've already experienced the quality of your ideas, and the answer to your "buy" invitation is more likely to be an enthusiastic "Yes!"

Make Your Buzz a Continuous Conversation

Remember, building buzz isn't a one-time event. It's an ongoing conversation between you and your audience. During your launch, you'll talk about your book a lot—some might call it shameless self-promotion. But that's what it takes to stand out in a sea of four million new books a year.

Don't worry about overdoing it. If your message is valuable, and your stories are genuine, your audience will cheer you on. And if a few folks say you post too much, they're likely not your ideal readers. Keep going anyway.

Getting the word out about your book is not about luck; it's about consistent hustle, creativity, and boldness. Don't let fear keep you small—be everywhere your audience hangs out. Remember: free methods + strategic paid methods + unstoppable enthusiasm = Bestselling Buzz that launches your book sky-high.

So, take the leap. Go on that podcast. Publish that LinkedIn article. Run that ad. Be unafraid to make a fool of yourself. Because if you hold back, you might rob the world of the transformational message your book has to offer.

Up next, I'll discuss Step 11—where we'll dial in your guaranteed launch strategy to fuel your climb to number one.

FREE GIFT: AI Content Plan + Promo Calendar

You don't need a big audience to market your book. This daily content calendar and prompt guide helps you generate buzz—without burning out. Find it at AuthorGifts.com or by scanning the QR code.

> "Our goals can only be reached through a vehicle of a plan, in which we must fervently believe, and upon which we must vigorously act. There is no other route to success."
> – Pablo Picasso

STEP 11: YOUR GUARANTEED LAUNCH

Becoming a #1 Bestselling Author

Imagine you're standing on the summit of a mountain you've spent months—maybe years—climbing. The air is crisp, the view is breathtaking, and every step you've taken has led here. This is the moment you've been waiting for—your book launch. You're about to unveil your message to the world in a way so magnetic that your readers won't be able to look away.

But make no mistake—launching is more than just uploading your manuscript to Amazon and hoping the world discovers it. It's about orchestrating an event so compelling that all eyes turn in your direction. You've spent these chapters crafting an incredible message, learning how to create buzz, and testing your voice on different platforms. Now, it's time to pull those threads together into a Launch Plan that catapults your book into bestseller territory.

Why a Coordinated Launch Matters

Here's the brutal truth—many authors stumble at the finish line. They think writing the book was the hard part, but launching it is the true test of their endurance and ingenuity. The most common missteps? Poor preparation, lack of clarity, and underestimating the power of a coordinated push.

As I've mentioned in previous steps, most authors have no idea what it takes to push a book to number one in their niche. They assume it'll happen by chance or that a publisher or a vanity press will do the required heavy lifting for them. Yes, traditional publishers do provide some marketing, but it's typically more traditional promotion such as press releases and paid media interviews. Many vanity presses and pseudo publishers will do the work of pushing your book to number one—but only for a very hefty fee that's often in the tens of thousands of dollars.

None of that will get you where you want to be. I'd rather show you exactly how to do the hard part by yourself. The plan in this chapter shows you *precisely* how you can make your book number one. And if it sounds overwhelming, don't worry! You can hire others to assist you. (Frankly, my team will do it for you.) But even then, I want you to understand the entire process. Our goal is your long-term success and prosperity—not short-term gains and "one-hit-wonder" style attention that will evaporate after a week or two.

Your launch isn't a quiet whisper into the void; it must be a resounding roar that echoes across the landscape of your niche. To achieve that, you need a plan—a Launch Plan. What you need is a focused, high-impact event—something that commands attention and makes your book unmistakably visible from day one.

Think of it this way: if you're hosting a birthday party, you don't simply tell a few friends the morning of and hope they drop by. You plan the party in advance, send out invitations, maybe decorate the place, and tease everyone with the promise of a great time.

> "Teamwork makes the dream work, but a vision becomes a nightmare when the leader has a big dream and a bad team."
> – John C. Maxwell

Your book launch deserves that same level of energy. In fact, it deserves a thunderous celebration—an all-out campaign that floods social media, email inboxes, and Amazon search results in a short but explosive wave.

It's not rocket science—it's more like event planning. You pinpoint a specific date, rally your supporters around one massive push, and create urgency through bonuses, limited-time discounts, or exclusive behind-the-scenes access. This pressure-cooker approach triggers Amazon's algorithms to notice your book and show it to an even wider audience. If it feels a bit intense—that's because it is. But it's also exhilarating.

"Coordinated" doesn't mean complicated. It just means timing your efforts—your social media posts, your email blasts, your special price promotions—so they all converge in a powerful crescendo. Instead of spreading your strongest marketing thin over months, you zero in on a short timeframe where every single person in your orbit sees your book, gets excited about it, and—this is the key—buys it. This concentrated burst of sales is what ignites the Amazon algorithm, nudging your book higher in the rankings faster than you might believe possible.

> "You're not truly a bestselling author until your mom buys 100 copies and asks if that counts."
> – Unknown

Why Amazon Is the Foundation for Your Bestseller

Let's be real: if you're serious about hitting number one fast, Amazon is your best bet. Traditional publishers might get you on bookstore shelves, but they can't match Amazon's instant, global reach—especially if you're just starting out. By listing your book on Kindle Direct Publishing (KDP), you're tapping into a colossal marketplace where tens of millions of readers browse daily.

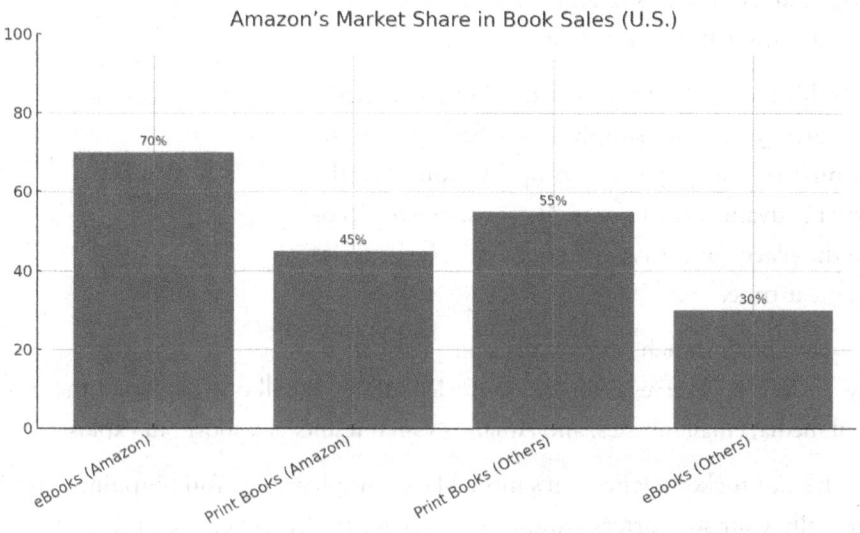

Amazon sells both digital and physical copies through KDP, and it wields colossal power for all book formats. According to various industry analyses, Amazon accounts for over seventy percent of the U.S. eBook market and is estimated to handle between forty to fifty percent of print book sales in many regions.¹ That kind of dominance means whether you're publishing a sleek paperback, a hardcover, or an eBook, Amazon is the grand stage to reach readers fast. Going this route also means you control your price, your promotional timetable, and how quickly you can update your listing. That's crucial when executing a high-stakes, short-window launch plan.

Why You Shouldn't Go Traditional—Just Yet

Here are a few top reasons that Amazon is a more versatile and effective way to publish your book and climb to number one:

- **Speed & Control:** A traditional publisher might take twelve to eighteen months (or more) to transform your completed manuscript into a book on shelves. On Amazon, you can go live in under a week. You also keep control over your pricing, cover design, and marketing angles—freedoms typically surrendered in a traditional deal.

> "If opportunity doesn't knock, build a door."
> – Milton Berle

- **Better Royalties:** Traditional publishers might pay a ten to fifteen percent royalty, while through KDP, you can earn up to seventy percent on eBooks (in qualifying price ranges) and a competitive royalty for paperbacks and hardcovers. If you're a first-time author, the financial difference can be game changing.

- **Global Reach:** With a single upload, your book appears across multiple Amazon marketplaces (U.S., Canada, UK, Australia, and more), potentially exposing you to millions of shoppers worldwide—all without you having to wrangle foreign rights or set up complicated distribution deals.

Does this mean you'll never go traditional? Of course not. But if your goal is to climb the bestseller charts quickly—and keep a solid slice of the profits—Amazon is the place to flex your launch muscles. Once you've proven yourself on the biggest stage online, doors to traditional deals or hybrid deals swing open more easily (if that's something you want).

---

1. "Six Takeaways from the Authors Guild 2018 Author Income Survey," *The Authors Guild*, Jan 5, 2019. https://authorsguild.org/news/six-takeaways-from-the-authors-guild-2018-authors-income-survey/

Maximizing Your Launch on Amazon

When you combine Amazon's built-in traffic with a strategic, concentrated launch push, you're essentially tapping a fire hose of potential buyers. That starts with setting up your metadata properly by picking specific categories, using strong keywords, and crafting a killer book description. Then, you orchestrate your email blasts, social media posts, and promotional pricing so that *all* of your efforts hit in the same brief window. The result? A powerful sales spike that can shoot your book up the bestseller charts for both physical and digital formats.

> "The delicate balance of mentoring someone is not creating them in your own image, but giving them the opportunity to create themselves."
> – Steven Spielberg

If you list on Amazon, you're stepping onto the largest book stage on the planet. The seats are filled with eager readers, you're standing in the spotlight, and now it's your turn to deliver. That's what Kindle Direct Publishing (KDP) is all about: giving you a backstage pass so you can seize that spotlight. Here's how to set up your Amazon listing:

Create a KDP Account

1: Head to kdp.amazon.com

Use your existing Amazon login or create one specifically for your author persona. Think of this like registering for an exclusive club membership; you want to be sure all the details are correct from the get-go.

2: Fill Out Your Profile

Yes, you'll need to give Amazon your tax and banking info. Royalty checks need to arrive somewhere, right? Handle this once, and then you'll be set for every new title you launch.

3: Survey the Command Center

Pop into your KDP dashboard—your new playground. You'll see tabs labeled "bookshelf," "reports," and "marketing tools." This is where you'll do everything from uploading your manuscript to running promotional deals. Get familiar with it so you can confidently pull the right levers when Launch Day hits.

Meet Author Central: Your Digital Autograph Room

Author Central is the official "author page" Amazon assigns you—the place where readers can learn more about you and your other books and even see your latest blog posts or tweets (if you connect them). Why should you bother with this step? Because readers often click your name on your book's listing page to decide if you're "legit" or not. A sparkling Author Central page could turn a "maybe" into a "yes"—especially if someone's already intrigued by your cover and description.

> "I tried waking up early to write. My creativity didn't get the memo."
>
> – *Unknown*

Here's How to Make It Shine:

- **A Friendly Photo:** Swap the stiff headshot for something warm and approachable. Be the author they'd like to have coffee with.
- **An Engaging Bio:** Share a piece of your story—why you wrote the book, the experiences that shaped you, and maybe a quirk or two. Readers love to know the person behind the pages. Write a "buy-o" and remember to include Marketing Words.
- **Optional Blog & Social Feeds:** If you run a blog, feed it here. If you're active on Twitter or Facebook, link them up. The more ways readers can follow your journey, the deeper their connection to you—and your book.

Upload Your First Title

You've refined your message. You've created a knockout book cover and interior layout, and you've been building your buzz on social media. When it's finally time to launch the first rocket on your Amazon journey, click "add new title" on your KDP dashboard:

1. **Choose eBook and/or Paperback:** You can do one or both. Just remember that each format has its own upload path in the dashboard.
2. **Enter the Details:** Title, subtitle, series name, language—this is where you start defining how your book appears to the world.
3. **Write a Book Description:** Think of it like a movie trailer for your book. We'll get into writing a killer description later, but know that this is a sales pitch, not just a summary.

4. **Don't Forget Pre-Orders:** If you plan a pre-launch strategy, KDP lets you pick a release date. Amazon will then show a countdown, letting readers "lock in" your book ahead of time. This can supercharge your ranking on day one if you've built enough anticipation.

Print Edition Considerations

Here are a few additional tips for uploading a print file to KDP:

- **Interior Files:** You can upload a properly formatted PDF prepared by a designer or use KDP's built-in tools to create one. If you choose to use KDP, give your margins, headers, page numbers and other formatting specifications the attention they deserve to ensure your book looks like a winner.
- **Cover Design:** KDP's Cover Creator is handy, but as I suggested in Step 6, a professional cover often pays off in credibility.
- **Proof Copies:** *Always* order a proof copy. You want zero surprises on launch day. If something's off, make sure you can fix it before your real audience sees it.

Select the Right Amazon Categories

When a reader stumbles upon your book page, Amazon reveals the categories—like "self-help" or "science fiction"—where your title competes. Each category is a little shelf in Amazon's massive bookstore. Position your book on the right shelf, and you'll be discovered far more easily by your ideal readers.

1. Zero in on the Perfect Categories

Choosing those categories wisely can be the difference between languishing on page seven or swiftly landing the number one bestseller spot. A smaller, more specific category—such as "personal finance > budgeting" rather than the broad "business and money"—is typically easier to dominate. When you spike in sales, the odds of grabbing that coveted orange "bestseller" tag are much higher. Here's how to do it:

> "The reward for work well done is the opportunity to do more."
> – Jonas Salk

- **Research Competitors:** Peek at books similar to yours. Scroll down to "product details" on their Amazon pages to see which categories they rank in. Notice if they're big, generic categories or narrow niches—like "parenting teenagers."
- **Look for Narrow Subcategories:** If you aim for "nonfiction > self-help," you'll battle thousands of established titles. But "nonfiction > self-help > creativity" or "nonfiction > self-help > stress management" might have fewer direct competitors. Don't shy away from a narrower path; sometimes dominating a small corner of Amazon is the swiftest route to a big, sweeping success.
- **Apply Hidden Categories:** Amazon only lets you pick three categories upon setup, but you can often request additional subcategories by contacting KDP Support. This extra layer can widen your net while maintaining your best chances for ranking.

2. Balance Relevance with Ranking Potential

Yes, going super-niche can help you hit number one fast—but it needs to make sense for your book. If you're forcing your relationship book into "health and fitness > injuries and rehabilitation," readers will be confused. Find the sweet spot: a category that's *truly relevant* yet not so broad that it's overrun by mega-sellers.

> "Being busy does not always mean real work. The object of all work is production or accomplishment and to either of these ends there must be forethought, system, planning, intelligence, and honest purpose, as well as perspiration. Seeming to do is not doing."
>
> – Thomas A. Edison

3. Plan for Ongoing Optimization

After launch, you can still tweak your categories. If you notice your book would naturally fit another niche (for instance, maybe readers keep mentioning it solves a different kind of problem) adjust accordingly. Amazon is dynamic, and your marketing strategy should be too.

4. Enjoy the Payoff of a Bestseller Tag

When you reach number one in your chosen subcategory, Amazon will slap that bright orange "bestseller" tag next to your title. The resulting boost in credibility is huge—browsing customers often click on books with that badge first.

Think of your Amazon listing as the stage lighting and sound system for your performance. If the lights are dim (incomplete details) or the mic is off (weak description, missing author info), your big show falls flat. But when everything is dialed in—metadata, cover, author profile—it's like flipping on brilliant lights and surround sound. Readers click into your listing and think, "This is top-notch—I'm in."

So, take a moment to get it right. When your listing is solid, Launch Day will go far more smoothly. Your fanbase can jump straight to the buy button, any press coverage can link directly to a polished product, and the Amazon algorithm is far more likely to reward you. In short, the foundation you lay now sets the stage for that incredible bestseller moment just around the corner.

> "Bestseller status means your book has been read, loved, dog-eared—and possibly used to level a wobbly table."
> – Unknown

Defining Your Launch Goals

You've got your Amazon foundation set—your cover, metadata, and Author Central profile are all in place. When it's time for your Soft Launch, you'll be ready to upload your book. Now, before you start orchestrating a flood of emails, posts, and ads, let's get crystal clear on *what* you want. If you don't define your target, you might still sell some books, sure, but you won't have that laser focus that catapults a launch to true bestseller territory.

Pick Your Number (or Rank)

The simplest question is, what does success look like for you? Maybe it's hitting number one in a specific Amazon category for at least twenty-four hours. Maybe it's selling one hundred copies in the first seven days. It could be both. Here are a few other possible goals to get you thinking:

- "I want to sell fifty eBooks and fifty paperbacks in the first week."
- "I want to reach number one in 'business and money' on Amazon for at least one day."
- "I want fifty reviews posted by the end of the second week."

Any of these goals will work. The key is to *choose* one or two so that your goals can guide every action you take.

Amazon Ranking Chart

Niche	Amazon Category	Estimated Daily Sales to Hit #1	Example Titles
Parenting & Family	Books › Parenting & Relationships	~10/day	What to Expect When You're Expecting by Heidi Murkoff; The Whole-Brain Child by Daniel J. Siegel
Cooking / Cookbooks	Books › Cookbooks, Food & Wine	~30/day	Magnolia Table by Joanna Gaines; Salt, Fat, Acid, Heat by Samin Nosrat
Christian / Spiritual Growth	Books › Christian Living	~200/day	The Purpose Driven Life by Rick Warren; Get Out of Your Head by Jennie Allen
Health & Fitness	Books › Health, Fitness & Dieting	~150/day	The Body Keeps the Score by Bessel van der Kolk; Outlive by Peter Attia
Children's Picture Books	Children's Books › Growing Up	~500/day	The Very Hungry Caterpillar by Eric Carle; Grumpy Monkey by Suzanne Lang
Business & Money	Books › Business & Money	~800/day	Rich Dad Poor Dad by Robert Kiyosaki; The Psychology of Money by Morgan Housel
Motivational / Success	Self-Help › Success	~1,000/day	Can't Hurt Me by David Goggins; You Are a Badass by Jen Sincero

Reverse-Engineer Your Way to #1

If a bestseller slot in a certain category is your dream, here's a quick way to estimate what it'll take to get there:

1. **Scope Out the Competition:** Search your chosen category on Amazon and note the current number one book. Check its "Best Seller Rank" (BSR)—often found under "product details."
2. **Estimate the Necessary Daily Sales:** Tools like TCK Publishing's BSR calculator or other online BSR estimators can give a ballpark figure on how many daily sales that rank equates to. For example, if the number one book typically has a total BSR rank of around two thousand in the Kindle Store, that might mean it sells (roughly) fifty to eighty eBooks a day.

3. **Add a Buffer:** If you aim to *beat* that number, plan to exceed it for at least a day or two. If the current book is selling between fifty and eighty books per day, shoot for one hundred sales in twenty-four hours.
4. **Calculate Reviews:** High daily sales often trigger new readers to leave reviews. Some authors see one review per twenty to thirty sales, so if you want fifty reviews in the first week, you might aim for one thousand to five thousand total buyers or ARC readers (with some being part of your pre-launch review team).

This isn't a perfect science—Amazon's algorithms are famously secretive—but it *is* a real way to get concrete about the numbers you need to hit. No more picking a number out of a hat or just guessing.

Use Specific Goals to Trump Vague Wishes

Saying, "I'd love my book to do well," is like telling a builder, "Just make me a nice house." You'll get *something*, but likely not what you truly want. Concrete targets—like "one hundred copies" or "number one in 'cooking and wine'"—act like magnets, aligning all your daily tasks toward a measurable outcome. Having a goal also means that you'll know when you've hit it, so you can celebrate with confidence!

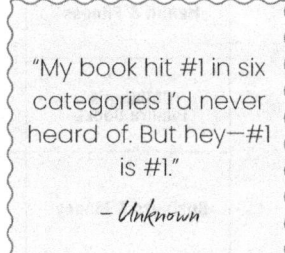

"My book hit #1 in six categories I'd never heard of. But hey—#1 is #1."

– *Unknown*

Use the SMART Framework

Most of us have heard George T. Doran's SMART[2] acronym about goal setting before, but here's how you can apply it specifically to your launch:

- **S** (Specific): Pinpoint an exact number, ranking, or review count.
- **M** (Measurable): Ensure you can track it easily with Amazon's rank updates, sales reports, or your own spreadsheet.
- **A** (Achievable): "Stretch" goals are great, but first do some basic math. If your email list has five hundred people, shooting for ten thousand sales in twenty-four hours might require a serious partner or ad campaign.

---

2. Doran, George T. "There's a S.M.A.R.T. way to write management's goals and objectives," *Management Review*, 1981.

- **R** (Relevant): Does your goal move the needle for your career? If you're aiming to build credibility as a business coach, a category rank in "business and money" might be more relevant than "self-help."
- **T** (Time-bound): Give yourself a window, such as within three days of launch or by the end of the first month.

Define Your "Why": The Emotional Driver

Goals without passion can quickly fizzle. So ask yourself, "Why do I really care?" Maybe you wrote a life-changing memoir that can save someone's marriage, or you're revealing a how-to system that'll help folks get out of debt. That "why" can be your fuel on the days you're tired of emailing or scheduling posts. It will also resonate when you talk about your book: readers will sense that you're not just hawking a product—you're on a mission. Here are some examples of a strong "why":

> "Let our advance worrying become advance thinking and planning."
> – Winston Churchill

- "I want my kids to know that with grit and faith, you can achieve anything."
- "I believe my story can help thousands of struggling single parents."
- "I need to establish credibility in my field so that the next time I speak at a seminar, I'm introduced as a bestselling author."

Put It All in Writing

Take out a sheet of paper—or open a note on your phone—and literally write your specific goals down, making sure each goal has a specific deadline. Here's an example:

1. **Primary Goal** – Example: "Sell one hundred copies in the first seventy-two hours."
2. **Support Goal** – Example: "Gather fifty Amazon reviews by day fourteen."

Pin these goals near your desk, make them your phone wallpaper, or stick a Post-it on your bathroom mirror. The more you remind yourself (and your supporters) of the end game, the more likely that every action will line up with it.

Creating a Successful Launch Plan

A Launch Plan is more than just a to-do list—it's your strategic playbook. It outlines every action you'll take, every deadline you'll hit, and every resource you'll need to ensure your book doesn't just launch—it *soars*.

Think of it like planning a wedding. You wouldn't just pick a date, show up, and hope for the best (or at least I hope you wouldn't). Instead, you'd coordinate the venue, caterer, guest list, and a hundred other details to make the day perfect. Your book launch deserves the same level of attention to detail because the stakes are just as high—this is your chance to make a lasting first impression.

Why Your Launch Plan Matters

Without a clear plan, launching your book can feel overwhelming, like trying to assemble a one-thousand-piece puzzle without the picture on the box. A Launch Plan brings clarity, focus, and structure to the process. Here's how:

- **Prevents Overwhelm:** Knowing what to do—and when to do it—keeps you from spinning your wheels or wasting time on activities that don't move the needle.
- **Maximizes Impact:** By aligning your actions with your audience's behavior and preferences, you'll ensure your efforts create buzz where it matters most.
- **Keeps You Accountable:** Deadlines turn dreams into reality. Your Launch Plan ensures you stay on track and hit every milestone.
- **Minimizes Surprises:** A solid plan helps you anticipate and prepare for challenges, so you can tackle them head-on rather than scrambling in crisis mode.

A good launch gets your book on the market. A *great* launch gets your book in the hands of people who rave about it, review it, and share it with their networks. The difference often comes down to strategy. Your Launch Plan is the foundation of that strategy, ensuring every effort is laser-focused on your ultimate goal: creating a bestseller.

> "You haven't truly written a bestseller until someone leaves a one-star review titled, 'Meh.'"
>
> – Unknown

The Anatomy of a Launch Plan

Every successful journey starts with a plan. Whether it's climbing Mount Everest or the bestseller list, preparation is everything. You made a Map to guide your writing process, and launching your book is no different. This is your Everest, and your Launch Plan is the blueprint that will guide you to the summit—a bestseller launch that gets your book in the hands of your ideal readers and beyond.

> "I planned to write the next great American novel. Instead, I alphabetized my spice rack. Same creative energy, different seasoning."
>
> – Unknown

Every step, every milestone of your Launch Plan is designed to build momentum and anticipation. Here's what your plan will look like in roughly chronological order:

1. Choose Your Launch Day

The cornerstone of this plan is your Launch Day. Pick a single day when all your promotional efforts will converge. Why just one day? Because urgency is rocket fuel. When your audience knows they have a short window to nab bonuses, deals, or a special price, they'll act fast. Better yet, Amazon's algorithms reward that sudden surge in sales by showcasing your book to even more shoppers. If you concentrate your pre-launch efforts around this date, you'll create the perfect environment for a chart-blasting debut.

2. Coordinate Your Pre-Launch

Plan a sixty- to ninety-day pre-launch phase to implement marketing strategies and ramp up your social posts. This is the ideal time to refine your compelling message, leverage influencer and podcast opportunities, send press releases, engage in media outreach, build urgency, and ensure that everything is in place for Launch Day.

You should also use this period to gather your launch team—your personal cheerleading squad who will amplify your voice across their own networks. Think early adopters, beta readers, loyal email subscribers, and supportive friends. With a bit of guidance (like pre-written social media posts or email templates), your team can spread the word on launch day, post reviews, and share that "last call" sense of urgency.

3. Run a Soft Launch

Your Soft Launch is the transition stage between your pre-launch and your Launch Day. This phase allows you to quietly release your book two to three weeks early to a smaller circle of readers, such as family, friends, and ARC (Advance Review Copy) readers, who can help you spot errors and provide you with the vital customer reviews you'll need to build confidence in prospective buyers.

Aim to gather at least twenty-five customer reviews in preparation for your Hard Launch. When prospective buyers see verified reviews for your book on Launch Day, they'll see that your book is a proven product, and they'll be eager and ready to invest their time and money to follow the buzz you've created.

> "Organizing is what you do before you do something, so that when you do it, it is not all mixed up."
> – A. A. Milne

4. Unleash Your Hard Launch

A Hard Launch is another name for your biggest moment—Launch Day. During your Hard Launch, all of your preparation, marketing, and social media efforts will ignite in one explosive event. This is the day to proclaim your message to your carefully prepared audience so they'll know it's time to buy your book. Coordinate this day carefully with increased social media posts and special bonuses that will intensify throughout the day as you climb toward your goals.

5. Track Your Success, Readjust, & Plan for the Future

Your book launch is something to celebrate, but don't get distracted. Just because you reached your initial goal doesn't mean you're finished. There are still thousands of readers who need your message. Don't forget to track successes and failures, readjust your strategies, and plan for future goals.

KEY PERFORMANCE INDICATORS

Weeks	Week 1	Week 2	Goal KPIs
Opt-In Rate	28%	32%	35%
Conversion Rate	3%	4%	5%
Average Order Value	$42	$51	$50

Taking Launch Day to Another Level

Your Launch Plan is more than a checklist. It's a powerful strategy—a symphony of anticipation that culminates in one triumphant moment when your book claims the spotlight. And the information found here is just the tip of the iceberg. Check out the free ninety-day launch plan at the end of this chapter, and I'll walk you step-by-step through building the necessary momentum to reach number one using your pre-launch, Soft Launch, and Hard Launch phases.

Amplifying Your Impact with Strategic Tools

Writing a compelling message is only part of the equation. The tools you use to share that message determine how far it travels and how effectively it resonates. At this point, you have a growing arsenal of tools at your disposal. Your challenge is to use them wisely, blending authenticity with strategy.

> "You don't have to be a genius or a visionary or even a college graduate to be successful. You just need a framework and a dream."
>
> – Michael Dell

Remember: your goal isn't to sell a book—it's to build a relationship with your readers. When they see you as a trusted guide, they'll not only buy your book but recommend it to everyone they know.

Take action today. Choose one platform, one tool, and one strategy to focus on. Master it, measure its impact, and then expand your efforts. Remember that you're not just launching a book—you're building a legacy.

Your Launch Toolbox

Launching a book is a monumental task that requires juggling multiple moving parts—emails, social media campaigns, text messages, website updates, and more. Keeping all these elements aligned can feel like trying to conduct an orchestra without a baton. This is where technology becomes your ally. To implement your Launch Plan effectively and amplify your efforts, you need more than a simple to-do list. You need a system—a powerhouse of organization and automation.

Enter MonetizePro, the ultimate all-in-one marketing tool designed to simplify and supercharge your book launch. Created for authors, coaches, and business leaders, MonetizePro is more than just software; it's your launch team's secret weapon.

MonetizePro centralizes your communication, integrates AI chat features to help with quick responses, and offers scheduling tools so you never miss a beat. You'll not only track your book's buzz in real time but also ensure no comment or question goes unanswered. Remember, the moment you respond is the moment you transform a casual reader into a lifelong fan—and a strong platform with automation can make that process feel effortless.

Why You Need a Tool Like MonetizePro

Let's face it: manual processes are slow, error-prone, and overwhelming. Without a centralized platform to manage your launch activities, you risk missed opportunities, inconsistent communication, and burnout. That's why I, my co-authors, and my Authors Accelerator students, rely on MonetizePro to execute seamless and impactful launches.

Here's what MonetizePro does for you:

- **Saves Time:** Automates repetitive tasks like scheduling emails and social media posts so you can focus on what matters most—your book and your audience.
- **Streamlines Communication:** Ensures consistent messaging across all channels, from email campaigns to social media outreach.
- **Amplifies Impact:** Combines AI-powered tools to help generate high-quality content and respond to leads instantly.
- **Organizes Chaos:** Provides a single hub to manage everything—launch websites, funnels, marketing campaigns, and more.

> "I'm a true believer in the strength of teamwork, in the power of dreams, and in the absolute necessity of a support structure."
> – Julie Payette

MonetizePro is your backstage crew, your marketing director, and your project manager all rolled into one. It's built on the trusted technology that's used by thousands, meaning you're leveraging cutting-edge software to give your launch an unbeatable advantage.

Putting MonetizePro to Work

Now that you understand the power of this tool, let's look at how to integrate it into your Launch Plan to achieve maximum efficiency and impact.

1. **Automate Your Launch Timeline:** Once you've mapped out your launch plan—emails, social media posts, pre-launch bonuses, and launch-day announcements—MonetizePro ensures everything runs like clockwork. Use its scheduling feature to pre-plan emails, text messages, and posts, so they're sent automatically at the right moments.

2. **Create Stunning Launch Pages:** A strong first impression is critical. With MonetizePro's intuitive funnel builder, you can design high-converting launch websites and sales pages tailored to your book's audience. Whether you're offering pre-order bonuses or creating a countdown page, MonetizePro makes it simple and effective.

3. **Engage Your Audience with AI:** MonetizePro's AI bots work tirelessly to interact with your leads. Picture this: someone visits your launch page and has a question. Instead of waiting hours for a response, an AI bot engages with them immediately, answering questions and nudging them toward action—whether it's pre-ordering your book or signing up for a bonus webinar.

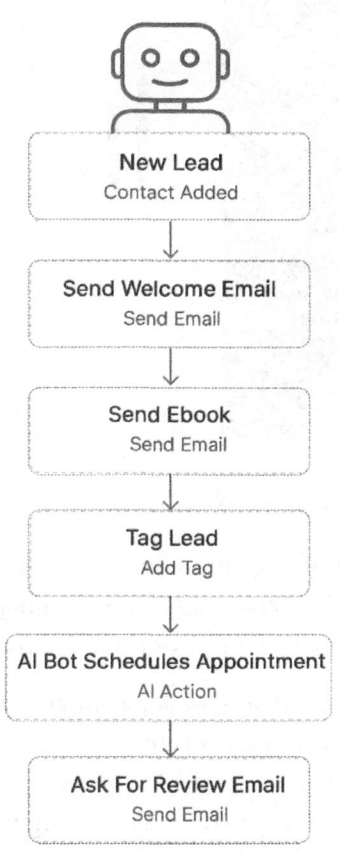

4. **Centralize Your Communications:** Stop switching between platforms to manage emails, texts, and social media. MonetizePro consolidates all your communication tools in one place, making it easy to track conversations, respond to queries, and keep your messaging consistent across channels.

5. **Track & Adapt in Real-Time:** One of the most powerful features of MonetizePro is its analytics dashboard. Monitor the performance of your campaigns, track clicks and conversions, and make data-driven adjustments to optimize your launch as it unfolds.

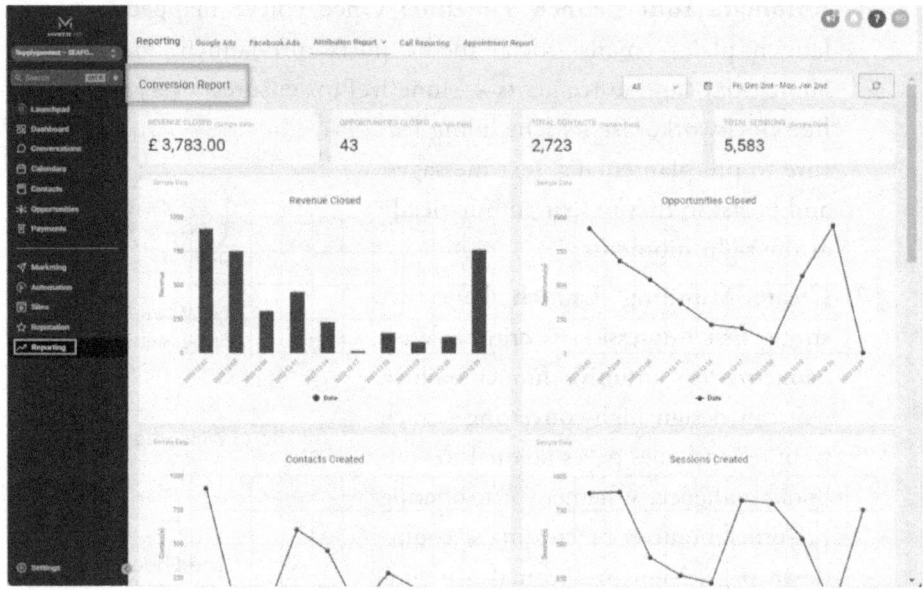

Your Next Step

You've spent months crafting your book, and your launch deserves the same level of precision and care. By integrating a tool like MonetizePro into your strategy, you're not just working smarter—you're amplifying every effort your team makes.

Ready to see it in action? Try MonetizePro for free and experience how this tool can transform your launch from stressful to seamless. Your book is a labor of love—let MonetizePro handle the heavy lifting so you can shine on Launch Day. Visit authorgifts.com/trial or scan the QR code with your smart phone to learn more.

You're Ready—Go Claim It

A launch isn't just a marketing stunt; it's your declaration to the world that your book matters. You're raising your hand and saying, "I have a story that can change lives. I have a system that can solve a problem. I have a vision that can spark new ideas." Believe it, own it, and let that conviction shine. Because once you reach number one, it's more than just a nice badge—it's a beacon that draws readers, media, and future opportunities your way.

One of our Accelerator members followed our exact launch instructions and reported her results:

> *Exciting news! Diary of a Soul Traveller has ascended to the number one spot in its category on Amazon! Thank you for your incredible teaching and insights. I followed your marketing strategies, such as giving out free books and asking readers to buy my book in the same hour, and the result was instant. Wow!*
>
> *– May Long, Bestselling Author*

Whether your dream is to land a big speaking gig, lock in a traditional publishing deal for your next project, or simply know that thousands of people are reading and loving your work, an effective Launch Plan can get you there.

Now, trust what you've built, rally your supporters, and make your book's debut an event people can't ignore. Then stand back and watch as the rank climbs, your inbox pings with new fans, and your author career takes flight.

You've *got* this. This is your moment—step into the spotlight and show the world what you've been working toward. When you look back, you'll realize it wasn't just about hitting number one; it was about becoming the writer—and the force for change—you were always meant to be.

FREE GIFT: 90-Day Launch Plan + Amazon Review Cheatsheet

Want to hit #1 and stack legit reviews fast? This step-by-step launch map and bonus review script will walk you through it. Download both at AuthorGifts.com or scan the code.

STEP 11 BONUS: THE SUPERFAN STRATEGY

The Underground Launch Tactic That Builds Bestsellers from the Inside Out

Let me give it to you straight—you don't need millions of followers. You don't need to be famous. You don't even need a big marketing budget. If you've got the right one hundred people—people who believe in your book, your mission, and you—you can create a surge of momentum that launches your book straight up the charts.

We call them Superfans—not because they're famous, but because they're fierce in their belief. They're the people who say, "I don't just want to read this book—I want to help share it with the world."

And when you organize those people into a team, give them a clear mission, and show them how to help… That's when things explode. Your book doesn't just trickle out into the market—it shows up like a tidal wave.

Let's break down exactly how to do it.

What Is the Superfan Strategy?
The 1,000-Copy Shortcut Most Authors Miss

The Superfan Strategy flips the traditional book launch on its head. Instead of trying to convince thousands of strangers to maybe buy your book, you focus on activating a small inner circle of loyal believers—your one hundred Superfans—who each commit to helping ten people in their world grab a copy on launch day.

That's it.

Not one hundred thousand people. Not a viral post. Just one hundred humans with a clear mission and a reason to care.

Do the math: 100 people × 10+ buyers = 1,000+ sales.

And when those sales all hit on the same day? That's how algorithms notice. That's how bestseller charts move. That's how launches ignite. This isn't a strategy for influencers. It's a strategy for impact-driven authors who know how to lead a mission—and rally their tribe.

No ads. No tech headaches. No big spend.

Just people, passion, and a plan.

Let's build yours.

What Do Superfans Get in Return?
How to Make Helping You Feel Like an Honor

Here's the truth: People want to be part of something bigger than themselves. But they need a reason to believe—and a reason to act.

So when someone raises their hand and joins your launch team, you don't just give them a task, you give them a role in your story. And that's where the magic happens.

Here's what your Superfans get:

- A signed copy of the book (it's more than ink—it's personal)
- Private "insider" updates during the launch—like they're in the control room with you
- A spot in your Launch Team Zoom Party (scheduled about 7 days before launch—details below)
- Their name printed in the book—immortalized forever in a special thank-you section
- A chance to win a bonus prize if they drive the most sales (optional, but adds friendly fire)

But here's the real reward: They get to say, "I helped make this book a bestseller." That's the kind of pride money can't buy. When you give your team a chance to feel seen, celebrated, and part of the win, they'll show up stronger than any paid ad ever could.

How to Launch the Superfan Strategy
The 5-Part Blueprint to Activate, Align, & Amplify Your Team

You've got your believers. Now let's turn them into a launch force. Here's the full system:

1: Lock In Your Launch Date & Make It Irresistible

Pick your launch day and protect it like gold. Everything revolves around this moment. Want a surge of momentum? Make the Kindle version ninety-nine cents for twenty-four hours only. This one tactic makes it easier for your Superfans to say, "It's just ninety-nine cents—grab it today!" This isn't just a launch. It's a flash event.

2: Extend the Invite (Like You Mean It)

This isn't a "maybe if you have time" favor. This is a real mission. Send a personal message, post a video, or reach out directly with heart.

Here's what to include:
- What the book is about (make it matter to them)
- Why it's important now
- What you're asking them to do:
  a) Join the launch team
  b) Help ten people buy the book on [insert date]
- What they'll receive in return (see previous section)

Frame it like they're getting access to something exclusive, not just being asked to help.

3: Host the Superfan Launch Team Zoom

This is non-negotiable. You must rally the troops in real time. Hold a Zoom meeting seven days before your launch and keep it to sixty minutes or less. This meeting turns helpers into advocates.

Your goals:
- Share the bigger "why" behind your book
- Explain exactly how they'll help

- Show them what to say, where to post, and how to follow up
- Let them ask questions
- Get them emotionally invested

4: Equip Your Team with Share Tools

You want zero friction. The easier it is to share your book, the more your team will do it. Send them,

- A short, swipeable email or text (see next section)
- 1–2 images they can post on social media
- Your Amazon link (short and clean)
- A countdown reminder to add to their calendar

This is what I call "Launch in a Box" because it includes all the tools and none of the overwhelm.

5: Follow Up with Precision

People get busy. Your message can get buried. That's why follow-up is not optional—it's strategic. Use this exact cadence:

- 72 hours before: "We're almost there! Quick checklist + reminder"
- 48 hours before: "Here's what to share + how to send it"
- 24 hours before: "Tomorrow's the day—let's go!"
- Morning of launch: "Today's the day. Every click counts. You've got this."

These reminders don't feel like pestering. They feel like leadership. And they'll keep the momentum from fizzling out at the finish line.

Follow up like a leader-not a nag.

The key to making this strategy work is clarity—clarity on what to do, when to do it, and why it matters. If you handle this right, your Superfans will feel energized, aligned, and ready to go to war for your book.

Superfan Sample Outreach Message
Copy, Paste, & Watch the Magic Happen

Your Superfans are willing to help—don't make them write from scratch. Give them a proven, high-converting message they can personalize in thirty seconds or less. Here's a template that works:

> **Subject line (if used for email): Need your help**
>
> Hey [First Name],
>
> Quick favor!
>
> I'm helping launch a book I really believe in, and today is the big day. For one day only, it's just 99 cents on Amazon.
>
> It's called [Insert Book Title], and it's written to help people [insert quick benefit/goal of the book — e.g., "turn their knowledge into a bestselling book" or "learn how to build multiple streams of income with just 30 minutes a day"].
>
> If that sounds interesting—or if you just want to support something cool that I'm part of—could you grab a copy today?
>
> Here's the link: [Amazon link]
>
> You don't need a Kindle to read it—the free Kindle app works on any device.
>
> Even if you don't read it right away, the 99-cent purchase helps us climb the charts so more people discover it.
>
> It would mean a lot.
>
> Thank you,
>
> [Superfan's First Name]

Pro Tips to Share with Your Team:

- Encourage them to text this message directly to ten people they know would support them.

- Give them easy-to-use graphics or stories to post on social (optional but powerful).
- Remind them: They're not "selling"—they're sharing something they believe in, and people want to support people, not just products.
- Why This Message Works
- It's low-friction and emotionally honest.
- The favor is small. (99 cents, one day, no Kindle required)
- The language is warm, not salesy.
- The CTA (call to action) is ultra-clear.
- It empowers the Superfan to feel helpful, not pushy.

Your 100 People Can Change Everything

This isn't a replacement for marketing—it's rocket fuel for what you're already building. Let's be clear: If you're serious about hitting number one, you'll likely be using a few tools:

- Social media? Yes.
- Paid ads? Absolutely—if budget allows.
- Email list? A huge advantage.
- Media appearances? Bonus points.

But no matter what else you're doing, the Superfan Strategy gives you something those other channels can't:

- Real people, personally invested in your launch.
- A concentrated wave of word-of-mouth and urgency—all on one day.
- A small but mighty force that acts like a lever, multiplying the impact of everything else you do.

You're not replacing your ads or content—you're supercharging them. Think of it this way:

- Your content spreads awareness.
- Your ads drive interest.
- Your Superfans drive action.

And action is what gets your book ranked. 100 people. 10 buyers each. 1,000+ purchases in 24 hours. That's not hype—it's math. So, here's what to do next:

- Build your team of 100
- Host your pre-launch Zoom
- Hand them the right tools
- Follow up on schedule
- Cheer them on
- Celebrate them like royalty

And yes—layer this strategy on top of your paid media, your posts, and your press. That's when your launch doesn't just succeed—it scales. Because books don't hit number one by accident. They hit number one when the right strategy meets the right people—and the spark catches fire.

And your Superfans?

They're the ones holding the match.

"You're a spark away from an explosion of prosperity."
— Robert G. Allen

STEP 12: YOUR EXPONENTIAL SCALABILITY

Adding Zeros

Now that I've shown you how to become a bestselling author, you have two possible plans to follow: Plan A—publish your book and hope someone buys it (good luck with that), or Plan B—build a book platform and info business that can provide you with lifetime streams of income. If you've read this far, I'm assuming you choose Plan B. So let's scale your profits and add some zeros.

First, we'll discuss the theory. Then, I'll share a practical example.

Scaling Profit

What does scaling mean? It means growing your profits faster than you grow your costs—or in other words, adding zeros to your income. Let's start small. We'll assume your first word-product (unit) is a bestselling book. How could you turn this into an income stream of at least $10,000 net dollars a month? I'm about to teach you how.

$1 Profit per Book

If your profit per book is $1, you'd need to scale it up from selling 100 to 1,000 to 10,000 books a month to reach your goal. That's a large number. You're new to this, and it might be beyond your belief threshold to think you could scale up that big. To make that number more believable, let's scale it down into bite-sized chunks: 10,000 books would be about 2,500 a week, or 333 a day.

"Hmm," you wonder. "That's still a big number. How could I market 300-plus books a day?" Don't worry—there are other options.

Play the numbers. Multiply the impact.

$10 Profit per Book

Let's scale up the profit per book to reach your goal instead. When you combine digital and physical book sales, a $10 average profit per book is realistic.

If the profit was $10, you would only need to sell 1,000 books a month. That's only 33 books a day to reach your $10,000 monthly target (30 days × 33.33=1,000). Could you sell 33 books a day? That seems easier. Still, selling 1,000 books a month would be a substantial, part-time side hustle. There's still got to be a better way.

$100 Profit for a Book & Info-product

Let's scale up the profit again and add another zero, from $10 to $100 in profit per book sale. Like you learned in "Step 9: Your Succession Stack," you can scale your profits by creating additional offers to enhance your readers' experience. For instance, maybe you could create a companion course to go along with your book. This might consist of ten sessions on Zoom in which you teach the book's content along with more advanced information. Since the content would be delivered digitally, the profit margin could be high, so $100 net profit for the book

> "The only place success comes before work is in the dictionary."
>
> – Vidal Sassoon

and the companion course is realistic. To make $10,000 a month, you'd only need to sell about 100 units per month, or about 3 units per day. Hmm. Does that seem doable?

$1,000 Profit per Unit

It's time to add another zero and scale up the profit yet again. Do you think you could sell a package of information units for $1,000?

Here are some examples of products you could package together:

1. A physical book and an eBook – $25 retail
2. A digital online course – $295 retail
3. A 90-day live Zoom group coaching program – $495 retail
4. A valuable 2-day seminar (live and on Zoom) – $995 retail

Total retail value –   **$1,810**

Special Promotional Price –   **$1,000**

In this scenario, you'd need to talk to fewer people, and they'd need to be more qualified. But you'd only need to sell ten a month. When you scale up the price by adding a zero, you can scale down the number of units sold and subtract a zero. (Now, keep in mind that this example isn't exact. Obviously, there would be expenses for delivery and marketing in this scenario. But let's keep it simple to illustrate a point.)

> "Trust yourself. Create the kind of self that you will be happy to live with all your life. Make the most of yourself by fanning the tiny, inner sparks of possibility into flames of achievement."
>
> – Golda Meir

Do you believe you could sell ten similar product packages based on the information in your book this month?

That depends. Would it be easier for you to sell 100 units at $100 or 10 units at $1,000? It's the same net profit. Some people are not great salespeople, and selling products at a higher price is more difficult. If that's the case, selling a higher number of units at a lower price point might be more attainable. But if what you're offering is something you *really* believe in—something you feel it's your purpose to share—then, yeah, you could probably work up your courage to sell ten packages a month at $1000 a pop, couldn't you? Would that interest you?

$10,000 Profit per Unit

Well, just for fun, let's say you raise the price and make $10,000 in profit per unit. You'd only need to make *one sale* a month! But wait a minute—what information could you provide that would entice someone to pay more than $10,000!?

Does anyone in the world spend that much for information? Absolutely! For exclusive access to a network of famous experts and their highly valuable information, some people spend $100,000 or more. (See? They've added yet another zero.) I know of some gurus who charge $1,000,000 (there's *another* zero) per year for an exclusive, one-on-one, intense, personal coaching experience. But that's extremely rare.

Your $10,000 product would most likely consist of a year-long, one-on-one coaching program with lots of bells and whistles. It would also require a lot of your personal time spread out over a year. I'm assuming you don't have a PhD or other powerful credentials. So, why would anyone pay "little ol' you" over ten grand? Are we starting to reach the limits of your "belief" threshold?

The question is, where do you want to enter this game?

Do you want to sell a *lot* of info-units at a *low* profit?

Or do you want to sell a *few* info-experiences for a *lot* of profit?

The answer is all of the above.

This is what I call the Million Dollar Matrix. There are a million ways to earn a million dollars with information, but let me show you at least seven ways.

The Million Dollar Matrix

1,000,000 units × $1 = $1,000,000

100,000 units × $10 = $1,000,000

10,000 units × $100 = $1,000,000

1,000 units × $1,000 = $1,000,000

100 units × $10,000 = $1,000,000

10 units × $100,000 = $1,000,000

1 unit × $1,000,000 = $1,000,000

> "You are not here merely to make a living. You are here in order to enable the world to live more amply, with greater vision, with a finer spirit of hope and achievement. You are here to enrich the world, and you impoverish yourself if you forget the errand."
>
> – *Woodrow Wilson*

Offer	Unit Price	Sales Volume	Revenue
Live Event Access	$10,000	100	$1M
Newsletter	$1	1,000,000	$1M
eBook	$10	100,000	$1M
Course Bundle	$100	10,000	$1M
Autographed Video Kit	$1,000	1,000	$1M
Elite Access	$100,000	10	$1M
One Superfan Gift	$1,000,000	1	$1M

To reiterate—the higher your profit margin is, the lower the number will be of units you need to sell. And vice versa. Isn't this matrix just another way of showing how the price of information increases depending upon the way it's delivered—from basic information to advanced content that includes personal interaction with the author?

The secret is to scale up and down the Millionaire Matrix to reach a set of numbers that cause you to believe you can achieve your goal. Once you reach those "belief" numbers, you then pick the timeframe to reach your desired total profit target.

The One Minute Millionaire

I'm the co-author of the very popular book, *The One Minute Millionaire*. Could you make a million dollars in a minute using the Millionaire Matrix? That's absolutely crazy, right? Well, think about it: How *could* someone make a million dollars in a minute? That depends on the number of names who are exposed to your offer. You could buy ads on radio or TV to reach a million people, but that's old school. These days we send email blasts to people's databases instead. Or we reach millions of people on social media and on podcasts. Here's how to use your database and joint ventures with other influential people to scale quickly.

> "If you think you are too small to make a difference, try sleeping with a mosquito."
> – Dalai Lama

Scaling Names on a Database

Your most valuable asset is your database of happy fans and customers. There are two kinds of databases. The metaphor I like to use for these is a lake filled with fish. The lake is a database, and the fish are the names in the database. Your lake is made up of people who have opted into your database, including your growing list of happy customers. So, there are two kinds of "lakes."

> "Life is like the monkey bars: you have to let go to move forward. Once you make the decision to leap into entrepreneurship, be sure to loosen your grasp on old concepts so you can swing your way to new ones."
> – Leah Busque

The first type of lake belongs to you. You have stocked your lake with fish. The population starts out small and grows steadily. Before long, the fish have matured, spawned, and became schools of hungry fish. If you want supper, you can go out on the shore of your own lake and catch at your leisure. You don't need permission from anyone, and no one else can fish in your lake unless you give them permission. This lake represents your personal customer database. You can fish in this database by sending out promotions.

Have you ever opted in to an excellent online promotion? They're a thing of beauty. You're aware that you're being persuaded, but you have difficulty resisting. Copy that style. Learn to master the persuasion process as you fish in your database.

> "Unity is strength... when there is teamwork and collaboration, wonderful things can be achieved."
> – Mattie Stepanek

The problem comes with doing *too* much fishing, or sending out constant promotions to your list so that your fish get sick and tired of your constant pitching. They opt out of your list and say, "NEVER email me again!" Have you ever unsubscribed from a list? If you have, you know what that kind of pestering feels like. Don't do that to your list. Don't make them want to unsubscribe.

Now, please forgive the metaphor. Equating catching and eating fish with "catching" customers is a bit gory. You're not really catching and eating your customers. It's just the opposite— you're actually enticing them into a more abundant life. You're serving them, supporting them, and guiding them.

Scaling through Joint Ventures

The second kind of lake is owned by other people who—just like you—have stocked their lakes with their own customers. Under the right circumstances, you can also gain access to this type of lake. You might ask, "How can these lakes benefit me if they belong to someone else? Why would these database owners let me send an email to their database of highly prized customers?" I'll tell you.

If the bait you offer is tasty and enticing, then you could probably find success by introducing it to other people's customers. But if *you* sent a message to *their* list, it would be spam. However, if *they* send it to their own list, or the message comes with their personal endorsement, it comes from a trusted source. If you offer to share some of the catch with the owners of other lakes, then they might let you fish in their databases. The lake (list) owner has customers who could benefit from your info-product. This is called a joint venture (JV) from which you both profit.

JVs are the fastest ways for you to profit because you get an immediate haul of fish and split the take with the lake owner. It's a natural fit for both of you.

The Power of JVing

One way to scale your business is to add a zero to your list of JV partners. From 1 JV to 10 to 100. When you're bringing consistent income to your bottom line—$5,000 or $10,000 to $100,000 or more—you're ready to *level up*. You have perfected a sales sequence that successfully "pulls" customers to your own database. Then, it's time to introduce your info-product to other JV info-marketers and their databases. Broadening your marketing in this way just multiplies your success by 10 or 100 or even 1000.

You can show your potential JV partners the exact promotion sequence that worked so well in building your own database of customers. You've assembled the detailed marketing metrics: revenue per click (RPC,) lifetime value of a customer (LTV), etc. When a new JV promotes your product to their database, then both of you split the profit. To the savvy JV partner, it's

> "Scaling is multidimensional. Different methods address different things."
>
> – Fred Ehrsam

free money. You deliver the product and the ongoing support, and the JV simply collects up to half of the revenue.

> "You must learn from the mistakes of others. You can't possibly live long enough to make them all yourself."
> – Sam Levenson

Then, you reciprocate. Your JV partner sends their proven marketing messages to your list, they deliver the product and ongoing support, and you collect up to half of the revenue. You both make money while you sleep.

JVs are the lifeblood of your business. They pay the rent. They can sometimes provide windfalls of needed cash. In the Authors Accelerator class, I'll teach you a proven system for cultivating these JVs into budding profit centers. Sometimes, when I help one of my students to create an irresistible info-product, I also let them fish in *my* lake. We JV together. Would you like that?

Here's the JV bottom line: If you want to scale, somebody's got to promote you. And you've got to promote other people. JVs are a must-have. Eventually, the profit from your JVs could exceed the profit from marketing your own products.

It might seem like a lot of hassle to track down other list owners and ask for permission to sell to their lists, but it's worth the hassle. With just a little research, you can find compatible list owners who might be interested in JVing with you.

One of my most successful students is Alfio Bardolla from Italy. He came to my home in California in 2006 and rang my doorbell because he wanted a mentor. He had been to many of my seminars and the programs of other "gurus" in America. I could tell he was going places! Ten years later, in 2016, he asked me to join the board of directors of his new publicly traded company in Milan, Italy. He had arrived—big time! His sold-out events in Italy are legendary. Thousands of people love his approach to moneymaking. One of my favorites of his many books is *Money Makes You Happy*.

Robert Allen and Alfio Bardolla

Alfio has a large database of happy customers. One of his friends is Vishen Lakhiani, founder of the famous online learning platform, MindValley. It turns out that Vishen had also read one of my books, *Multiple Streams of Income*. That book, he told me, was a catalyst in launching the early iterations of MindValley. So, it was natural for us to form a joint venture: my database, Alfio's database, and the massive database of MindValley. We held a seminar in London called the Financial Freedom Summit that was attended by thousands online and offline. Eventually, as your brand grows, you'll be forming similar joint ventures. It's how you scale.

Now, let's add some more zeros.

Alfio Bardolla, Vishen Lakhiani, and Bob Allen

The Ultimate JV

Suppose you and I have been invited to be on *The Joe Rogan Experience* podcast or *Oprah* or some other program with a famous host. Rogan has a database of over fifteen million listeners. How can we use the metrics of scaling to make millions for Joe Rogan's favorite charity? Let's say we promise Joe that we can do it in just sixty seconds, and he's intrigued. We encourage him to make a special offer to his viewers, and I agree to send a special message to my own email database of a million targeted entrepreneurial fans.

Joe and I agree to devote a weekend to teaching our closely guarded secrets to a very select group of one hundred people—out of millions, only one hundred. There will be a hefty tuition, but the experience will be worth it. There will be time for photos and videos and autographs and fun meals. The networking with this highly qualified group of one hundred would be priceless. And one hundred percent of the money will be given to Joe's favorite charity.

We announce the event on Joe's live podcast and my email database. Only one hundred lucky buyers will be selected. And they will only have *sixty seconds* to respond. The first one hundred will be charged $10,000 for the opportunity to be part of this special group. Do you think we'd find one hundred people? Duh! Only one person in ten thousand needs to accept the offer! Those are very good odds. And one hundred attendees multiplied by $10,000 equals a million dollars for Joe's charity.

> "Defeat is not the worst of failures. Not to have tried is the true failure."
> – *George Edward Woodberry*

After these special participants are selected, what about the millions of others who weren't selected? Let's raise even more money for Joe's favorite charity using the Millionaire Matrix. We could launch a weekly newsletter for only $1 a year. Would a million people opt in for a buck? Yes, I bet they would.

1,000,000 × $1 = $1,000,000

Next, we could create an eBook of the entire experience for only $10. Would 100,000 people be enticed to buy it? I think so. There's another million.

100,000 books × $10 profit = $1,000,000

Then we could offer an online course summarizing the lessons of the $10,000 premium experience into an info package of books, online downloads, and audio programs for only $100. Would 10,000 people buy this valuable package? That's yet another million.

10,000 online course buyers × $100 profit = $1,000,000

The video of the weekend with Joe could be packaged into a personally autographed, beautifully packaged learning system made available for *only* 1,000 people. The price? A mere $1,000. Would Joe agree to sign his name to 1,000 info-packages if it would raise another million for charity? Slam dunk.

1,000 autographed learning systems × 1,000 buyers = $1,000,000

Now let's revisit the exclusive weekend event for only 100 people:

100 attendees × $10,000 = $1,000,000

Would 10 of those participants pay $100,000 for a special package of benefits? Done!

10 power partners × $100,000 = $1,000,000

And is there *one* super fan out of millions who would pay a million dollars cash just to be the *one* in a million?

1 in a million × $1,000,000 = $1,000,000

All told, that's over seven million dollars stemming from seven different price points. And the database of this entire experience could offer endless combinations of products for millions more over the next five years.

This whole idea might sound crazy, but if you pay attention, it's happening all around you. Just think about how some people buy a more professional looking hardcover book at a higher price to put in their library and other people wait until the book comes out in paperback at a much lower price. These are two completely different types of customers from the same database of buyers. In the same way, we can make seven completely different offers using the Millionaire Matrix. Some people satisfy their curiosity for a dollar. For others, price is not an issue. They have an urgent problem or a burning passion, and they are willing to go "all in" for the full experience.

> "Competition has been shown to be useful up to a certain point and no further, but cooperation, which is the thing we must strive for today, begins where competition leaves off."
> — Franklin D. Roosevelt

This is the power of making the right offers to the right database. If you *believe* it and *desire* it, you can *acquire* it.

Enough theory. Let's look at a real example.

$137,000 in 45 Days Starting from Scratch

Not too long ago, a student of mine named Nikki sat in my seminar called *Cracking the Millionaire Code*, and then she cracked it. Here's how:

She was listening to one of the speakers at the seminar—the marketing guru Jay Abraham. He was showing the attendees how to find a product to market. Yes, that's right—you don't even need your own product. There are millions of products out there already in some warehouse or online website just waiting for you to come along and offer to help sell them. Talk about low hanging fruit! It's hanging all around you.

Every business needs help selling. Some need it much worse than others. Some businesses are terrible at selling. They love to create products, but they're lousy at marketing them. You can come to their rescue.

Jay Abraham suggested that the participants find a product category that matched their purpose—things that they would love to sell because they *believed* in them.

This is something you can try too. Think about the purpose for your best-selling book. Google that purpose and see what products you find. Everyone is fighting for their products to appear in the top ten pages in a Google search. Let's do just the opposite in our Google search. Instead of going to the top of the Google results list, go to the *bottom*, or at least deeper than two or three hundred pages in the results search, where only a few people browsing the internet ever go.

> "You don't start out writing good stuff. You start out writing crap and thinking it's good stuff, and then gradually you get better at it. That's why I say one of the most valuable traits is persistence."
> – *Octavia E. Butler*

What do you find at the bottom of the search results? You'll find many people and companies that don't know how to sell their products. They need help. Search through the list and find ten that have some information you really connect with—something that you'd actually love to sell. Contact the seller and ask if they'd like to sell you a bunch of their products below wholesale cost—at *their* cost. Maybe they've got a warehouse full of items that they'd love to get rid of to generate some cash. You're looking for info-products you can acquire for an outstanding bargain—something that's just a step removed from a free giveaway.

Research a dozen companies and narrow them down to one or two possible candidates. Out of a dozen companies, at least one will likely be a perfect fit. Keep in mind that I make this sound easy, but don't expect these product owners to be thrilled with your offer. Only a few in a hundred will be open to your proposal, so it'll take some time to find the right one.

Now, you won't have to warehouse the product. It's already being warehoused. You don't have to ship it. They'll ship it for you as long as you pay for it. They've already created some marketing information that you can use. It's ready to go. You haven't spent a dime, and you're in control of a million dollars' worth of product.

Are you still with me?

This is exactly what Nikki did. She found a company at the bottom of Google's search results with a CD that contained special software and hundreds of valuable special reports for stay-at-home moms. It was extremely valuable, but it only cost $1 to reproduce. Nikki acquired the unlimited, non-exclusive rights to market this CD with her name on it for an investment of only $1,000. The info owner could still market it, but Nikki could also sell it and keep all the profit. Did you get that? Someone sold her the right to market their product for only $1,000.

> "We cannot seek achievement for ourselves and forget about progress and prosperity for our community... Our ambitions must be broad enough to include the aspirations and needs of others, for their sakes and for our own."
>
> – *Cesar Chavez*

Now she had the words to market—the info-product. But how did she find the names—the database?

At a party in her city, she stumbled upon two college students who had been studying database building in a college computer class. These nerds had been able to build a database of 500,000 double opt-in email addresses. (We assume they got an A in the class.) Nicky asked them if they would let her send a promotion to their database if one hundred percent of the money would be donated to her favorite charity—an orphanage in Mexico. She has a very soft spot in her heart for orphans. The young men thought that would be cool.

The email went out to 500,000 people. Here was the offer: "Send us $100 for this incredibly valuable CD. We'll donate ALL of the money to our favorite orphanage. All of it."

> "Without leaps of imagination, or dreaming, we lose the excitement of possibilities. Dreaming, after all, is a form of planning."
>
> – *Gloria Steinem*

Guess how many people on that database took her up on her offer?

Here are the results: 99.66 percent of the people on the list said no to her offer. Only one-third of 1 percent responded. But that tiny percentage from such a huge list still generated 1,370 people!

Yes, 1,370 people sent in $100 for the CD knowing that all their money would be donated to the orphanage. The total earnings were $137,000 in cash. Starting from nothing. Nikki did this in only forty-five days after learning the concept.

Now, *you* have just learned it. How soon can you earn your first dollar? It's time for you to organize some words (info products) and offer these words to some names (a database).

> "We don't stop playing because we grow old; we grow old because we stop playing."
> – George Bernard Shaw

You see, scaling is just playing with numbers:

units sold × profit per unit × number of names exposed to your offer = your bright future

Could you create something—a newsletter, a book, a course, a seminar, a one-on-one coaching session, or an info-product?

Play along with me, here—just say, "Yes!"

You cobble together your own list of names with 1,000; 10,000; or 100,000 people. Then you set up multiple JVs and gain access to their lists of 1,000; 10,000; or 100,000 names. And now you're in business. So crack the code. Find a way to sell it. Go up and down the Matrix and start selling advanced versions. Refine your marketing metrics.

How Do You Keep on Scaling?

Moving up and down the Millionaire Matrix is how you go *deep*. Let's scale even more by going *wide*.

Once you've conquered the internet, you can also scale up and add a zero by reaching ten new marketing avenues. There isn't time in this book to explain all the marketing methods that I call Multiple Streams of Marketing. But spend some time studying the graphic on the next page:

> "Even when you are marketing to your entire audience or customer base, you are still simply speaking to a single human at any given time."
> – Ann Handley

If you have an in-demand info concept, you could spend decades rolling out endless variations of products through multiple marketing channels—deep and wide. That's what I've done for almost fifty years. I've done TV and radio.

I've done teleconferences and Zoom classes. I've done direct mail and dozens of newspapers all over the nation in full page ads. I've done JVs.

Once I conquered the United States, I scaled wider by adding a zero to reach ten other countries all over the world, then twenty countries, and then thirty. I have JVed with dozens of seminar promoters from China to the UK to South Africa to Italy—in over twenty-five countries worldwide. The JV partner in each location I visited did all of the work to "put butts in the seats," and I delivered the message. They delivered the names, I delivered the words, and we both profited.

That's the beauty of scaling. If you've figured out a way to market a hot product in North America, the rest of the world is just waiting for it. The possibility for growth is exponential.

IF IT WORKS HERE... IT CAN WORK EVERYWHERE.

Being an info guru might not be your dream, but I've helped launch "gurus" in the United States, Canada, Italy, the UK, Japan, Taiwan, China, and Singapore.

Handing Out the Diploma of Done

Do you remember the Diploma of Done? Now you know how to write a book that people will want to read, and you know how to turn it into a bestseller, but being successful at selling words is not enough. When your readers have paid the money, you've got to deliver. No more upselling. It's time to follow through on your promise and educate them enough to generate results.

You promised transformation—so transform them! Take your readers all the way to the end of the row. Teach your heart out. But don't just teach *how* to do it—*watch* them do it. Your seminar needs to be a "do-inar." The harvest of your crop is not money. Your harvest is the success stories of your students. Then, when they give you a testimonial, it will not be about what they've learned but what they've *done*. The diplomas you offer are not just about how smart your readers have become. These diplomas are about,

> "Happiness lies in the joy of achievement and the thrill of creative effort."
> – *Franklin D. Roosevelt*

- How much weight your readers have lost.
- How much money they've made.
- How much success they've achieved.
- How much more love they now enjoy.
- How much more they get done.

Your success is knowing that your readers and customers are now healthier, smarter, richer, and happier.

We don't have time in today's world to learn things. We need to get things *done*. This is your diploma—the Diploma of DONE.

Lifelong Fans

Helping people get things done creates true lifelong fans. True fans like to buy everything that their teacher creates. Brands spawn fans. Give your fans a reason to keep fanning the flames of your fame.

Your *best* fans can become part of your inner circle. They hang with you and play with you at the highest levels. They become peers and friends.

And then, if you treat them right, they leave you testimonials like this:

> "Robert Allen was instrumental in helping me start from ground zero in my business. Before I met him, I had been struggling for three or four years. I was in debt. I took a leap of faith and invested in him and his training, and it was one of those pivotal moments of my life that really changed everything. He surrounded me with this attitude that, 'You can do anything,' and, 'I'm here to help.' Within a year and a half of working with him, I had a six-figure business ($100,000+), a year later, a seven-figure business ($1,000,000+), and now I have an eight-figure business ($10,000,000+.) I have over twenty people on my team. I have this amazing life with my business and with helping people, and it all started with Robert Allen. Now it's an honor to call him a peer and a friend."

– Greg Poulos

When you achieve any success—from writing a book to creating and marketing a bundle of info products, please share it with me at support@robertallen.com.

Scaling Onward

The world of marketing information is changing at warp speed. There are marketing methods on the drawing boards of today that will be the new Googles and Facebooks and Xs of tomorrow. You'll be constantly learning and testing new ways to reach your avatars.

Will you be able to step away from the whirlwind to reap a residual lifestyle in your remaining years? That would be nice. So, set up your empire in a way that it can send you checks when you want to take a break for a week or a decade or a lifetime.

But, as my friend, Lisa Sasevich says, "Don't die with your book still on your hard drive!"

> "Effective communication is twenty percent what you know and eighty percent how you feel about what you know."
>
> – Jim Rohn

Once you've learned this bestseller system, I bet you'll have trouble stepping away from your keyboard or microphone. It's just the nature of the game. Can you imagine Celine Dion ever wanting to stop singing? I heard Julio Iglesias say on a stage in Las Vegas, "When I go, I want to go on stage in the middle of a song."

If you have a message, you'll want to write it, speak it, or sing it for as long as you breathe. Most employees who are pulling down a job can't even imagine a world where there is no retirement. For an infopreneur, it's not a job—it's a joy. If you feel that it's your purpose to improve the planet with your message—if you get joy and fulfillment and satisfaction in watching the words flow—then, why would you ever want to retire?

> "Sometimes I've called writing a disease. If so, I'm glad that it caught me."
> – Charles Bukowski

Still, the time will come when you'll be forced to retire. You'll be summoned to another world to sing your word songs to bigger audiences. So, as you prepare to step onto the eternal stage, make sure that your empire here keeps scaling even when you are no longer here to scale it. Make sure your avatars can still be moved by your messages in the same way that we still thrill to Elvis and Michael.

It's your empire. Your way. Your message. Your wealth.

Onward, my friend—onward. ☺

FREE GIFT: AI Empire Builder – Revenue Coaching Toolkit

If you want to turn your book into a full business, I built a toolkit with AI-driven systems, offers, and monetization strategies to scale fast. It's free at AuthorGifts.com or via the QR code.

"Talent is nothing without dedication and discipline, and dedication and discipline is a talent in itself."

– Luke Campbell

30 MAGIC MINUTES

Your Commitment to Succeed

Do you really want to an author—a bestselling author—a number one bestselling author? Can you dedicate thirty minutes a day to your goal for at least the next ninety days? Is that a "yes"?

So, prove it. Go to your calendar right now and block out thirty minutes. Schedule it every day at the same time for the next ninety days. This time will be inviolable, sacred, non-negotiable. Tell those around you not to bother you during these special minutes. Find a time when you will not, cannot be distracted, bothered or interrupted. This is your Bestseller Time.

You've wanted to write a book for years. This is your time to write up or shut up.

The twelve steps in this book will guide you. As you begin your journey to the top of the bestseller lists, plan sixty seconds every day as you start your thirty-minute bestseller session. For sixty seconds, imagine what it will be like when your book hits number one in your niche on Amazon. Consider what it will feel like: a surge of pride, a sense of humility for the sacrifices you made to get here, a boost of self-respect. You did it!

When you introduce yourself as a number one bestselling author, people will look at you differently from that moment onward. They're envious. They've always wanted to do what you've accomplished, but they wouldn't sacrifice those thirty minutes a day like you did. They'll admire you as a member of a very special, highly unusual, successful clique of bestselling authors.

You belong to a minuscule minority of thought leaders who have persevered to get a book written and driven to the top of the bestseller lists. Soak in that feeling. You deserve it. You let nothing get in the way of your thirty minutes a day—starting with those special sixty seconds as you imagine the bestselling results.

So, let's begin. For thirty minutes a day, study this entire book from cover to cover to get a complete overview of the entire process. Don't let yourself feel overwhelmed with all the information that you'll eventually need to implement. Just remember, that you can accomplish anything in thirty minutes a day if you keep putting one foot in front of the other thirty short minutes at a time. Here's a little review on how to focus your efforts:

> "It was character that got us out of bed, commitment that moved us into action, and discipline that enabled us to follow through."
>
> – Zig Ziglar

Step 1: Your Irresistible Message

As you re-read this chapter, ponder what you really want to say to the world. At first, your message will be ordinary, basic, even clichéd. Ask yourself, "How can my message be said in a new, fresh, interesting way?"

Try out your elevator pitch with anyone you meet over the next few weeks. If someone asks you, "What do you do?" Tell them, "Well, in addition to (blank), I'm writing a new book. Here's the working title." And then share it with them. How do they respond? If they say, "Wow, how can I get a copy?" then you know you're onto something. But if they avert their eyes and say, "Hmm, that's interesting," then you know you've got some more work to do. Spend the next thirty-minute sessions refining your message.

Step 2: Your Perfect Avatar

Imagine that someone in the world has an urgent problem or a burning passion. They're googling to find more information about it right now. Imagine who that person might be in detail. Give them a name. Imagine talking to them and sharing information that they urgently seek of deeply desire. Write you book for that person. If you can locate them somehow, they'll buy it. They need it—NOW. Spend one or two of your daily thirty-minute sessions getting clear on who they are.

Step 3: Your Success Map

Create a metaphor you can use to communicate your entire message in one clear picture. If a picture is worth a thousand words, then your Map is worth as many as fifty thousand words because your book will probably contain thirty to fifty thousand words. You want your reader to see the entire content of your book immediately in one visual Map. Look at our bestseller map for this book. The process is clear, with twelve steps to the top of the bestseller list. Follow these steps, and you'll be there.

Step 4: Your Revolutionary Brand

Take a few thirty-minute sessions to read and ponder your "brand." The hardest part of the bestseller process is coming up with a unique concept—a fresh way to present your "take" on your subject. There will be a thousand other books on a similar topic. You want to stand apart from them in an exciting new way. Just keep asking yourself, "How can I make my information different—revolutionary?" You don't need an immediate answer. Just plant the seed, let the idea simmer, and move on to the next step.

"We use metaphors to express our own truths.""
– *Lynn Nottage*

Step 5: Your Word Forge

Here's where the rubber meets the road. If you have your concept and your Map, you can lay out the steps for your reader to achieve the result you promise. Each step in your book is a chapter of information designed to lead your reader to the end result. Organize your steps into chapters headings. Then ask yourself, "What three basic chunks of information do I need to teach my reader in each step so they move closer to my promised result?" In this way, a table of contents is just a list of steps. And in each step, there are three chunks of content. A ten-step book will have about thirty chunks of content. That is your outline. It may take several thirty-minute sessions to get your outline together. Don't start writing until your outline is complete.

It will probably take you about thirty days to complete these first five bestseller steps and complete your outline. Then, with your outline in front of you, start laying down words at five hundred words a day. During each new thirty-minute session, revise what you wrote the day before and lay down five hundred more words. Get into a rhythm. You'll eventually produce a full-length book in as few as ninety days. Just keep writing (or talking or AI-ing) for thirty minutes a day, until your rough manuscript is finished. Then, run your words through ChatGPT. It'll clean up your words into a smooth, flowing document. Now the words are done. Next, we'll be shifting toward gathering the Names. But first, let's get a killer book cover.

> "My editor said, 'Cut 10,000 words.' I said, 'But those were the words I suffered for!' She said, 'Exactly.'"
>
> – Unknown

Step 6: Your Bold Book Cover

Now you need a bold book cover. You started back at Step 1 by testing out your "working title" with everyone you met. You've probably sifted those titles down to two or three possible titles. It's time to test them with your database.

Then, go to Fiverr.com or 99designs.com and hire an artist to design a cover for you. If your budget is tight, spend your thirty-minute sessions on Canva.com creating your own cover for free. But don't stop until your front cover is done. Then, shift to the back cover where you'll list a summary list of the concepts in the book plus short endorsement blurbs from ten of your successful friends or chosen experts. Getting these blurbs may sound like a lot of work, but it's worth it. So, take thirty minutes a day to track down and build a list of at least ten back-cover blurbs.

Step 7: Your Impressive Layout

You've been working on your words. Now it's time to layer different bestselling concepts throughout the words to make the words more visual and interesting. Here are the first few layers to get you started.

For thirty minutes, track down two or three testimonials about your process from successful clients or early readers and insert them in the text of each chapter. Contact real people, get them an advance digital copy of your book, and ask them for a genuine testimonial. And maybe even a four- or five-star review on Amazon. Write some sample testimonials for them to review. They can select one of the ones you wrote, if they prefer, or write one of their own.

For thirty minutes, insert visuals throughout the book, such as charts, graphs, and illustrations. ChatGPT can help you with this. This step will probably take several sessions to complete. It will turn your wall of words into a visual display of ideas. That's how you make each chapter more "sticky."

For thirty minutes, track down twenty-five of your favorite quotes on your subject to sprinkle throughout the text of your book. (Notice the quotes we've sprinkled throughout this book.) Insert these quotes into the text of your book.

For thirty minutes, go to ChatGPT and ask for twenty-five humorous thoughts on your book's topic to sprinkle throughout the text of your book. Don't spend too much time laughing!

Step 8: Your Opt-In to Wealth

Layer some "gifts" for your reader into your book content so you can send them to your opt-in page and build your database.

Then, focus your attention on Step 9: Your Succession Stack until you have created a list of your upsells. Then, layer those upsell "seeds" throughout your chapters to let your readers know subliminally that you offer higher educational opportunities for the few who want to go deeper.

Then, shift to **Step 10: Your Bestselling Buzz**, and on to **Step 11: Your Guaranteed Launch**. Then, finally to **Step 12: Your Exponential Scalability**.

You get the idea! Continue through each step and follow the instructions faithfully—thirty minutes at a time. There's no magic. It's just committing to focus for thirty minutes at a time.

Set a kitchen timer or your digital watch or phone for a thirty-minute focused interval. Don't be distracted. Don't doodle or dawdle. Just focus on accomplishing the tasks in the next step until you can check them off your list. You'd be amazed at what you can get done in an intensive thirty-minute sprint.

> "An illustration is a visual editorial—it's just as nuanced. Everything that goes into it is a call you make: every color, every line weight, every angle."
>
> – Charles M. Blow

Follow this plan, and we know you'll join us at the top of the bestseller lists!

The End (But, Really—Your Beginning)

You've made it. You've reached the end of this book—but what's really waiting for you on the other side is the beginning of your bestseller journey.

Whether you're writing your first book, launching your fourth, or just now daring to believe that this dream is possible, now you know—now you see how it's done. Now you have the road map!

What comes next is all about taking action.

If this book helped you get unstuck, if it gave you a burst of clarity or confidence, or if it lit a fire under you to finally get your message out into the world, then promise us this:

> "I don't focus on what I'm up against. I focus on my goals and I try to ignore the rest."
> – Venus Williams

Don't stop here.

Books don't change lives sitting on the desk. Bestsellers don't write themselves. And your audience? They're waiting.

LET'S STAY CONNECTED

If this book helped you, inspired you, or gave you the kick you needed—we want to hear about it:

- Snap a photo of you and your copy of this book (digital or printed), share it on your socials, and tag us so we can cheer you on!
- Join our Facebook group for authors so our community can support your upcoming book launch. Just scan the QR to the right with your smartphone.
- Tag us using the hashtag: **#1BestsellerBook**

JOIN THE FACEBOOK GROUP

Have a question? Stuck on a step?

Send us a note. We read every single message: **hello@robertgallen.com**

Know someone who needs this book?

If you know someone else with a book in their heart—a coach, speaker, expert, or entrepreneur who's sitting on a message the world needs to hear—please send them to **www.numberonebook.com**. We'd be honored to help guide them, too.

Need help with your launch or want to work with us?

If you're serious about hitting bestseller status—and want help getting there—we'd love to support you. Whether you need,

- Expert help marketing your book,
- A clear plan to build your author platform,
- Or the opportunity to partner directly with Robert, Lyndsey, and Aaron on your next book, we've built something just for you.

This is your shortcut to expert support, strategy, and bestselling-level execution—without wasting time, money, or momentum. Visit **AuthorGifts.com** or scan the QR code to get started.

Whatever stage of your journey you're in,

- You now have the tools.
- You now have the Steps.
- You have what it takes.

We believe in you! Let's make your book more than just a book—let's make it a movement.

To your success,

Robert, Lyndsey, & Aaron

OUR DEEPEST THANKS

Some people are with you from the first breath. They see your light long before the world does. They hold your hand in the dark… and never let go.

To our families—our original, forever fans.

You've been the heartbeat behind everything we do. Your love, your belief, your presence—it's sacred. You've celebrated our wins. You've stood through our storms. And through it all, you made us feel like we could do anything.

Robert's family: Daryl, Aimee, Aaron, and Hunter

Lyndsey's family: Bill, Patty, Amy, Jenny, and Kara

Aaron's family: Sherry, Tracy, Nattie, Carissa, Derek, Brilee, Davin, and Mason

You are our roots. You are our why. You are everything.

And to our extended family—our beloved community of Superfans…

You may not share our last names, but you've stood with us like family just the same. You championed this project with your time, your energy, your voice—and your hearts. You reminded us what community really means.

Your names are stitched into the fabric of this book:

Adreina Adams, Kevin Anthony, Rema A, Jenna Ayoub, Hamza Abbasi, Paula Banks, Carey Barnett, Caroline Bate, Karen Nelson Bell, Bonnie Best, Jason Bird, Anne Elisabeth Bisgaard, Bindu Bodanapu, Myra Britt, Dan Britton, Krystal Bryant, Kippax Byronwilliams, Nancy Camardo, Bill Campbell, Natividad Carrillo, Lyton Chandomba, Noema Chaplin, Steve Chapman, Doris Chen, George Christenakis, Dolores Christian, Jl Clark, Melissa Claybrook, Monica Cuneo, Virginia Da Silva, Dr. Opal Dailey, William Dambach, Stephen Deats, Joseph Descans, Irene Diamond, Idriss Adama Diaw, Ivan Dowdell, Dan Durrant, David Frost, Tiffany Feinstein, H Marie Gagnon, Robert L. Galke, Trenique Baugh Garrett, Steven Golden, Yvonne Gonzalez, Lokeshchand Goolchand, Howard Gray, Sayed Haider Abbas Sa, Catherine Hanson, Fazl Haque, Dr.

Victoria Hart, Shonya Hattley, Gertrudis Hernandez-Cohen, Robert Hite, Stephen Huggins, Sandra Jacks, Juanita Jackson, Teresa Jhalli, Doris M. Jones, Chaplain Gayle Jordan, Albert Klamt, Christopher Kohler, Bob Kokott, Sara King, Sallie Kraus, Joshua Ledesma, Megan Lehto, James Lemire, Charles Lewis, Gabriel Lopez Galvan, Tammy Lowe, Sheila Macarthur, Joe Marques, Hiroto Matsushima, Carol Maupin, Dwight Mccaulsky, Debbie Mcgrann, Matthew Mcintear, VNL Mision, Dara Mitchell, Shi Moulton, Amanda McCown, Jim Mullins, Veronica Newbern, Sajil, Shaswat Kumar, Sohail Noorani, Judy Bushy, Paul Costa, Elizabeth Ainsworth, Georgia Francis, Christine Martin, Edwin Atlas, Ogonna Nwajiobi, Dennis Ondrejka, Daniel Ortiz, Ryan Paige, Leon Pickett, Thomas Painter, Maria Angeles, Maureen Palmer, Wyatt Payne, Andrea Peponakis, Romina Pineda, Ron Plummer, Michele Plunkett, Dolores Priegnitz, Alan Pryor, Samuel Ismael Pulido Navarro, Matthew Radmanesh, Marlie Rae, Brett Reina, Olmeca Rich, Jeanette Rivera, Corinne Rodin, Satya Saini, Stacy Salam, Lonnie Sanders III, Jeffrey Sanow, Lola Schappell, Stephen Scott, Darren Scrubb, Gilbert Segovia, Jay Selva, Nalini Sheosankar, Yalawnda Sidney, Fred Siegel, Chuntianle New Power Art, Hatem Sleem, Diane Smith, Tonya Spencer, Deeanne Stiles, Tom Stout, Heidi Strohbeen, Saulius Stu, Philip Sullenberger, Timur Tazhetdinov, Brian Thomas, Djuro Tomic, Evelyn Traylor, Val Ukachi, Ann Urich, PJ Vandervort, Al-Hafiz Virani, Angelica Wagner, Francisca Walters, John Warner, Earl Waud, Curt Wellumson, Anna Williams, Taranja Griggs, Armin Willis, Carolyn Wilson, Thomas Alan Wintering, Robert Wortham, Lana Wuolukka, Regina Wuthe, Nabila Feroze, Lacy O'Leary, Marcelina Emefiene, Ann Promise, Elijah Golden, John Jarrell, Cid McDonald, Cynthia Bowers Smith, Jason Oswald, Steve Bates, Bonnie Kogos, Griselda Samara, Lawrence McNair, Jane Kelly, Jaye Miller, Matthew Selhorst, Neil J. Paterno, Lizther Kaye C. Rufin

And so many more.

We carry you with us always.

With love and gratitude,

Robert, Lyndsey & Aaron

Made in the USA
Monee, IL
02 September 2025